THE **ART** OF
SCREEN TIME

THE **ART** OF **SCREEN TIME**

Digital Parenting Without Fear

Anya Kamenetz

PUBLICAFFAIRS
NEW YORK

PublicAffairs
Hachette Book Group
1290 Avenue of the Americas, New York, NY 10104
www.publicaffairsbooks.com
@Public_Affairs

Printed in the United States of America

First Trade Paperback Edition: July 2020
Published by PublicAffairs, an imprint of Perseus Books, LLC, a subsidiary of Hachette Book Group, Inc. The PublicAffairs name and logo is a trademark of the Hachette Book Group.

The publisher is not responsible for websites (or their content) that are not owned by the publisher.

Print book interior design by Linda Mark.

The Library of Congress has cataloged the hardcover edition as follows:
Names: Kamenetz, Anya, 1980– author.
Title: The art of screen time : how your family can balance digital media and real life / Anya Kamenetz.
Description: First edition. | New York : PublicAffairs, [2017] | Includes bibliographical references and index.
Identifiers: LCCN 2017037331 (print) | LCCN 2017046204 (ebook) | ISBN 9781610396738 (ebook) | ISBN 9781610396721 (hardcover)
Subjects: LCSH: Internet and families. | Internet and children. | Information technology—Social aspects. | Internet addiction. | Families.
Classification: LCC HQ784.I58 (ebook) | LCC HQ784.I58 K36 2017 (print) | DDC 004.67/8083—dc23
LC record available at https://lccn.loc.gov/2017037331

ISBNs: 978-1-61039-672-1 (hardcover), 978-1-61039-673-8 (ebook), 978-1-5417-5089-0 (paperback)

LSC-C

10 9 8 7 6 5 4 3 2 1

*For Elvera Stone, who has brought us
hope and light from her very first day.*

CONTENTS

ACKNOWLEDGMENTS

THANKS TO MY EDITOR, BENJAMIN ADAMS, FOR TAKING ME TO LUNCH TO TALK about the next book. It has been such a delight working with him and the team at PublicAffairs a second time.

Jim Levine has been everything you could want in an agent.

Thanks to my teammates at NPR Ed past and present—Steve Drummond, LA Johnson, Lauren Migaki, Elissa Nadworny, Claudio Sanchez, Cory Turner, Eric Westervelt, and Sami Yenigun. You inspire me every day, and your support helped make this possible. Special thanks to Pamela Hurst-Della Pietra and her organization Children and Screens: Institute of Digital Media and Child Development, as well as to Carnegie Mellon University, for help and support with this research.

This book stands on the shoulders of so many amazing researchers and thinkers, many of whom are also, and not incidentally, mothers. Thank you thank you, danah boyd, Justine Cassell, Sonia Livingstone, Alicia Blum-Ross, Mimi Ito, Mitchel Resnick, Kathy Hirsh-Pasek, and so many more. And to the whole motherboard!

All gratitude and a bowl of soup to Adam, my partner in parenting and in life.

And thanks to Lulu, for being herself.

PREFACE

I'M WRITING THIS PREFACE DURING A MOMENT THAT FEELS LIKE A PREFACE—the first chapter of a bewildering new reality. It is April 1, 2020. My three-year-old daughter is sitting next to me, drawing in a notebook. Her Montessori school is closed, just as schools are in 185 countries around the world; 89 percent of the world's children have no school to attend and most of them will be out for the remainder of the spring term. And of course that's not all. Societies have shut down, economies ground to a halt, in an unprecedented collective effort to fight the spread of the novel coronavirus.

I called this book *The Art of Screen Time*, but *time* is an increasingly limited shorthand for thinking about humans' use of digital devices. An immediate consequence of the pandemic is that strict screen time limits—which were always largely the province of more privileged families—are going out the door, everywhere. In the first two weeks after most children in the United States were kept home from school, traffic to children's apps and digital services increased by 70 percent. Most schools, from preschool to college, began to offer some form of distance learning.

Except for the many essential workers, from nurses to supermarket clerks, who were put directly in harm's way, we were sealed within the cordon of the household. As a result, the Internet became our life-line to friends and family, workplaces and commerce, churches and temples, neighborhoods and the wider world. By the time you read these words, this time that we've spent, together, apart, will inevitably change our relationship with technology.

As you'll see in chapter 3, I talk about harm reduction, which is an approach to public health that recognizes that fully avoiding risk or danger may be impossible. Harm reduction should be our mantra because we are in the process of recovery from a global crisis. These are not ideal conditions. They call on us to be adaptive, flexible, and as forgiving as possible of ourselves and others.

Based on what I've learned about screen time, the following are my suggestions for how to do less harm to yourselves and your children while adapting to your new relationship with technology.

Guard Sleep: Strive to create margins of screenlessness before bed-time and after waking up in the morning. The effects of screens on sleep are well established, and we need a chance to get good rest to confront the exceptional stresses of these times. This applies to both children and adults.

Nurture Emotional Intelligence: What I've come to realize after reflecting on the findings in this book for the past few years is that so many of our problems with technology really come from a disruption and alienation that creeps into our own relationships with ourselves and others, as we allow our experiences to be mediated by media. The antidote is connecting to our feelings, with the assistance of loved ones who make it safe to do that.

From their births, we soothe our children with our own bodies. From the time they start to have words, we can help them build their vocabulary and awareness of emotions, so they can learn to soothe themselves. Check in with your children, ask them how they're feel-ing, and help them locate emotions as physical feelings in their body. Together, start developing a toolbox of coping strategies they can use when they feel overwhelmed, scared, or sad—a special soft blanket, a familiar song, or a hug.

Teaching children to identify emotions and listen to their bodies has never been more important than in this age of pervasive anxiety.

My older daughter, now eight, is starting to understand that her eyes get tired when she stares at a screen too long and she needs to take breaks. She's also learning that when she spends too much time playing video games, her mood gets cranky and squirrelly in ways that the rest of the family notices.

Watch for Behavioral Reactions to Screen Time: Explosive emotions when the screens turn off are very common. Sometimes the severe behavioral reaction to too much screen time is an issue of quantity, and sometimes the problem is the type of activity. Especially vulnerable are children with ADHD, autism, or other behavioral or mental health issues.

Ideally when this starts to become a problem, try to limit the kinds of screen time most associated with those behaviors. It could be the time of day that matters most to your child, or the length of time, or a certain kind of show or game.

At other times, especially these days, you might fail at limiting screen time. Or you might choose not to limit screen time because you or your child are sick, or you have work to do, or you have a plane ride to get through. None of us is perfect, but you will need a plan B. Prepare for and weather the tantrum and/or zoned-out feeling that follows with some physical activity, hugs, or a snack, or all of the above. Talking to your child in advance about the screen hangover can help pre-empt it, especially as they get older and more self-aware.

The special culprits in terms of kids' behavior and emotions are violent and exceptionally fast-paced video content, many casual video games, including mobile games, and, unfortunately, many children's apps. A 2019 study by Dr. Jenny Radesky, who is cited throughout this book, found that 95 percent of the most popular apps for young children included ads that were often "manipulative," "disruptive," and as distracting as possible. These interruptions destroy attention spans and equilibrium. This was true even of paid and educational apps, including those associated with beloved children's book characters.

Maintain Human Connections: Connecting with other human beings is the most life-affirming use of screens. As virtual reality expert Ken Perlin tells me in the last chapter, "All we care about is whatever is going on between me and another person. Any medium that enriches that is successful. Any medium that replaces that is a failure." Translation: lean into video chat and real-time interactions. During this time of sheltering in place, so many people discovered and quickly adapted to new ways of connecting. In just the first few weeks, via video chat, we have connected in many different ways: lit the Shabbat candles and held a Passover Seder with friends and family around the country; had art lessons and story time with the grandparents; participated in live family yoga and ballet classes; attended Sunday school and preschool circle time and show-and-tell; held dance parties; and much more. My daughter Lulu and her best friends get on FaceTime almost every afternoon and play Roblox together or do a YouTube workout video, and they even had virtual sleepovers (a marathon chat session that lasted until they both fell asleep).

Designate Time without Screens: Screens are a disembodied experience. We need to take care of our bodies really well. Screens can be a catalyst, inspiration, or companion for physical activity. But we all need to take breaks, go outside, stretch, and be in the sunshine. Try to have the whole family put away screens during mealtime because you'll eat more mindfully and enjoy the food more. Look away from the screen and rest your eyes regularly.

Screens offer endless diversion, so we have to mindfully cultivate boredom. Try to plan for unstructured, screen-free play breaks, as well as reserving space in the morning and before bedtime.

Teens and the Screen: The dynamic between screen use and teenagers' mental health, in particular, is complex and multidimensional. While stuck at home with their families, teens inevitably lean on their virtual connections to peers more than ever. The lockdown accelerated trends among young people that older generations were in the habit of criticizing, viciously: they don't drive, they don't go out, they're content with a wholly vicarious life. Ironically, these habits have kept them one of the lowest-risk generations in decades, according to indicators such as drug use and pregnancy, as I talk about in chapter 2. And suddenly they were under public orders to stay home to save their own lives and others'.

As I've become more immersed in the debates over teens, screens, and mental health, I'm angry on behalf of our young people. We're handing them a ravaged environment and a wrecked economy, interrupting their educations and canceling their proms. And then we have the nerve to get on their case because of how they choose to socialize and express themselves? They deserve our protection and for us to lift up their voices.

When it comes to media use and mental health, I think we can all model for our teens awareness and intention rather than being prescriptive and critical. Remind them that when they are feeling sad or anxious, scrolling aimlessly through social media is unlikely to make them spontaneously feel better, but texting a friend for support or consulting a specific uplifting site or account might do the trick. One thing I've noticed since the pandemic began is that it's become far more "okay to say you're not okay," as Cambridge researcher Amy Orben put it to me. This openness about mental health will surely save lives.

I'd like to think that when families are forced to be home and spend more time together, they will get to know each other better and soften toward each other. I know some families will turn on each other and tear each other up, but I hope the former is more common.

Practice Good News Hygiene: Don't let the radio or TV stream in the background. I try hard to be apart from my kids when I read the news because it can be so upsetting. I would suggest that you designate specific, separate times with everyone in your household, including children from elementary school onward, to check in and discuss what's happening in the world. Help them process their emotions and take the opportunity to address any misconceptions they may have come across.

Be Aware of Your Own Screen Habits: Consider your own media diet and how it may affect your ability to be present with your kids when they need you. My email, text messages, and social media are full of people's intense emotions that I can't always respond to while at the same time giving my kids the stability they need. It's not easy to maintain those boundaries, but it always pays off when I do.

✧ ✧ ✧

One day we will be able to open our doors and go outside without fear.

We will reemerge, blinking like Dorothy taking in the Technicolor Oz of three-dimensional everyday life. Hugs from friends, playdates, sports practices, and birthday parties will be part of our children's everyday experiences once more.

When it comes to our kids and screens: Is there any hope of getting back to a healthier balance when all this is over?

I think the strategies laid out in this book will help you do that. But there is no rushing a recovery. For years to come, many of our efforts as a society will be devoted to this recovery in all kinds of ways. The truth is, as kids get older, screen rules and agreements need to change all the time anyway. So as the world starts to come back, keep the lines of communication open with your kids. Help them reflect on how they feel when they spend too much time online or with certain kinds of online activities; talk with them about what they've enjoyed about their virtual lives and what they haven't. And then agree together on what kinds of new boundaries make sense for the new world.

You will be reading these words a few months after I write them. You, reader, know more than I do about how the pandemic turned out: how much we managed to flatten the curve. Reopening dates. Economic relief plans. New social movements. Scientific breakthroughs. Cultural responses. Acts of heroism and iniquity that history will not forget.

Body counts.

But here's something I can tell you that is true today and will be true into the future. Media and technology profoundly affect our lives. They're not going anywhere. Taking a thoughtful, balanced approach to them can salve our minds, hearts, and bodies. We can experience their benefits while limiting their harms. Using media and technology in a healthy way within our family circles is more important now than ever. And after sharing this book with thousands of readers across the country, I can tell you that the methods outlined in this book will help you do that.

PART I

Kids and Screens

1 DIGITAL PARENTING IN THE REAL WORLD

You picked up this book because you are curious, and let's face it, a little anxious about kids and screens. I am too. I wrote it to help us both get past that anxiety. To cut the guilt, turn down the volume, tune out the noise, and look deeper. Then we're going to make a plan.

But first, a story.

Late one night in the early 1980s, I was a towheaded little girl in a nightgown perched on the foot of my parents' bed watching TV. The screen showed a towheaded little girl in a nightgown, perched at the foot of her parents' bed, watching TV.

On the television within the television, the credits rolled. The parents were dozing. My parents were dozing. The broadcast day ended on the televised television. The national anthem played over a shot of the American flag. The little girl scootched closer to the screen. I scootched closer to the screen.

Then a terrifying mass of green ectoplasm burst out of the screen within the screen. The movie was *Poltergeist* (1982).

In that moment was born a lifetime phobia.

Not of ghosts. I love ghosts. I even went through a middle school se-ance phase, appropriate to the bayous of South Louisiana where I was reared. No, I was deathly afraid of closing credits. The fear has faded over time, but to this day, when a movie ends I prefer to hustle up the aisle. When a TV episode is over I have to minimize the window before the Netflix countdown gets to the next episode.

A quarter century later, my older daughter's introduction to inap-propriate content came on the potty. We had tried everything we could think of to get a toddler to sit down long enough to go number two. And as suggested by a number of other parents, the only bribe that really worked was the offer of a short video on our phones.

We found plenty of kiddie-approved potty training material on YouTube: a catchy ditty about washing your hands from PBS's *Daniel Tiger's Neighborhood*; a nice instructional skit from Elmo; a hyperen-thusiastic Japanese-speaking panda. Then one day, I happened to click on a five-minute cartoon. It was called "Potty Training." It had mil-lions of views.

It turned out to be an episode of an incredibly filthy, obnoxious car-toon web series, apparently intended for dimwitted adolescents. My daughter loved it, of course, and asked for it again and again.

A quarter century from now, my daughters may be raising kids of their own. If the forecasters are to be believed, we'll all be plunged into a gently glowing alphabet soup of AR, VR, AI, MR, and IoT—aug-mented reality, virtual reality, artificial intelligence, mixed reality, and the Internet of Things. We'll be inhabiting the bodies of avatars 24/7, exchanging GIFs with our sentient refrigerators, and using virtual as-sistants to ward off telemarketing bots. Digital experiences will be so immersive and pervasive that Yellowstone National Park will look like today's Times Square. By then the existence of screens as separate en-tities, with borders and off buttons, will be a quaint, half-remembered state of affairs.

The terrified little girl inside me asks: How worried should we re-ally be about kids and tech? Where is all of this heading? And what should we actually do about it—now, in the "real world," a phrase that as of the early twenty-first century still has some meaning?

These questions have resulted in the book you're reading. It's a book that I wish I'd had when my firstborn daughter arrived: a clear, deeply researched, and nonjudgmental take on an issue that faces nearly every parent today. I hope it will be a good resource for you as, together, we try to navigate the rocky shoals between fear and hype and untangle the growing role of digital media in our family lives, and in our lives, period.

I'm not presenting myself to you as an unassailable expert. I'm just a parent, one with a solid research toolbox, trying to work this stuff out as best I can. I've been writing about education and technology for over a decade. I became a parent in 2011. I belong to the first generation of parents who grew up with the Internet. And I'm now raising two members of the first generation growing up with screens literally at their fingertips.

Children today first engage with digital media at the average age of four months—or almost as soon as they can focus past the end of their noses. In the 1970s, the average age was four years.

According to a Pew survey in 2015, almost half of parents of school-aged kids say that their children spend too much time with screens. On average, children in the United States spend as much time daily with electronic media as on any other waking activity—including school.

Astonishing. But so what?

As parents, we find ourselves without traditions or folk wisdom— or, crucially, enough relevant scientific evidence—in answering that question. Traditional authorities, covering for real gaps in knowledge, fall back on tired tropes.

I think the self-proclaimed experts have let us down in our attempt to make sense of this incredible new reality. In the absence of Grandma's advice or a wealth of up-to-date research studies, the source of knowledge that we consult to resolve not only these conflicts, but seemingly every question and hiccup in our children's lives and our own, is, ironically, the Internet. Dr. Google is the new Dr. Spock.

But the digital information ecosystem that we're all living in has an inherent bias toward clickbait. That means the existing books, articles, video segments, and blog posts out there about kids and screens all seem to portray worst-case scenarios, to push our buttons so we will keep pressing Like, Share, and Play.

And that in turn means that the crucial questions of digital parenting aren't only about our kids. They're about our use of digital media too. Are you embraced by the virtual village or menaced by the virtual mob? Is the phone a magical work-life balancer or a constantly bleeping attention-sucker?

Some of this tension is not new. Moralists raised the alarm over radio, cinema, and then television, all of which in their turn arguably changed childhood just as much as, or even more than, today's tiny screens.

But today's devices are mobile, meaning we're bringing them everywhere all the time, and they have touchscreens, making their interfaces intuitive even for infants. These two new aspects have intensified existing anxieties about the influence of older media like television and video games, with their power to lull, to obsess us, to "overstimulate or... inappropriately stimulate developing brains," in the words of pediatrician Dimitri Christakis, and to transmit messages to our children in our homes that are out of our control as parents.

In the twenty-first century, few parents escape without considering their children's use of screens. It's part of our model of what makes a good, conscientious parent. If you don't ration and control screen time like candy, you can at least have the decency to act guilty about it. But is screen time really the new sugar?

This is an exploration of the real world of parenting in the digital age. I surveyed over five hundred parents to find out how parents just like you are really making, and breaking, screen time rules. And I talked to the researchers. I can tell you not just what the experts are saying, where they agree and disagree, but at home, when no one is looking, what they're actually doing as parents with their own kids. The best-known expert recommendation about screens, until very recently, was the American Academy of Pediatrics (AAP) rule of "no TV before age two." It was based on little evidence. Nine out of ten parents do not follow it. In 2016, it was significantly altered—but still without very much evidence for the new version.

The research landscape, it turns out, is marked by large gaps, and much hotly contested territory. Still, the best evidence we have currently suggests that if you are functioning well as a family otherwise, there is a huge amount of leeway in the screen radiation your kids can absorb and still do just fine. TV is not DDT. In fact, many of the observed negative effects of screen time are utterly confounded by the realities of social inequality in America. Simply put, the children of lower-income, less-educated parents are both more exposed to screens at younger ages and more subject to a host of other ills. Also, a lot of the issues that come up with screens and kids, both physical and emotional, are traceable to a single effect as old as electric lights.

Technology is ubiquitous. The air we breathe is saturated with Wi-Fi signals. Outside a few tiny subcultures, there is no control group. This is our reality. If you're looking for a book that beseeches you to turn your back on all that and move to the wilds of Maine, this is not that book. (It's been written a couple of times, anyway.) Instead of nurturing escape fantasies, let's think like scientists. I wanted to unpack my own irrational fears and look at them in the light of day. And I want to help you do the same. I'm going to give you an algorithm of sorts so you can figure out the screen strategy that best suits your family today. Don't fear unknown poltergeists.

First, look for evidence of harms related to proven risks. These include attention problems, weight problems, sleep problems, and academic or emotional issues. They can relate to screen use in general or certain occasions or types of content in particular. I'll go over the questions to ask when your child encounters screens at school and with peers, and what you as a parent should know about privacy, marketing, sexting, bullying, and other common concerns.

Next, explore your own feelings about where media fits into your family. You may rely on screens as a babysitter. Device use may cause you guilt or contribute to family conflict. It may feel uncomfortable to negotiate and set boundaries. Or, screens may be a warm family hearth; a source of fun, wonder, and excitement. Sometimes all of the above. I've started advising other parents on how to create and own realistic boundaries and revise them in a reasonable way when circumstances change. One point that psychologists and family therapists stand firm on is that hypocrisy and inconsistency in boundary-setting, on any issue, makes for confused, sometimes angry kids—and lots of conflict.

Finally, hash out your own use of screens. Maybe you feel constantly on call, harried and distracted. Or maybe it's your partner who seems preoccupied. Maybe devices help you get more things done, or maybe they're an escape hatch from the pressures of home. Social media could be a source of invaluable parenting wisdom and support or a locus of extra conflict. The Internet and social media can be a powerful, necessary source of support for parents, but when it gets out of control it can be equally disruptive and damaging.

I've lived the positive side. I spent two years struggling with infertility before conceiving my first daughter and went through another year of treatments and procedures with my second. During those times, online message boards and Facebook groups formed a vital, virtual support group for me. The women there were fully engaged with all the gory details I didn't want to talk to anyone else about—not my husband, not my family, not my friends. I couldn't have gotten through conception or pregnancy without them. I will never know most of their real names or identities.

Yet the platforms we use to make these kinds of connections are neither benign nor neutral. As a journalist covering technology for years, I'm all too aware that one of the world's most powerful industries is keen to capture our attention and direct our choices as parents. As the adage goes, if you're not the customer, you're the product.

You might want to change your practices online, or pull back altogether. Once you've taken stock, you may try to shift your family's habits, as we have, limiting use by time, place, occasion, content, priority, and/or specific activity or type of media use. I'll give you workable solutions to choose from, based on the real-world decisions that other families have made and stuck to, with good results, and starting at any age.

What may be even more challenging is the next step: discovering and unleashing the joy of screen time with your kids. Yes, I said *joy*. Particularly when shared, screen time can have meaningful benefits: creative, emotional, and cognitive. For modern, far-flung families, or the many dealing with divorce or other separations, screens can weave family bonds more tightly. With a little attention, you can choose habits of social media and Internet use that help you be the parent you want to be. Part of what this book is about is how to manage research and weigh evidence and advice when making decisions, not just about screen time but about most things. It's important, now more than ever before, to be curious and critical about your sources of information and where to place trust.

Parents, prospective parents, grandparents, educators, and mentors, this book is for you. Use it as a springboard for discussion and reflection, to discover how you feel and to decide how to approach parenting in the digital age.

✧ ✧ ✧

Given what we do know, and how much we still don't know, what is the best analogy for how to understand the impact of screens on children?

On the one hand, some would have you believe that screens for kids are like smoking: There is no safe level of exposure. Every little bit could hurt. One father confessed to me that he has that feeling that every minute his toddler is engrossed in a screen is adding to his "bad-dad debt." I think a lot of parents share this feeling, especially since the one doctor's recommendation that has made its way into public consciousness says "no screens before age two."

The second scenario is that screens are like food. Yes, there are endemic problems that come with excess. Yes, there is junk that should play a small part in anyone's life. But it's overkill to imagine that any single bite, or byte, is toxic. Unless, of course, you are part of a sensitive minority with a severe allergy—and I think equivalent populations may exist, particularly when it comes to certain media products like violent content or video games. At the same time, we can recognize that food is necessary, and the right foods can be powerfully pleasurable, healing, and life-enhancing. By being thoughtful about what behaviors you model and how you introduce foods to your kids, and by sharing the creation and consumption of great meals with them, you can lay the groundwork for joyful lifelong habits. And the same is true for media.

Research can help us draw better-quality distinctions. Activists can push for better labels. Public education efforts and regulations can all make a difference. Slowly, habits can change, at least among those with the privilege to make better choices. But it won't be easy—because our deep evolutionary systems are challenging our very will to choose, because structural inequalities in our society make it difficult for many people to change.

I ran this comparison by Dr. David Hill, an amiable man who favors bow ties. He is responsible for communicating the American Academy of Pediatrics' various positions to the media. He said, "With diet, harm reduction measures seem to be turning the tide of the obesity epidemic. With tobacco, on the other hand, there really is no safe level of exposure at any age. My personal opinion is that the diet analogy will end up being more apt."

We don't yet have a set of solidly evidence-based recommendations that say, "Healthy screen time looks like this." But I have come up with my own take on food writer Michael Pollan's famous maxim: "Enjoy screens. Not too much. Mostly with others."

2

THE (SOMETIMES) SCARY
SCIENCE OF SCREENS

THE LAST MAJOR PIECE OF FEDERALLY FUNDED RESEARCH ON CHILDREN AND media in the United States was titled "Television and Behavior." It was published by the National Institutes of Mental Health. In 1982. Needless to say, quite a few new questions have presented themselves since then. The world of research on kids and touchscreens especially, and on the social impact of new media more generally, is young, hotly contested, and full of drama. Enduring a tantrum-prone toddlerhood, if you will.

It's not just we parents who are confused. The experts are talking past each other. And they disagree, often dramatically. "The real challenge is finding what constitutes healthy screen use and a healthy amount of it," says Dimitri Christakis. (I first met Christakis and many of the other researchers named in this chapter at a 2015 convening at UC Irvine organized by Children and Screens: The Institute for Digital Media and Child Development. Children and Screens is working to create a new, interdisciplinary research agenda on these topics.)

Christakis, affable with graying temples and glasses, is a professor of pediatrics at the University of Washington and the director of the Center for Child Health, Behavior and Development at Children's

Hospital in Seattle. He's also an author of many foundational studies about the impact of electronic media on young children. And he's the co-author of the one rule most people are familiar with about kids and screens: the American Academy of Pediatrics' 1999 recommendation to avoid television viewing under age two. In 2016 that recommendation was officially revised—more on which later.

If media is something like food, it makes sense to hear what the doctors have to say about its effects on body and mind. As I quickly learned after plunging in, the bulk of the existing scientific literature on children and media really reads like a list of the top anxieties that keep any parent up at night: obesity, low-quality sleep, aggression, attention disorders. Part of this barrage of anxiety reflects a systemic bias across scientific disciplines and subjects, first in how experiments are designed and conducted, and then in what research is published and subsequently covered in the media.

Dan Romer is the director of the Adolescent Communication Institute at the Annenberg Public Policy Center at the University of Pennsylvania. "Any time there's a new technology, . . . it raises concerns," he tells me. "A lot of the research, in order to get published, they focus on the harms." This observation applies to all the areas we'll discuss in this chapter and the next one: experiments that show correlations between screens and negative effects receive more attention than experiments that show nothing conclusive, and those that show benefits are less likely to be conceived or conducted in the first place.

"We can make preliminary recommendations, but it's based on such limited evidence," says Melina Uncapher, a young, rising-star neuroscientist at the University of California at San Francisco. Glamorous in cat-eye glasses, she is involved in setting a national research agenda around kids and screens.

And here's the rub. To a large extent, Uncapher tells me, the ability of science to discover the truth about kids and screens will continue to be hobbled in the future. Not just because of a lack of funding or industry opposition, but because of the very nature of the question.

The gold standard for scientific evidence is the randomized controlled trial, in which researchers divide subjects randomly into two groups. One group gets the treatment (a pill, or an exercise, or whatever) and the other gets some kind of placebo, or nothing. In this way researchers can account for unobserved differences between groups.

But with human subjects, randomized tests aren't always allowed. You can't randomly assign pregnant women to use crack cocaine just to find out what effect it has. And, it turns out, you can't randomly assign babies to watch television.

"If the initial studies show a relationship between x and y that is negative—say, heavy media multitaskers seem to be more distractible—that suggests a negative relationship that could be causal," says Uncapher. "And no ethics board in the country would allow you to put kids in a condition that may cause negative cognitive changes."

Children are vulnerable. Screens may very well be harmful. So you can't do a controlled study in which you subject children to more screens. As a result, "most of the research out there is all correlational. We can't really say a lot about the causality."

If you can't do an intervention study where you give kids more TV to watch, what about a study where you ask families to limit TV?

Christakis has tried this. It didn't work. "In the past we've done media reduction studies," he says. "They're painful because you spend an enormous amount of effort and you achieve an effect size of around twenty minutes a day. Say from four and a half hours to four hours, ten minutes." In short, it was too hard to get many families to alter their lifestyles for science. As a researcher, he says, this is profoundly frustrating. "It's like, what the hell have I really accomplished?"

Okay. So what about natural experiments? There are groups within our society that limit screens: the Amish, for example. Orthodox Jews, at least one day a week. Other religious groups, like evangelical Christians, might eschew mainstream commercial media but have developed their own competing electronic media (*VeggieTales*, anyone?). Families at Waldorf schools and some homeschoolers strive to limit screens. These groups have something else in common: they are out of the mainstream in many ways—culturally, politically, economically—all of which makes it difficult to generalize any effects of being screen-free from that population to the typical kid.

Starting with infants, we're allowing engagement with screens to become the single identifiable activity that takes precedence above all others. What's happening all over the world is a giant experiment. And there is essentially no control group.

Taking that into account as much as we can, this chapter reviews the best-established scientific findings, and the biggest remaining questions, in what's called "media effects research."

There's also a laundry list of emerging mental, social, developmental, behavioral, and emotional issues that have less evidence but still have researchers keeping an eye out for links to growing screen use. That's in chapter 3.

Immediately afterward in chapter 4, we'll look at the positive evidence about how young people are adapting resiliently to the ubiquity of digital technology, and how technology can help children overcome deficits, learn, create, and connect with others. So—it gets better.

THE BOOB TUBE

The bulk of evidence we have about kids and screens, dating back decades, concerns television. In a way that's all right, because children still do more essentially passive video watching than any kind of interaction with screens. But researchers suspect that interactive media, such as games, apps, and social media, is very different from TV. They just disagree about whether it's generally more harmful or more benign—or whether it's even useful to generalize. Certainly from the average person's perspective, the smartphone and tablet era feels different from what came before. It's all-consuming and all-encompassing. We are within inches of screens at every waking moment.

On the one hand, the screens are more individual and less communal than the electronic family hearth that was television. On the other, they can be tools for communication and creation, not only portals for passive absorption. Even when our kids are supposedly doing the same thing we used to, say, watching *Sesame Street,* they're watching very differently: choosing clips with their favorite characters on YouTube, skipping commercials, streaming episode after episode (after episode) on demand.

While we're on the topic of research difficulties: parental education, parental income, and parental self-efficacy (the belief and confidence that you are an effective parent) are all correlated with less screen time for kids. If richer, more educated, more confident parents are more likely to have the wherewithal to limit screen time, it follows that less screen time is going to be correlated with more positive outcomes for kids regardless of the direct impact of the media itself. Researchers can attempt to control for this confounding factor, but they can't always succeed perfectly, especially when ethics in many cases prevent randomly assigning children to imbibe different amounts of media. This also means that if we are concerned on a societal level with excessive screen time, mitigating it probably involves more social support for low-income families, particularly those headed by single working mothers.

TIME

The first fundamental shock in the literature is about time.

About as soon as our babies start discovering their own toes, screens are part of their world. My younger daughter smiled at her grandparents over Google Hangouts at just eight weeks old.

Television has been with us for a long time, of course. And some researchers suggest that overall viewing hours have been stable for the past fifty years. But having constant access to screens while out of the home is a new phenomenon. Most of the upward trend in screen exposure has occurred not gradually, over the last forty years, but suddenly, over the last fifteen.

A 2011 survey covered nine thousand preschoolers. On average, these children, between ages three and five, spent 4.1 hours in the company of screens daily. "Preschoolers' cumulative screen time exceeds recommendations and most previous estimates," the report observed, quite an understatement. And that's by parents' and caregivers' own reports; presumably they'd often be motivated to understate the total.

These are children who sleep, usually, twelve hours a day. They may not see working parents for more than two hours on a weekday.

I asked Yalda T. Uhls, a child psychologist and author of *Media Moms & Digital Dads: A Fact-Not-Fear Approach to Parenting in the Digital Age,* to put that figure into context. "There are media-light families that barely use it at all," she says. "But at the same time there's a lot of different kinds of families. A lot of people come home and that's what they do. They turn on the TV and leave it on. . . . The vast majority of America is in the middle and that middle number is four to five hours a day."

A 2003 study found that two out of three children age six and under live in homes where the TV is left on at least half the waking hours, even without viewers present. One-third live in homes where the TV is on "most" or "almost all" of the time—children in this group appeared to read less than other children and to be slower to learn to read.

Turning on the television is the simplest and easiest way to keep a young child occupied and thus physically safe with minimal intervention. So who's going to leave the TV on? When are we going to leave it on?

- People with multiple children to look after.
- People who can't afford lots of toys or books.
- People who are tired, infirm, or busy, or who need to do work or housework.
- People who are not trained for, are not being paid for, or do not have any choice about spending time with a child.

I can afford to order my sitter not to turn on the TV because I'm paying her a decent hourly wage to ferry my kids to playdates, paint pictures, bake cupcakes, read stories. But if I were instead asking my neighbor to pinch-hit and watch them as a favor? You bet that TV goes on.

Viewing goes down a tiny bit when children enter school and have less free time, but by the end of elementary school it's joined by increasing levels of smartphone use, texting, music, video gaming, video messaging, and more, plus schoolwork done with a computer, often all at the same time. The most widely cited national census of children and teens' media use, last conducted by the nonprofit Common Sense Media in 2016, found that 94 percent of teens and tweens were using at least some screen media daily. Good old TV was still the leader: three out of four teens watch, and those who do watch more than two hours a day.

DOSE MAKES THE POISON?

So, we know that kids are spending a lot of time with media. But we don't know what a healthy limit is, or how much is dangerous.

Christakis argues that because kids are spending so much time with screens, it makes sense to think of media risks in two categories: direct effects of exposure, and "displacement effects," whereby spending more time with screens means spending less time with something else. "Even if it's healthy or harmless it could be bad at the extreme if it displaces other important activities," he told me. "That's true for adults, and it's especially true for young children who are vulnerable to the addictive properties of screens." (We'll deal with the addiction issue a little later on.)

"This is a gap in the research," says Victor Strasburger, another co-author of the original AAP recommendation. A bit more blustery than Christakis, he's a professor emeritus at the University of New Mexico School of Medicine and another major voice in the field. "We have no good idea about what the media diet should be if you include computer time, smartphones, iPads, that sort of thing. Maybe it's four or five hours a day. Maybe computer time for homework shouldn't count, or does count. We simply don't know."

BIFF! BANG! POW!

So our kids are spending more time with screens than any other single activity, and that's certainly true of adults as well. Two more big questions present themselves: Why? So what?

As for the why, Christakis and others who study these questions posit that TV screens and touchscreens tend to be habit-forming for very different reasons.

When it comes to TV the phenomenon is pretty simple. Humans have something called an *orienting reflex*. When we see a novel sight or hear a new sound, we turn our heads and look to see what's going on. The evolutionary reason for this is pretty plain: to alert us to danger or potential rewards in our environment.

Younger humans are less able to inhibit this reflex. Their responses to a stimulus in general are more involuntary. They are more easily riveted. If you've ever locked eyes with an infant, you know what I'm talking about. But their attention spans are short, and television offers loops of endless novelty within a repetitive framework.

When the Children's Television Workshop was creating *Sesame Street* in the 1960s, they did tests to see what would best hold children's attention. The answer: quick cuts. Children's television today has editing cuts, pans, or zooms an average of every one to two seconds. So for TV, what compels the youngest viewers is basically wondering, "Where did that thing go?"

By the time children hit age two or so, they can recognize Dory the fish on a screen and imitate her actions in the real world. They start watching television the way the rest of us do, only more so—following characters and stories, watching their favorites over and over. Young children in general are obsessed by repetition. They crave order and routine. It helps them learn new words and concepts and provides touchstones of predictability within a chaotic and sometimes scary world. Electronic media, whether records, reruns, or replays, satisfies this need for repetition like nothing else.

Preschoolers immerse themselves in pop culture with an enthusiasm that outgeeks any otaku cosplay anime freak. Some media researchers posit that kids have "parasocial" relationships with characters, seeing them as *superpeers*—charismatic and highly influential, whether they are solving problems with a hug or hitting their sisters.

As child psychologist Bruno Bettelheim described in his groundbreaking 1976 work on fairy tales, *The Uses of Enchantment,* young children's emerging psyches have hard work to do, and stories are crucial. They're in those wonderful and terrifying phases of imagination and identity formation. They're forming, naming, and grappling with strong emotions, developing social awareness, and spinning fantasies of power and control in a world where they remain small and weak. Superheroes, princesses, and talking animals become fodder for their dreams and nightmares. But some worry that the surround-sense input of filmed stories, unlike the stories our great-grandparents spun around the fire, overwhelms the workings of the inward eye of imagination.

With active screens, like games and apps, Christakis believes, the appeal is one step more complex. Children are doing an action and getting a result. It's not too different from throwing a toy off the high chair and having someone pick it up, except it's faster, more regular, more relentless. The dopamine pathway in the brain is activated, dopamine being the neurotransmitter associated with seeking rewards.

Finally, for tweens and teens, electronic media is a lifeline to the experiences they crave most: thrills, a space to explore independently, and 24/7 access to peers.

So that's the *why* of media's appeal, more or less. The *so what* is more complicated. "Studying media is like studying the air we breathe," notes Strasburger. "The media are ubiquitous and it's very difficult to sort out their exact influence."

THE MOUSE IN THE CASINO

Christakis urges us to consider the "profound implications" of exposing children to the intense stimulation of digital media during the months and years when their brains are forming a peak density of connections and developing core functions such as attention and memory. "Is it possible to overstimulate or inappropriately stimulate the developing brain?" he asks rhetorically. He and other researchers suspect that it is, but they don't know.

Early childhood is when the brain is developing most rapidly. If there are significant brain changes in response to screen media, you'd be likely to see the most powerful impact in response to exposure before age five. Between birth and age two, synapses, the connections between neurons, go through a process of "blooming and pruning." To oversimplify dramatically, we form an overgrowth of connections based on our earliest experiences and then start a process of cutting back, refining, and reinforcing that continues into our teens and beyond.

And children are never too young for media to be truly "over their heads." In his talks, Christakis highlights experiments in which classical music is played for newborns, who show distinct patterns of breathing in response to the calming phrases of Mozart or the frenetic strains of Stravinsky—at one day old.

To get a better picture of what extreme screen stimulation might do to developing brains, Christakis has forced mice to spend their entire childhoods watching mouse TV. For six hours a day, forty-two days straight, starting at ten days of life, they were blasted with endless chirping music and flashing colored lights, an environment looking and sounding much like a Vegas casino.

After a merciful ten-day break, the mice were then given what's called the *open field test*.

If you put ordinary mice in a wide-open space, they'll make their way cautiously around the perimeter, sniffing and pausing to listen and watch, with only occasional, brief forays into the center, where they are far more vulnerable to predators.

The casino-reared mice, by contrast, went wild. They hyperactively zigzagged across the floor, heedless of risk. Their paths across the space looked like a crazy scribble. This indicates a difficulty inhibiting reflexes, what some would call a problem with executive functioning.

What does this mean? It's suggestive, little more. So are preliminary brain studies in humans, like one showing a decline in "white matter," or loss of density in brain connections, from young people who were habitual heavy media multitaskers.

PEANUTS

Okay. From the point of view of a mom who does not want to freak out: don't freak out. Yes, kids spend a lot of time with screens. Yes, they find media powerfully appealing. Yes, this exposure, like every other experience they have, is influencing their developing brains.

What we really want to know is, what does the research say about the possible effects on the average kid, and the worst-case scenarios? And what warning signs should you look for to figure out if your kid is averagely resilient or particularly sensitive?

Sonia Livingstone, who researches these topics at the London School of Economics' Department of Media and Communications, draws an important distinction between risks and harms.

To say that there is a known *risk* of severe injury for a child not to use a seat belt doesn't mean that physical *harms* result from each and every car trip taken without a seat belt. That risk accumulates for every trip, yet there still may be no harm done.

Other risks vary by individual and can be observed. There is a serious risk of giving peanuts to a child whose allergy status is not known, but if a child eats them once and suffers no harm, the risk becomes much, much smaller.

Finally, risk assessment, technically, is a matter of combining the likelihood of any particular event with the severity of that event and weighing those potential costs against the benefits of a course of action.

With that taxonomy in mind, the best-established negative relationships in the scientific literature of media effects are sleep, obesity, aggression (violent media), attention disorders, cognition generally, and school performance in particular. In the next chapter, we're also going to discuss some less established but potentially grave risks: serious psychiatric disorders such as addiction; interaction with autism spectrum disorders; and narcissism, anxiety, and other emotional difficulties.

And let's keep these risks in perspective. Having your kid inside watching TV and playing video games, even for eight, ten, twelve hours a day, is safer *for most kids and in most cases* than having them play unsupervised in traffic; it's safer than having them inhale second-hand smoke or ride in a car with no seat belt.

Researchers also suspect that individual differences play a huge role in determining who will succumb to the worst negative media effects. In other words, for lots of kids, a peanut is just a peanut.

The best-established positive relationships are school readiness, general cognitive performance, improvements in autism and attention disorders and other learning disabilities, and other positive social and emotional outcomes. None of these occurs in relation to media use in general, but rather with exposure to certain kinds of media.

These lists suggest that some of the same problems caused by digital media in some experiments are solved by different, purpose-designed digital media in other experiments. All of these findings, reassuring and scary, converge on one message: children most definitely are learning from and being shaped by media. "This isn't rocket science," says Strasburger. "Children are like little sponges. They learn from the media." That means it may matter very much, not only how much time our kids spend hooked in, but what they consume and how. "There has really been nothing since the 1982 NIMH report," Strasburger says. "Which I think is scandalous. It is difficult to believe that when kids spend seven to eleven hours a day with a variety of different media, we're not looking much more closely at the impact of that time spent and how to maximize the prosocial, and minimize the negative aspects."

SLEEP

The most striking correlation in the research on kids and media use is the relationship between screens and a basic life necessity and common parental battleground: sleep. Lauren Hale of State University of New York at Stonybrook has been researching this interaction for over a decade. As she sums up the evidence, "As kids and adults watch or use screens, with light shining in their eyes and close to their face, bedtime gets delayed, it takes longer to fall asleep, sleep quality is reduced, and total sleep time is decreased."

One representative survey of 2,048 fourth- and seventh-grade students showed that those with electronic devices in their bedrooms slept an average of 20.6 minutes less per night than those without. Similar research in adults corroborates the idea that the nearer your smartphone is to your bedside at night, the less and worse sleep you're going to get.

"Sleep is one of the most fundamental things for learning," pediatrician Dr. Jenny Radesky told me. It particularly affects the consolidation of memories, which is especially important for kids. "You need to put the Jell-O in the fridge overnight and let it set."

Strengthening the case for the effect of screens on sleep, researchers have a good handle on the precise brain mechanisms involved. There are two. One is that exposure to light, especially blue-spectrum screen light, which mimics daylight, inhibits the production of melatonin, a hormone made by a gland in your brain. (That's the pineal gland, located directly between your eyes, in case you like a little symbolism with your science.) The closer the screen is to your eyes, the more light gets in.

Being exposed to this light for hours after sunset, in turn, throws off circadian rhythms, the body's clock, making it harder to fall asleep at an appropriate time. Gazing at your phone or laptop when waking up in the middle of the night, which is much more likely to happen when it's on your nightstand, is even worse in terms of promoting wakefulness.

The second sleep-depriving mechanism that comes along with screens is overproduction of cortisol, the stress hormone. Here, the focus is not simply on the screen itself but on the exposure it offers to emotionally arousing or exciting experiences: a snarky Facebook comment, an exciting car chase. Cortisol is also produced by the body in response to fatigue, creating a rebound effect where we go from tired to wired. If you've ever seen a kid bounding around the room way past his or her bedtime, that's cortisol.

"What do you think of when you think of a napless child?" Rebecca Spencer at the University of Massachusetts, Amherst asks me. "They're either grumpy or giddy." She's been conducting a five-year study of an economically diverse group of six hundred children, beginning when they were in preschool, to try to discover correlations between their sleep patterns early on and their school performance later. She quickly discovered screen time as a factor. Over 65 percent of the children in Spencer's study have a TV in their bedroom. And while some preschool classrooms keep naptime sacred, others allow children who aren't sleeping to play on a tablet instead. Sleep that's lost in early years can't necessarily be made up later, Spencer says. "It's the cumulative loss that can affect how these kids perform," says Spencer. "We need to apply this science to kids more frequently than we do."

Poor-quality sleep is connected, by reams of research, to a cascade of physical, emotional, and mental issues—depression, anxiety, obesity, poor school performance, attention deficit, irritability and short fuse, and even lowered immunity. Except for that last one, it's more or less the exact same bad-news checklist that you see with screens. So if poor sleep correlates with all these negative outcomes, and screen time is correlated with poorer sleep, many of the negatives that researchers connect to screen use may be simply and neatly attributed to a lack of sleep.

This is why sleep researchers like Hale sometimes feel like they're screaming in a mattress-padded cell. "I do feel like it's overlooked," says Hale. "There is part of me that is like, wait a minute, somebody needs to be defending sleep. It's one of the main pathways through which we're seeing outcomes in children change." These results also suggest that banning screens for at least an hour before bedtime, and keeping them out of the bedroom altogether, may be the most important and effective screen rules to enforce in any house, whether you have children or not.

While we're on the topic of eyes, myopia or nearsightedness has increased by two thirds in the US since the 1970s, and even more in Asia. Scientists aren't sure of the mechanism, or ready to blame screens for it. But spending more time outdoors as a young child has been found in multiple studies to protect against the condition. In a related vein, eye doctors have been raising the alarm about *computer vision syndrome,* or eyestrain caused by staring unblinking at the light of a screen, and they urge children and adults alike to take a twenty-second break from their devices every twenty minutes to stare at least twenty feet away.

OBESITY

After sleep, the second-best-established negative correlation in the research on kids and screens is between screen time—primarily television use—and childhood obesity.

The facts: across populations, more than two hours a day watching TV doubles the risk of obesity in kids. And remember, the average for preschoolers is four hours a day.

This isn't about fat shaming or fat panic. A wide range of body types can be healthy, and fluctuations are normal as children grow. This is about weights that put children at risk of chronic disease and shortened life spans. Obesity rates have doubled in children and quadrupled in adolescents over the past thirty years, and children are getting sicker because of it. Type 1 diabetes, the genetic kind, which used to be known as child-onset diabetes, isn't called that anymore, because so many young children are presenting with type 2 diabetes, which is linked to lifestyle. "If you spend more than two hours a day in front of a screen, there's a significant risk of obesity that carries through from when you're very young into adolescence and adulthood," says Strasburger.

How do screens make kids fat? Unlike with sleep, researchers don't exactly know. Surprisingly, they haven't been able to substantiate the most obvious explanation you might think of, the so-called couch potato hypothesis. That is, there isn't clear evidence that kids who watch more TV spend less total time moving their bodies or playing outside. Coloring with crayons and reading books are sedentary activities, too, as Christakis points out. Though Tom Warshawski, a pediatrician in Canada and founder of the Childhood Obesity Foundation there, told me that the deeply passive state of watching videos actually burns fewer calories than any other waking activity.

The potential explanations for the link between screens and weight, however, are more subtle, complex, and interacting. This turns out to be a common theme when researching media.

One hypothesis is that kids tend to snack more while watching videos. I've heard many a parent of a picky toddler admit to turning on the iPad during mealtimes in order to distract kids while they shovel food into them. It's a quick fix, but there's a danger that you're setting them up for mindless munching.

It's also possible, researchers told me, that children with a genetic tendency to be overweight also somehow have an inborn preference for watching more videos than average. Maybe they have very thrifty metabolisms and tire more easily.

Researchers believe that another significant factor in the screen-body connection is the commercials. "Children eat *while* they watch and they eat *what* they watch," says Dr. Warshawski. "TV was invented as a medium for marketing. And ninety percent of the foods and beverages marketed to kids are unhealthy. They have too much fat, salt, and sugar."

"We can see from food preferences and food requests that messages matter—kids pick up on them, very much," agrees Ellen Wartella, a researcher at Northwestern University who's been on several government-funded committees to make recommendations on the issue of media and obesity. Her policy work has focused on getting the food industry to self-impose restrictions by reformulating its foods and menus, like adding whole grains to Goldfish crackers or fruit to McDonald's Happy Meals. There have also been rules and voluntary protocols saying that popular "superpeer" characters would only be allowed to advertise healthy, or at least healthy-ish foods: SpongeBob SquarePants can sell vitamin-fortified fruit snacks, say, but not Pop-Tarts.

Child obesity rates have leveled off very recently. Some researchers suggest that the supplanting of video by apps or games is partly to credit. The reason is a bit silly: they keep the hands occupied, making mindless eating logistically more difficult. And the ability to skip TV commercials when watching on-demand video may have something to do with it as well.

But Wartella's not ready to declare victory yet. Even as DVRs and video streaming have conquered the candy commercial, junk-food companies are striking back with online and mobile "advergames" like *Oreo Extreme Creme Control* and targeting young teens with viral videos and social media marketing. "They're getting children engaged and interacting," says Wartella. "These are techniques that we have less data on."

Kathryn Montgomery, a communications professor at American University who has long been involved in lobbying for stronger restrictions on advertising to children, points out that advertisers have plenty of data on the effectiveness of various approaches to marketing to kids, but independent researchers do not. "It's just a constant struggle to try to keep the industry, particularly the food industry, accountable," she says. "The messages are cross-platform, pervasive, and coming at children from different angles."

SCARED, SAD, LAZY, CRAZY

Obesity and sleep are the areas where researchers have the most confidence about media effects. In the rest of this chapter I'm going to talk about stuff that every parent worries about and that experts are looking into but are less certain about.

- Attention deficit/hyperactivity disorder (ADHD)
- Lower scores on standardized tests of math and reading

- Worse school performance
- Aggression
- Depression

Does screen time cause these or make them worse? Does the wrong kind of material cause them or make them worse? Study after study says maybe—but if so, only a very little, barely detectable, bit. The relatively small size of associations holds true across most of these complex areas of human behavior. And as always, it's difficult to prove causation.

AGGRESSION

Let's talk violence as an example. When it comes to emotional and mental responses, historically, the most studied set of effects in media is the connection between violent content and aggressive behavior. It's also, no surprise, one of the most contentious topics in the field.

Douglas Gentile at Iowa State is one of the foremost experts on the topic. Self-effacing, in wire-rimmed glasses, he resembles *The Simpsons'* Ned Flanders a bit in manner. "I'm a child psychologist," he cracked when I met him. "I know, I look older."

But he is deadly serious about one thing. "We know a lot about this. We've been studying it for fifty years. The NIH, NSF, AAP, AMA, APA, and several other organizations are all on record saying the evidence is clear that media violence causes aggression."

In science, he points out, that word, *cause*, is a big deal. It's not just that aggressive kids have an inborn preference for violent media. It's not just that aggressive kids come from neglectful homes where no one is policing their media use, and so end up watching slasher films and playing first-person-shooter games. It's not just that aggressive kids have aggressive parents who enjoy violent media and expose their kids to it more often and at younger ages. All of that may, in fact, be true.

No. The reason scientists like Gentile use the word *cause* is in part thanks to Bobo the clown. Bobo was an inflatable doll used in a series of studies beginning in the early 1960s with the work of Albert Bandura, Dorrie Ross, and Sheila Ross. Children who were shown movies of the poor clown being punched or kicked were more likely to beat up on the doll themselves in real life when given the chance, just afterward. So there is pretty good experimental evidence that exposure to media violence produces violent imitative behavior immediately, in addition to a whole bunch of more long-range surveys showing small correlations in large populations and over time.

As with sleep, researchers also have good data on what is going on physiologically when people watch graphic representations of violence combined with quick cuts and loud music. Heart rates and respiration go up, pupils dilate. Brain images reveal signs of a fight-or-flight response. Your senses are enhanced as if you were looking for a threat, and thoughts race. Immediately afterward, impulse control is down; you are less likely to think before reacting to a perceived slight.

But, Gentile says, *cause* doesn't mean quite the same thing in a scientific sense that it does in a legal sense. And this is an important distinction for the public-health battles to limit kids' exposure to media violence. Violent videos and games are at most an environmental factor, like lead in the water. Their influence is relatively small. They can't be blamed for any one violent act. They don't take away people's agency or culpability. Several legal decisions, including by the US Supreme Court, have made that clear.

"Video games didn't make Dylan Klebold and Eric Harris start shooting at Columbine or Adam Lanza in Newtown," sums up Strasburger.

It's also important to point out, as Michael Rich, a Harvard pediatrician with a Hollywood background and the nickname "the Mediatrician," did to me, that aggression isn't even the most common effect of exposure to media violence. "Of the three outcomes that have been consistently measured, increased aggressive thoughts and behaviors are the least prevalent," he said. "The most prevalent is desensitization to the suffering of others." Having gone through the physiological responses to simulated violence, people's bodies and brains then show a muted response to real-life violence. And, Rich says, the second-most-prevalent reaction to media violence, "particularly in younger kids, but across the board," is "fear and anxiety."

That is, for every child who watches *UFC Fight Night* and picks a fight on the playground the next day, there are many more who shrug their shoulders and turn away from that playground fight, and others who will wake up with bad dreams and, Rich says, "the belief that the world is a mean, scary place."

The connection between violent media and violent behavior, fear, and desensitization comes closest to feeding my free-floating anxiety as a parent that even a minute of accidental exposure to the wrong thing is going to have toxic effects.

But there may be some comfort in the indication that this problem doesn't appear to be getting worse. Neither the adoption of mobile technology nor graphics innovations producing increasingly immersive and realistic first-person-shooter games have had any measurable impact on trends in murder, suicide, or antisocial behavior.

Mass shootings are a deplorable social phenomenon. The perpetrators, like Klebold, Harris, and Lanza, tend to be young men, a demographic that also enjoys violent video games. But that doesn't change the fact that overall murder rates are at historic lows. There is zero evidence that the net level of flesh-and-blood violence has increased in any way over the past two decades. And when you look cross-culturally, there are many countries where children consume essentially the same media diet as ours, yet those countries have much lower rates of violence than ours.

If you want to translate the experimental evidence on violence into policy, then, you'd have to argue that less exposure to media violence among a sensitive subset of kids would lead to lower levels of aggression and perhaps of alienation in society more generally. That's a hard idea to target or enforce.

Media violence researchers, like obesity researchers, are saying things that large, deep-pocketed industries decidedly do not want to hear. Gentile was careful to make sure I understand that he and his fellow researchers don't use terms like *ban*. They are staunch supporters of the First Amendment, he says. Strasburger, too, mentioned several times that he is a huge supporter of the arts, being a published novelist himself.

What researchers are looking for is not restrictions, necessarily, but a set of ratings based on the best possible evidence, so parents can make better decisions to protect their kids, especially the sensitive ones. But we probably won't get that.

The television, movie, and video game industries are basically self-policing. The Classification & Ratings Administration rates movies, the TV Parental Guidelines system produces television ratings, and the Entertainment Software Rating Board (ESRB) rates video games and apps, with some oversight from the Federal Trade Commission. All these systems are a little bit different.

"Do you know what the eleven different symbols in the TV Parental Guidelines system mean?" Gentile asks me. I admit sheepishly that I barely even know what that is. "Why don't you understand it? Because it's not particularly easy to understand. Why would it be created that way?"

All the ratings systems are indeed fairly complex. Moreover, they are explicitly designed to satisfy consumer and industry interests rather than those of scientists. Few media researchers are worried about kids' exposure to foul language, brief nudity, or fart noises ("comic mischief"), for example. But the ESRB game ratings specify all of these, which obscures the presence of real concerns.

"Parents have the responsibility to monitor the games, their content, and time their children spend with them," says Gentile. "In order for parents to be able to do this, the industry has a responsibility to be honest about the effects, to maintain a reliable and valid rating system, and to educate people why it matters that parents use it. And the game manufacturers have a responsibility to clearly label the content of the games and to advertise them appropriately."

Patricia Vance is the president of the Entertainment Software Ratings Board. It took me several months to get an interview with her. When I did, Vance maintained that the organization doesn't take a position on whether media actually poses risks to kids. "The evidence is so diffuse," she said. "It's been disputed for years. To take a position one way or the other would be not particularly wise on our part. We're about meeting consumer expectations."

At the same meeting, her PR person also presented me with a thick folder of industry-sponsored communication that calls linking games and violence "a fallacy." "We just want to make sure you have both sides of the story," said Vance.

DANDELIONS VS. ORCHIDS

Making solid decisions to keep kids safe, given such a miasma of contradictory evidence, is tough even for experts and policy makers, let alone us poor parents.

Patti Valkenburg, a widely respected media effects researcher at the University of Amsterdam, has a theory to explain the generally small size of media effects. It comes from the field of developmental psychology and is known as *differential susceptibility.* Or, dandelions versus orchids.

The idea is that most children are dandelions. They are hardy, resilient. They can thrive in a wide range of settings. A few children, however, are orchids. They're highly sensitive to severe consequences if their environment is less than optimal. They also have a greater-than-normal sensitivity to excellent nurturing. "In my opinion, the most plausible cause for the small correlations that we repeatedly find in large samples is that media effects are conditional," Valkenburg said. "They do not equally hold for all children."

With that caveat in mind, the next chapter will talk about the less well-established effects of media on some of our more delicate, orchid children.

3   EMERGING EVIDENCE

AS EXPLORED IN THE LAST CHAPTER, IMPAIRED SLEEP, OBESITY, AND AGGRES-sion currently qualify as the best-established relationships in media effects research. This means that even if you have a typically developing, fairly resilient, dandelion kid, you might want to be cautious about devices in the bedroom, snacking while watching, and age-appropriate content choices. Now let's move to the category of low probability, high risk. This chapter covers emerging areas of concern about young people and media, where the evidence is newer and many questions remain regarding addiction, severe brain and behavioral disorders, autism spectrum disorder, and less well-defined but worrisome social and psychological issues.

ADDICTION

At three in the morning, there was a knock at the door of Noelle's house in Orange County. Two burly ex–police officers had come to escort her fifteen-year-old son, Griffin, to the first wilderness-based treatment program for technology addiction in the United States.

"I went and woke him up and shared with him that his dad and I had done all we could, and we made a decision that he needed to go get some help," she says. "He's a very nice, sweet young man. He was cooperative. At that point he had resigned to the fact that yes, I have a problem. I'm going. He didn't fight it at all."

Noelle had known for a while that something was awry with her son. Griffin, always quiet, had become increasingly withdrawn and introverted. He had switched schools. He was struggling with depression and anxiety. He wasn't sleeping well.

But she didn't immediately finger his iPhone use or video gaming as the culprit. And, she says, neither did their family therapist. "I would bring it up to the therapist that we might have some addiction going on. But he didn't go, oh, red flag. It's so hard even to this day to find a therapist that recognizes [media addiction] or that knows a whole lot about it."

"I started playing [video games] when I was around 9 years old," Griffin told me via email, which he chose over a phone interview. "I played because I found it fun, but after a while I played mostly because I preferred it over socializing and confronting my problems."

Noelle has been divorced twice. The first time was when Griffin, her middle child, was three years old. He has an older sister and a younger brother. Both she and Griffin's dad are small-business owners—he's a car wholesaler and she owns a spa that specializes in eyelash extensions. Both households were busy.

Griffin would come home from school, to either Noelle's house or his father's, and play video games, usually first-person-shooter games, for hour upon hour. If it wasn't the Xbox, it was Netflix on his laptop. Then he got his own iPhone, and it was games and Netflix streaming, all day long, everywhere. "He was even hooked on watching Netflix on his phone if we'd be out," she says. "He'd say, Mom, I'm really into this series." Over time, she got suspicious, then convinced, that screens were a big part of her son's problem. But she didn't know what to do about it.

"My first two years of high school were the worst with my technology addiction because I had so many problems and didn't do anything about them," Griffin says. "I just sat inside and played on my computer whenever I could. So I guess I liked how all my problems were gone for the short period of time and I could feel happy without having to worry about anything."

Noelle found her way to help by an unlikely path. The man she was dating at the time was an actor working as a voiceover artist for video games. He observed Noelle's younger son playing the same games he was working on, some of them very violent.

"He'd witness my eleven-year-old playing, and he was shocked at the difference in his behavior afterward. He hadn't seen the end result of what he was working on. And he was like, I'm not [working on games] anymore. So he made an announcement on Facebook that he wasn't going to do it anymore, and these were the reasons why."

The Facebook post spread. A woman involved in the nascent Internet addiction treatment community reached out and thanked him for his bravery. She also put the family in touch with Jason Calder, who used to run the Unplugged program in Utah.

"I was like, oh my God, this is exactly what Griff needs," says Noelle. "We were feeling really lost in terms of treatment. We didn't realize there was one specifically for Internet addiction."

Calder, who sports a goatee and a sincere, gentle manner, got on the path toward youth counseling as a former troubled teen himself. "My second time in juvenile court the judge ordered me to go to counseling. I just happened to luck out and get matched up with a counselor who helped me see my value, my potential, my worth." Calder now directs a residential treatment center; his previous organization, Outback Expeditions, runs wilderness programs for teens with depression, anxiety, and drug abuse and alcohol problems. He came to the organization in 2014 and started a program aimed at teens with "problematic levels of digital media use."

Calder got interested in this area through his work with youth on the autism spectrum. Based on what he's seen as a clinician, he believes that "for various reasons individuals on the spectrum are more prone" to problems with screens.

He'd see teens, overwhelmingly boys, so wrapped up in video games that in-person relationships were gradually "pruned away." They'd stop hanging out with friends, stop talking to their families, stop coming downstairs for dinner, even stop going to school.

By the time families find the Unplugged program, their children have typically transformed into near-total recluses with terrible personal hygiene and diets of junk food. Barely sleeping, never exercising, they are pale and either undernourished or overweight or both, says Calder. "We see students who have thirty Mountain Dew bottles in their room filled with urine because they don't take the time to go to the restroom."

When Griffin got to Utah, the first order of business was a full medical checkup. The program officials needed to make sure he could manage hiking in the high desert while carrying his essentials in a pack. He turned over his iPhone to be put in a lockbox and was driven out into the country, about forty-five miles from the nearest electrical outlet. He stayed out there for six weeks.

It was a harsh adjustment. Griffin said one of the worst parts was switching from a junk-food-and-soda diet to drinking plain water and eating dinners of beans and couscous that the teens carried and cooked themselves. Outback participants dig their own latrines, build frames for their backpacks out of juniper branches they gather on the trail, and learn how to start a fire with sticks and friction, a method known as bow drilling. He'd never even been camping before.

On the plus side, he said, were the people. "They were so nice and caring, not just the adults, but the kids as well. I felt like I fit in so well and it was amazing."

Four weeks into the program, his mother flew out to visit him. They sat down with a therapist. "It was the most productive therapy session to date," she says. Griffin was open and focused. Back at home, she'd had trouble getting him to look up from the screens long enough to say where he wanted to go for dinner; now he was able to be present for tough conversations. "He was just taken away from everything."

When she came back to get him for good, she compares the feeling to bringing her first child home from the hospital as a newborn. "It felt very vulnerable, very scary."

A few months later, though, she said progress had been slow. "It's gonna take much longer than eight weeks to solve or even stabilize these conditions," Calder says. "In about eighty percent of cases we recommend additional inpatient treatment," such as a specialized boarding school. But that seemed unaffordable and extreme to Noelle.

She hasn't turned her house into a monastery. Her younger son still plays Xbox, though she says she's cut the hours way back and often takes it away entirely by locking the game system in the car overnight. Griffin's souped-up video game setup is gone, but he still has a regular laptop, still watches streaming shows, still has an iPhone. The only new rule is no video games. "His therapist suggested getting him a flip phone," with fewer features and no Internet access, "but I feel for him with his peers," she says. "I wouldn't want to walk around with the flip phone." Griffin says he uses the phone to "keep in touch with friends and plan things" and his laptop "for school, and for Netflix when I have nothing to do."

Noelle is very aware of what people's reactions are likely to be to her family's story. At first she was wary of granting me an interview. "It's easy to pass judgment and say, where's the parent?" she tells me. "But it's the reality today—you're single, working, busy with other kids. We all live in this really busy society. And this seems so benign. It's in your home. You say, okay, we'll let them play. Hours go by and the kid is sitting there. It's so easy to not even notice."

Does the riveting quality of screen media make them addictive in a clinical sense? In the television age, few worried much about this. There were outlier voices, like Jerry Mander's 1978 cult bestseller *Four Arguments for the Elimination of Television,* which called TV "an invasion of the mind, which altered behavior, altered people." But in general, in our broader culture, people don't seem to take the prospect of tube addiction too seriously. "Binge-watching" is a national pastime, not the sign of a serious problem.

We already have a word for someone who watches television alone, even in the daytime, for hours on end, to the neglect of job, school, family, friends. That word is *depressed.*

But with the growth of video games over the last twenty years, and the near-ubiquitous access to the Internet available over smartphones and tablets just in the last decade, the scientific consensus is changing. The word *addiction* is coming up more often, particularly with regard to children and youth.

Doug Gentile, the child psychologist, told me, "I came to this issue out of a place of deep skepticism: addicted to video games? That can't be right." But, he said, "I've been forced by data to accept that it's a problem. Addiction to video games and Internet use, defined as 'serious dysfunction in multiple aspects of your life that achieves clinical significance,' does seem to exist."

According to polls, nine out of ten American children under age eighteen play video games. And of those who do, Gentile says, about 8 percent meet enough categories on an addiction checklist to suggest that up to 3 million kids in the United States may be affected to some extent.

These are the types of questions clinicians ask to determine whether someone has a problem with Internet and video game use:

- How often do you find that you stay online longer than you intended?
- How often do others in your life complain to you about the amount of time you spend online?
- How often do your grades or schoolwork suffer because of the amount of time you spend online?
- How often do you snap, yell, or act annoyed if someone bothers you while you are online?
- How often do you lose sleep due to Internet use?

The clinical term is "problematic *or risky* Internet use," of video games, smartphone applications like social media or texting, or the Internet in general. These symptoms are associated with other conditions such as being on the autism spectrum, attention disorders like ADHD, depression, and anxiety, particularly social anxiety. And they're more common in boys than girls.

In the United States, professionals are currently debating whether digital media overuse should best be considered and treated as a stand-alone mental disorder or a manifestation of something else, like depression, anxiety, autism spectrum disorder (ASD), or obsessive-compulsive disorder (OCD).

That debate has money attached. If digital addiction gets listed as a standalone disorder in the *Diagnostic and Statistical Manual of Mental Disorders* (DSM), the bible of the psychiatric profession, it has a higher potential of being covered as a diagnosis, and treatment paid for by medical insurers. It may also lead to a legal requirement of special accommodations for students in school, which is increasingly relevant as more schools adopt laptops for all students.

Awareness of the issue is much higher in East Asia. In Japan, China, and South Korea there are treatment centers, and digital addiction is recognized as a public health problem. Taiwan has even gone so far as to legally prohibit screens for children under age two.

For mothers like Noelle the issue was clear. She saw her son's technology use as a specific problem that needed to be handled directly. "I do see this as something very real," she says. "I know there's a lot of controversy right now, but my experience is, it is real."

THE NIGHTMARE SCENARIO

Victoria Dunckley is a child psychiatrist in Los Angeles and the most extreme anti-screen scientist I've personally come across. Her 2015 book *Reset Your Child's Brain* argues that screen exposure is inherently toxic for kids. (The 2016 book *Glow Kids,* by psychologist Nicholas Kardaras, makes similar arguments, focusing on the dangers of addiction.)

For the very reasons that AAP member Dimitri Christakis says interactive media may be less harmful than passive TV—that they engage children and produce a response—Dunckley and Kardaras argue that interactive media may be more dangerous, at least to a vulnerable few.

This belief is not based on experimental evidence but on clinical experience. Dunckley prescribes her children and teen patients a four-week program of screen abstinence she calls a *digital detox.* She advises it for a dizzying variety of severe mental, neurological, and emotional problems: post-traumatic stress disorder (PTSD), autism, ADHD, obsessive-compulsive disorder, ticcing and Tourette's, bipolar disorder, psychosis, and newer symptom clusters for which children are routinely being prescribed psychoactive medications, such as oppositional defiant disorder (ODD), and disruptive mood dysregulation disorder (DMDD), to name a few.

The origins of her theory came when she first finished her training. "I was working in residential group homes with kids who had been abused and neglected," Dunckley explained. She kept reading behavior incident reports like *Jacob hit Robert over the head while they were playing a video game together on Saturday*. Or a kid would behave well all week, be rewarded with video game time, and proceed to act out. "Finally one of the [group residences] agreed to remove video games, and lo and behold, the incident reports went down by thirty percent. That was my first experience."

She has seen severe cases of ADHD; children who were diagnosed bipolar and put on powerful medication; OCD children who were handwashing dozens of times a day; even what looked like the onset of psychosis. All reversed when video games and handheld devices were taken away entirely for a period of a few weeks, and reintroduced slowly in tiny doses. "I started to get a reputation for taking on really difficult cases of kids who hadn't gotten better with conventional treatment. [A screen fast] was my secret weapon." Some of these children, she says, had been misdiagnosed in the first place and symptoms resolved completely; for others, "symptoms were easily cut in half."

Dunckley has a theory to explain this miraculous remedy. It is that interactive screen time overstimulates two signaling systems in the brain: the stress-cortisol response and the reward-dopamine response. The same two systems, in other words, that sleep researchers have identified.

Dopamine is released when the brain seeks, detects the possibility of, and receives a novel reward. Video games are designed to simulate that seeking and reward at an incredibly fast pace.

"They've done brain scans of a child playing a video game, and the amount of dopamine released in the brain is similar to what's seen with cocaine use," says Dunckley. Hooked on that surge, Dunckley says, children become less likely to seek out the milder, more intermittent dopamine rush of, say, social interaction.

Studies showing the release of dopamine in video game players' brains date back to at least 1998. Though it's often linked to drugs, in similar studies, dopamine releases have also been recorded in response to less controversial pleasures like physical exercise, listening to music, and relaxing in a tanning bed. Anything that feels good can cause the release of dopamine.

That said, dopamine levels in the brain are indeed connected to tics and even hallucinations. That's one of the mechanisms of the drug LSD, for example. If you've ever played a video game for any length of time you've probably had a video game dream—I remember having Tetris dreams as a kid. If you follow the dopamine hypothesis, this might be better understood as a video game flashback.

Games balance artificial rewards with imaginary peril. This, along with the typical bright, flashing lights and unpredictable, loud noises emitted by devices, Dunckley theorizes (and sleep researchers also find), raises levels of cortisol, the stress hormone. She writes about kids acting strung out, explosive, and weepy after a screen marathon. "They are stuck and are going to stay in that revved-up state until the overstimulation is removed."

Borrowing another page from the sleep researchers, Dunckley is especially concerned about screen use at night. That tends to happen more when kids have televisions in their bedrooms, or when older kids are sneaking under the covers with phones or laptops, in a practice sometimes known as *vamping* (for vampire). "Children get into a cycle where they sleep shallowly. The next day they're tired, so they release a lot of adrenaline to stay awake. That puts them in a state of arousal, so they seek out screen time because they already feel stimulated."

Excessive hours of screen use late into the night, among Dunckley's patients and also in the research literature, is correlated with depression and suicidal and self-harming behaviors like cutting.

Being stressed, quite often sleep-deprived, and habituated to screen overstimulation, in turn, she says, makes children regress in their ability to tolerate frustration and regulate arousal levels. This regression can mimic serious disorders or exacerbate tendencies that already exist for other reasons.

Talking with Dunckley is frightening. I try to keep in mind that there's no way of knowing how much the results that she has found with vulnerable, traumatized, and otherwise brain-impaired kids are generalizable to typically developing children. Dunckley doesn't have any lab evidence to point to, much less randomized controlled trials.

She doesn't have long-term follow-up results for her own patients. It could all be overblown panic.

Yet, I've seen my kid get weepy and angry in an exaggerated way when the cartoons are switched off. Other parents I know have seen that too, and other researchers have documented the relationship.

Dr. Jenny Radesky, a developmental behavioral pediatrician at the University of Michigan and lead author of the American Academy of Pediatrics' 2016 screen time recommendations, is interested in the connection between children's more ordinary difficult behavior and their media exposure. Her first study on the topic compared parents' responses to the *infant-toddler symptom checklist,* a validated measure of issues like difficulty falling asleep or overly intense emotional reactions, at ages nine months and two years, to their child's reported screen viewing at age two.

Overall, children in the study were watching 2.3 hours per day of media at age two. Those with persistent behavior problems were more likely to be consuming media, and they consumed more. Infants rated by parents as harder to calm at nine months watched an average fourteen minutes per day more TV at age two. Small, but significant. A follow-up study showed the same dynamic at play with difficult toddlers.

"That was one of the first studies that showed the connection" between behavior problems and media use, Radesky says of her infant study. "These are the kids that we may be putting in front of media more because we want a break or it's the only thing that calms them down." But ironically, they may be the very kids who are most vulnerable to excessive screen use.

Radesky is currently working on a second follow-up study to see how this pattern of fussy behavior and more media use interacts over time.

She sees the causal arrow traveling in many possible directions. Maybe fussy babies and children have parents who are less confident and more stressed, who need a break more often. Maybe their restless brains glom on more solidly to the stimulations and repetition of TV.

Like Patti Valkenburg, Radesky believes in the importance of differential susceptibility. "There might be kids who have great executive functioning skills, positive, happy temperaments," who can handle a couple hours a day of TV no problem.

"There might be some," like in the fussy-babies study, "who have very intense temperaments. These latter kids need more explicit instruction on how to calm down, focus and complete tasks, and problem-solve through difficult moments, and more media use might be displacing their opportunities for learning these skills through play, boredom, and parent-child interactions." Yes—boredom is a valuable opportunity!

The job of the researchers, she says, is to figure out "which of the kids we need to be most worried about," and be more vigilant in protecting them.

That's our job as parents, too.

ON THE SPECTRUM

Again in the category of low probability, high risk, a tiny group of researchers, far outside the medical mainstream, are floating the notion that early and excessive screen time has a problematic relationship with autism spectrum disorders (ASD). ASD diagnoses have skyrocketed in the last generation. Experts attribute much of this rise to expanded diagnostic criteria and greater awareness of the disorder. But they haven't entirely ruled out some underlying environmental cause.

Researchers, parents, and clinicians will tell you that children on the spectrum are even more drawn to screens than the general population. As Jason Calder, for example, told me, based on what he's seen as a clinician, he believes that "for various reasons individuals on the spectrum are more prone" to problems with screens. There is support for this in the literature: in one study of 2.5-year-olds, the typically developing group watched about two hours of television a day; those on the spectrum, over four hours on average.

Most researchers thus far haven't tried to show a causal relationship or suggest that more screen time could be a contributing factor to an autism diagnosis or symptoms, rather than simply correlated with it. However, in 2006 a single paper was published that analyzed large data sets to show two things:

- When comparing several counties in Washington, California, and Oregon that had changeable weather, researchers found that periods of heavy precipitation were correlated with a rise in autism diagnoses a few years later. On days when it rains heavily or snows, previous studies had established, children generally watch about thirty extra minutes of TV.
- Children who grew up in individual counties with relatively high cable subscription rates in the 1970s and 1980s also exhibited higher autism rates than those in counties without the same access to a wide variety of TV channels.

This paper—suggestive, not conclusive—was not received rapturously by the medical establishment. Rather, it provoked a huge backlash. Partly that was because the author, Dr. Michael Waldman at Cornell University, was an economist, not a doctor. Also, it's generally radioactive to suggest that parents might be doing something preventable that could cause or exacerbate ASD. And having nonspecialists speculating about preventable risk factors for autism raises the specter of the unfounded panic over vaccines, which has cost lives.

Nevertheless, others are asking the same questions as Waldman. Karen Heffler, an ophthalmologist and the mother of an autistic adult son, authored a paper in 2016 in the *Journal of Medical Hypotheses* laying out the case and appealing for further research.

Heffler believes that in children with a genetic predisposition to autism, who tend to have problems with sensory processing, screens provide a visual and auditory stimulus that is repetitive, predictable, and hypnotic. Heffler is concerned that these children's affinity for screens can cause a "crowding out" of more desirable experiences. Children who spend an extreme amount of time looking at screens may have correspondingly fewer interactions with caregivers and others. They spend less time learning to read human faces and human emotions and give appropriate responses. This in itself may be enough to exacerbate some symptoms of ASD. "I'm very passionate about helping families and children that may be at risk," Heffler says. "If there is an environmental risk factor it's very important to find out."

Dr. Radesky brings up this same theory unprompted, based on her clinical experience working with kids with autism. "This is very controversial," she says. "Some of my patients—two, three years old—have really severe autism symptoms and the only way they can chill out is to have a screen. That child is missing out on everyday interactions." And a child with autism especially can't afford to do that, she says.

The prevalent therapy for autism is called *applied behavior analysis.* It's a form of behaviorist conditioning or cueing, using rewards, to essentially train patients to engage with people and control problematic forms of acting out. Radesky says she coaches her patients' parents to be the front line of therapy. "Everyday interactions—getting dressed, or having a tub or singing songs together—these all contain tiny little pieces of intervention." For example, when you wait for eye contact before handing a child a towel, or prompt him to say "thank you" in exchange for a bite of food, you're reinforcing social interaction and language use.

"So my feeling is that when a child is using a lot of media, maybe because it's one of their restricted interests—like a patient obsessed with Thomas the Tank Engine—that's where excessive use of screens may be impacting the child's course of development or displacing other desirable activities."

When a parent puts on a favorite video or uses an app to get through mealtime or bathtime, Radesky argues, children are missing out on an opportunity for connection. Over time a child's tendency to withdraw from interactions could be reinforced. Symptoms may get worse instead of better.

Not everyone, clearly, is on board with this hypothesis. I spoke to Shannon Rosa, an author, blogger, and advocate for autistic people's rights. She has a teenage son who is on the spectrum. When I asked about a potential relationship between screens and autism, she laughed bitterly.

"This is indicative of a social bias against autism and stigmatizing rather than understanding it," she says. She cites prevailing research that autism is determined at least prenatally, if not 100 percent genetically.

Furthermore, Rosa and other advocates in what's called the neuro-diversity movement are very critical of applied behavior analysis. It's seen as a punitive, even abusive, attempt to control autistic people's behavior rather than work to accommodate their needs.

Rosa agrees with the underlying premise that autistic people often prefer screens because they have difficulty interacting with people. But she argues that this affinity is better seen as an accommodation than a problem. "When my son needs to chill he takes an app where you tap on photos and it plays the sound of that picture—say a violin, or a dog. He'll tap on that for about ten minutes just to decompress." Radesky concurs with Rosa that specific uses of digital devices can have positive applications for some children with autism, even while others may make symptoms worse. "I work a lot with parents to limit repetitive screen use (e.g., streams of YouTube videos, repetitive games) and pick apps that are focused on developing specific social or communication skills."

The positive side of the connection between ASD and screens is epitomized by the family of Ron Suskind. The *Washington Post* writer published a best-selling memoir that became a documentary film, *Life, Animated,* about his son Owen's obsession with Disney movies. He would watch and rewatch them, parroting the dialogue. Over time, with the help of therapists, the family took advantage of their son's "restricted interest," impersonating the characters and acting out the dialogue along with him. In this way, they were able to reconnect with him. Over time he recovered the ability to speak.

Even if the affinity some autistic people have for media doesn't prove to be a smoking gun, it is a prompt to consider how both our own and our kids' screens might serve as either a barrier or a bridge to other human encounters.

A small but intriguing 2014 study reinforces this idea. A team of UCLA researchers led by Yalda T. Uhls, a child psychologist mentioned earlier, gave two matched groups of preteens a test on their ability to infer people's emotional states from photographs and videos. Then one group spent five days at an outdoor nature camp, where all digital media was banned. The two groups took the test again, and the campers showed significant improvement on the emotional identification task compared to the group that stuck to their normal habits and environment.

There are lots of caveats. This is just one study, with a small sample size of just fifty-one kids in the treatment group. Maybe the improvements came simply from being at camp, hanging out with friends all day long, or being in nature, outside one's normal environment. Nevertheless, I think we'd all want our kids to be more emotionally attuned, rather than less, and to make sure they have plenty of opportunities to connect with others, online and offline.

PRINCESSES AND NINJAS

Moving away from the realm of medicine and into social science, over the decades researchers have repeatedly raised concerns about the influence of media on children's imaginations and identities.

In the 1970s, laws limited toys from being marketed based directly on children's television shows. The Reagan era of deregulation coincided with my early childhood. All of a sudden there were *Star Wars* tie-ins in Happy Meals and even entire cartoon series, like *He-Man* and *Strawberry Shortcake*, based on lines of toys (both of which I enjoyed very much).

During that time, two professors of education in the Boston area, Diane Levin and Nancy Carlsson-Paige, began hearing from classroom teachers about changes on the playground. They conducted a series of observational studies and published several books documenting changes in children's play showing the influence of media.

With the new convergence of toys and TV, teachers saw young children's play becoming more limited, even seemingly scripted, and more stereotyped. Children were more likely to hold to rigid sex roles laid out by Disney princesses and Ninja Turtles. Boys' behavior got more aggressive, with more weapon play.

When I talked to Carlsson-Paige, now a professor emeritus at Lesley University in Cambridge, Massachusetts, I questioned whether it's really so bad for children to imitate their favorite TV characters. I was feeling a little defensive—I used to do it all the time, and so does my daughter. "From the point of view of child development it's a pretty serious issue," she told me. "Play is important for healthy child development. It should be original and no two children's play should look the same. It's got to be relevant to a child and arising from her imagination. That's how it serves inner resilience and builds up social and emotional concepts."

A representative study in this field, published in 2016 by Sarah Coyne at Brigham Young University, looked at approximately two hundred preschoolers. Sixty-one percent of the girls played with Disney princess material at least once a week; those who did were more likely a year later to choose gender-stereotyped toys and to avoid behaviors stereotyped as boyish, like rough and tumble play. Eric Rasmussen at Texas Tech found a similar relationship in a separate study between boys' superhero viewing in preschool and violent play and play with weapons at older ages.

As I've been repeating ad nauseam, studies like these don't address causation. Maybe girlier girls are more into princesses and aggressive boys more into superheroes in the first place. Or maybe parents who buy a lot of princess toys or toy guns are invested in rigid gender roles that they reinforce in other ways.

Intriguingly, the Disney study also found that the small number of little boys who played a lot of princess games had more positive body image and were rated by others as more helpful.

Imitating stories, Carlsson-Paige argues, isn't a problem in itself. Visual media can be. "Storytelling is wonderful. It's a way to touch those archetypes that are within all of us as human beings, and then we may use them to spring off of as we invent our own stories. But seeing images constructed by someone else doesn't leave enough room in the child's imagination."

This strain of research tends to be based on small sample sizes and parents' or teachers' reports of children's behavior. There's also a lack of longitudinal evidence about whether kids whose play is highly inflected by media as children grow up to be emotionally unhealthy adults in some way. Surely some of those movie-obsessed kids grow up to be Steven Spielbergs. But this research is still worth mentioning as we start to think about what media effects we'd want to foster or try to limit in our own children.

TEENS AND SCREENS GONE WILD

By the time kids these days get into double-digit ages, they're amazingly obsessed with their phones. The newfound ability for tweens and teens to connect with peers, and of course strangers, 24/7 has fed a textbook moral panic. It encompasses all the things we usually worry about with regard to teens and young adults—sex, drugs, crime. And especially what used to be called the "virtue" of young girls.

"The dominant force in the lives of girls coming of age in America today is social media. What is it doing to an entire generation of young women?" reads the marketing copy for a 2016 book by Nancy Jo Sales, *American Girls*. A similar 2016 book by Peggy Orenstein was titled, more directly, *Girls & Sex*.

Both books are based on interviews and anecdotes. And they're engrossing, if alarming. But here's the thing to keep in mind. By most measures teens, especially middle-class teens, are doing pretty okay. If anything they have been doing better, or at least no worse, since the dawn of the Internet. College-going rates are rising and high school graduation is at an all-time high. Teen car crash rates are down since 1999, and so are traffic deaths. Dangerous drug and alcohol use has plunged since the 1970s. Teen pregnancy rates are down 44 percent since 1991. Compared to the 1990s, fewer high school students have had sex, are having sex, and started having sex before age thirteen. HIV rates are down, although less serious STDs are up slightly among teens. The Crimes Against Children Research Center reports a 62 percent decline in sexual abuse of children between 1992 and 2010, which they believe reflects a true decline in the prevalence of abuse, not just changes in reporting or emphasis on such crimes. Similarly, the Bureau of Justice Statistics reported a 64 percent drop in sexual violence against women between 1994 and 2010. Arrests of teens for all crimes also plunged dramatically—over 60 percent—between 1996 and 2014. The incidence of eating disorders appears stable. On a national health survey given annually by the CDC there's been little change since the 1990s in parents who reported a serious emotional or behavioral difficulty in their kids.

And by the way, only about 7 percent of teens in one large survey reported that they had created sexually explicit images of themselves and shared them over social media. In a second, retrospective survey that came out in 2015, a larger proportion of college students (one in four) recalled any incidents of "sexting" during their teen years. In most cases they shared images of themselves with a romantic partner and, to their knowledge, no one saw them other than the intended recipient.

Similarly, in the most recent nationally representative federal survey, just 7 percent of teens reported experiencing any form of cyberbullying, compared to 21 percent who experienced the old-fashioned, in-person kind. In a second national survey published in 2016, 58 percent of teenagers reported that people online were "mostly kind."

What is social media doing to the entire generation? Nothing much that we can measure.

"If there is a digital revolution, it's not bending the trajectory downward sufficiently to start worrying," concludes Dan Romer, to whom I am indebted for this line of reasoning. He spends a lot of time thinking about how adolescents are doing, as the director of the Adolescent Communication Institute at the Annenberg Public Policy Center at the University of Pennsylvania. He suggests we are all to some extent victims of the fact that doom and gloom gets clicks and eyeballs. "The news media [focuses on harms]. Which is reasonable, because if there are harms we should know about them. But those [negative reports] tend to drown out the overall pattern."

Romer also subscribes to the dandelion versus orchid theory. "Kids who spend too much time on some screens doing some things are probably not doing well. But they're a minority. We need to watch out for them and help them if we can. The typical adolescent is not encountering those kinds of problems, which is a good thing."

Moral panic, particularly about the sexual mores of teenage girls, has a long history. It comes along with every new form of technology— the telegraph, the telephone, the car. "My favorite example of this is the sewing machine," says danah boyd, the author of *It's Complicated: The Social Lives of Networked Teens* and an internationally recognized authority on social networks. "The idea was that girls' legs would be rubbing up against each other," thanks to the pedal action, awakening lascivious thoughts.

"There has been a lot of uproar about girls being abducted: [the idea that] the Internet allows access to our daughters. The same thing, to the word, was said about the telegraph and the telephone," points out Justine Cassell, the associate dean for technology strategy and impact in the School of Computer Science at Carnegie Mellon University. Just as in previous generations, the real threat to our nation's youth hardly ever comes from strangers, Cassell points out. "Look at the statistics: who are committing crimes against girls? The same people as ever: family members, sadly enough."

She makes a point also covered in boyd's work: that the identity formation and experimentation that happens partly online for teens today happened in a physically far riskier way in previous generations—in Cassell's case, by dressing scantily and hanging out in the East Village.

For example, part of the reason there's been a decline in traffic accidents in this age group is that teens are doing less driving, and some argue that's because they can stay home and meet up with their friends online instead. "The big conversation I keep having with young people about sexting is: 'Everybody keeps telling us not to have sex. We're told we're supposed to have safe sex. Well, sexting sounds like great safe sex!'" says boyd.

When it comes to reports of how teens feel, as opposed to how they behave or what happens to them, some relationships are worth paying attention to. Reports of online harassment are worrying, even if the numbers are small. And more social media use correlates with higher levels of depression and anxiety among young people. There has also been a striking rise in self-reports of narcissism and a decline in empathy among American college students since the 1970s, with the steepest drop in concern for others and perspective-taking since 2000. The same survey that found that teens said people were "mostly kind" online also found that nearly half of them had been called ugly names at some point online.

But again the causal arrow can point both ways. It could be that socially isolated youths spend more time on social media exactly because they don't have real-life friends. We don't have Bobo the clown–style studies that connect following Rihanna on Instagram, say, and getting an eating disorder.

Sara Konrath at the University of Michigan, the lead author of a large study about the decline in empathy, told me it was the media that "pulled out the idea of social media as the cause." But once again, the idea of a cause is not supported by the science, she says. "We said we could not come up with causes, because that's not the paper we were doing." However, she does not dismiss the possibility that the two phenomena are "somehow related," especially since separate studies show that more narcissistic people tend to post on social media more often.

Her research group has been trying to fight fire with fire. They are testing programs that promote prosocial behavior by sending text messages throughout the day reminding people to, say, reach out to a friend who is having a hard time. If new media can promote self-absorption, she reasons, it can equally be harnessed to strengthen social ties and empathy.

Other research bolsters the point of view that the inherent design of social media platforms can in turn affect their users' mood and behavior. For example, in a University of Michigan study released in 2015, undergraduates using Snapchat reported being in a better mood than those who used Facebook or Twitter. Researchers speculated that Snapchat, a place for exchanging video messages that expire in several seconds, felt more spontaneous and personal and required less "self-presentation," or faking something for an audience.

Yes, there are kids out there whose lives are made miserable by cyberbullying, sexting, porn, and even a desperate need for digital validation. Their stories need to be told. There are certainly concerned parents, educators, and others who might want to try to limit some young people's access to technology in some contexts. More broadly, we might all work to change community norms and promote better digital citizenship.

What we don't have is any concrete evidence that the mere availability of new communications technologies is, by itself, exacerbating risks, harms, or trends of antisocial behavior in the real world, rather than channeling some of the darker sides of growing up that have always been with us.

Assimilating these scary but still speculative ideas about harms associated with kids and screens is tough to do. You want to pay the right amount of attention to potential dangers, but not overreact. When thinking about my simple nutrition framework, it strikes me that a good analogy is to populations with allergies: kids with attention disorders, addictive tendencies, autism spectrum disorders, or other brain issues may be able to tolerate only very small servings, or have to avoid certain types of media altogether. Parents need to be watchful and good role models, particularly in the early years when they have more control over their kids' experiences.

NO SCREENS BEFORE AGE 2?

Given all that we know, all that we don't know, and all that we may never know, it may seem bizarre that scientists are relaxing official screen time recommendations. But that's exactly what's happening.

There's one single expert recommendation that everyone has heard when it comes to kids and screens: no screens at all before age 2, according to the American Academy of Pediatrics. First uttered in 1999, the rule was reissued, essentially unchanged, in 2011.

Dimitri Christakis was on the committee that wrote that rule. He also conducted much of the research behind it. He no longer believes it to be true. "If we took the publication at its word, that would mean that an eighteen-month-old shouldn't Skype with grandparents or read a book on an iPad. That's clearly ridiculous both scientifically and practically."

Victor Strasburger, another author of the policy, feels differently. "I wrote the statement years and years ago that babies shouldn't be watching screens until age two. There was NO evidence—none! We made it up. And we caught holy hell. And it turns out now it is evidence-based. There are a dozen or more studies showing language delays," from too early and too much screen exposure.

The AAP issued revised guidelines in the fall of 2016. The "no screens under 2" rule went out the window. The AAP now says that video chat, and other social purposes like looking at family pictures together, is probably okay for children younger than age 2—even tiny babies. They didn't cite positive evidence to shore up that recommendation, though a couple of small observational studies suggest that infants as young as six months old can tell the difference between a live Skype exchange with Grandma and a prerecorded video of her. This would imply that video chat could be a way to form the foundation of learning to talk.

And as for cartoons? Starting as young as eighteen months, the recommendation is now for no more than an hour a day of media. Christakis says they arrived at that number in an admittedly unscientific way: that's the amount of time that toddlers are likely to engage with anything in the toy box at that age.

And, importantly, the emphasis now is to avoid *solo* media use. "Shared media use was a new emphasis," says Jenny Radesky, lead author of the new recommendations, "because we know parents are meaning-makers for young children, and we need parents to be creative, curious, and kind role models while using their own media, and also to use media together with children to show them that media use is not only a solo activity." The AAP cites some small studies showing that even toddlers fifteen months old can learn from an educational video if, and only if, adults are there to repeat, highlight, and reinforce what's on the screen.

The desired limit is still 2 hours a day for children older than preschool, and caregiver involvement is still ideal for older kids. And doctors are trying to shift to making recommendations based on content, context, and the type of engagement, emphasizing active over passive and social versus solo.

In Christakis's view, interactive digital media may, under certain circumstances, be as healthy as any other kind of play. When there's an actual person on the couch or on the other end, research shows, even young toddlers can learn and get social interaction from screens. The big idea is to move media use to preferred activities like reading an ebook together or video chatting with relatives, and to balance it out with other preferred forms of play or activity.

Here's the caveat, though. The AAP didn't frame the updated recommendation based only on the evidence. Doctors like Christakis are part of an emerging consensus within the scientific community that advocates a "harm reduction" strategy for kids and screen time.

Harm reduction is a public health approach more commonly associated with illegal drug use. Harm reduction takes for granted that authorities don't have the power to eradicate a given behavior from the population. So it's more practical to bring the behavior into the sunshine, so to speak. An example would be offering drug users resources to reduce the risks: free addiction counseling, if they choose to try to get clean; or clean needles and a safe place to take drugs, if they don't.

We're talking about kids watching cartoons, not a derelict shooting up in an alley. Still, harm reduction does seem like a more pragmatic approach than prohibition when an activity is extremely common. Christakis wanted scientists to come up with "a thoughtful, nuanced set of guidelines" because "ninety percent of parents were ignoring" the old ones. That's a real figure—nine in ten children currently see some television before age two. And the scientific establishment is feeling pressured to answer the burning questions of parents like you and me, before there's a full body of scientific evidence showing exactly what harm is caused from exactly what dosage of what kind of content under what conditions.

The "burning question," Radesky says, is how to go about translating the nascent research into actionable and accessible recommendations.

But that doesn't mean that an interventionist philosophy is no use, Dr. David Hill of the American Academy of Pediatrics says. "There was a time when eliminating smoking indoors, removing lead from gasoline and paint, and restraining children in cars were all seen as unrealistic recommendations that no one would ever follow. And yet each of these practices has been widely adopted with profoundly positive effects on child health."

Victoria Dunckley, the psychiatrist who prescribes digital detoxes, believes members of the harm reduction camp, such as Dr. Christakis, are muddying the waters with statements that interactive media might be fine even for young infants and that more study is needed. "A lot of us 'in the trenches' saw a huge fallout from Christakis's statement—or more precisely, how it was portrayed by the media and marketers. Because the stakes are so high, we have to think about not just what we're saying but how people—including parents and the media—interpret it, as well as the potential repercussions of interpretation."

Christakis responded: "To withhold or misrepresent information because we do not have faith in how it will be interpreted betrays the public trust and undermines our credibility."

My takeaway from all this is that raising kids away from all screen media is impractical if not impossible. And there's no way to have perfect foresight about the impacts of our choices. While researchers lobby for more funding and clinicians try to give better advice, the best we can do as parents right now is share information, watch for danger signs, and rely on enduring values.

To return to our diet analogy briefly, research gives us some ideas about healthy quantity and quality of screen time. Average exposure to screen media across the US population—four hours a day for young kids, six to seven hours for older kids—is probably enough to be suboptimal. A more moderate intake would be two hours a day for children over four, and just thirty minutes a day for babies and toddlers. Time of day matters too, because of the effects on sleep.

It's hard to get a full "nutritional" content breakdown, but we do know that violent media can have negative effects on some highly sensitive children. There may be some basis for believing that children are likely to be influenced by advertising, including ads for junk food, and sexist, racist, and other antisocial messages found in media.

4 YOU HAVE THE POWER: POSITIVE PARENTING WITH MEDIA

I TOOK MY OLDER DAUGHTER, LULU, TO SEE HER FIRST MOVIE IN THE THEATER on a very rainy Saturday. She was three years old. Our pick was *Inside Out,* the rainbow-hued Pixar tale starring the warring, personified emotions inside one girl's head. Red was the color of Anger, blue was Sadness, green was Disgust, purple was Fear, and glowing gold was Joy, in charge of it all.

I talked up the movie theater in advance as I do with most of Lulu's new activities.

"It's a very big screen," I said.

"We have a big screen here, Mama," she said.

"Yes, well this one is even bigger! And you have to get there at a certain time . . . and you have to be quiet during the show . . . and you can't get up too many times . . . and there are other people there . . . no, not our friends, just strangers . . . "

Wow, I thought. What on earth is the purpose of going out to a movie theater anymore?

But I love the movies. So does my husband, Adam. So did Lulu, from the start. She was captivated by every frame. She didn't get scared at the scary parts or upset at the weepy parts. The movie showed a family just like ours at that time: a stressed-out, stubbly dad with a startup. An exhausted mom trying to keep everything together. And one dark blonde, goofball little girl.

"Is that all?" Lulu asked when it was over. She didn't want to leave. It was cute for a minute. Then her rage reached titanic proportions not typical for her at that age—what Dr. Victoria Dunckley might call an "explosive" reaction, discharging the energy and excitement of the movie. She was clinging to the door of the theater and screaming as people filed past.

"I guess the red guy is coming out, huh?" said another mother sympathetically.

I knelt down next to Lulu and hugged her as she sobbed. Her face was flushed under the slightly crooked bangs I'd cut for her. I held out a leftover M&M. "Remember when the imaginary friend, Bing Bong, was crying pieces of candy?" "Yeah!" Just like that she cheered up again. It was a tough moment in an otherwise great day. And ever since then, we haven't missed a kids' movie in the theater.

Thus far we've been dwelling on the scarier aspects of media and kids. I spent a great deal of the previous chapter describing what researchers know and don't know. Much of the research, as well as much of the media coverage of that research, is focused on risks and harms. There are good reasons that the conversation tilts this way. But one unfortunate result is that at this point, many parents—or at least the relatively affluent, anxious types who buy most parenting books—see their role as primarily being to restrict kids' media use, or divert it to preferred forms of content. That's not enough.

POSITIVE EFFECTS

Nearly every media researcher I talked to was careful not to be painted as an anti-screen zealot (exceptions noted). They all mentioned that all the negative evidence on kids and media has a flip side. "The research is all over the map," says Heather Kirkorian, director of the Cognitive Development and Media Lab at the University of Wisconsin, who casts herself as more "media positive and parent positive" than most researchers. "Some types of content are harmful, some have the potential to be beneficial."

For one thing, she says, educational television really is educational. In several huge studies, watching *Sesame Street* has been found to be almost as good as attending preschool. Children ages three to five can effectively get ready for school by learning vocabulary, body parts, numbers, counting, letter sounds, and how to sound out words from viewing cute Muppets. This is good news, since a relatively small proportion of US children have access to preschool.

And the benefits persist over time. "Children who watch *Sesame Street* are more ready to learn," Kirkorian told me. "They get higher grades in English, math, and science in high school. They are more likely to participate in extracurriculars."

In fact, she says, "The research suggests that preschool-aged children, three-plus, can learn all kinds of things from traditional TV: academic, prosocial, or antisocial." This is yet another good reason to pay attention to the messages in the media your kids are watching.

A newer study by Eric Rasmussen, a co-author on the Disney princess study cited in the last chapter, has demonstrated that the PBS TV show *Daniel Tiger's Neighborhood,* which is designed to reinforce social and emotional lessons, can improve preschoolers' empathy, confidence, and ability to recognize emotions—provided that parents are in the habit of discussing television content with their kids.

Research on the efficacy of educational media for young toddlers is a very new field. In the past decade and a half, studies by Kirkorian and others have shown that children are able to transfer knowledge, such as how to put together a toy, from television to real-world contexts by about age two—perhaps as early as fifteen months with extensive repetition.

But there's more. Many clinicians have harnessed the compelling power of video games for therapeutic purposes. In fact, purpose-built games, simulations, and other software applications can ameliorate some of the problems that are made worse by conventional games and software.

Fast-paced video games have been shown to improve reading speed in dyslexic children. They work as well as or even better than much more difficult, and less enjoyable, traditional reading drills and exercises.

Fast-paced video games can also help improve attentional control and focus, potentially making people better learners in a broad sense.

Active video games such as the Wii or Kinect can successfully motivate children with obesity or cerebral palsy to engage in light to moderate physical activity. And video games that resemble biofeedback simulators have been used to treat ADHD, helping children develop attentional control. One, a driving game developed by Adam Gazzaley at the University of California, San Francisco called NeuroRacer, is currently in FDA trials.

Jeremy Bailenson at Stanford University has shown that taking part in specially designed virtual reality simulations can cause young people to improve on measures of empathy and altruistic behavior. In one game, instead of crashing a fast car, breaking windows, or mowing down people with a submachine gun, you play a superhero who flies through rooftops to rescue a sick child.

Other VR simulations are being tested as safe forms of pain relief for children with sickle cell anemia and burn patients, transporting them to a peaceful visualization while they undergo painful medical procedures. (In a less futuristic mode, my friend who is a pediatric ER doctor keeps a slew of funny videos and video games on her phone to help distract kids who need stitches or a painful exam.)

And in some applications, from preschool up to college, learning software has shown improved outcomes compared to traditional teaching methods alone, which we'll delve into further in the chapter on screens at school.

Shannon Rosa, the autism advocate, often writes about iPad apps that people with autism, learning disabilities, and other issues can use in a variety of ways, such as to communicate, reduce stress, and learn how to recognize emotions. A friend of hers has a nonverbal autistic son who had been assumed to have a learning disability and is now doing work at grade level with the help of apps that help him access math concepts, for example, primarily visually.

Even if there weren't so many examples of positive applications of technology, limiting and monitoring would be an inadequate response. We live, and are raising our children, in a digital media–saturated reality that we have created and that we choose every day. "Technology is neither good nor bad; nor is it neutral," in the famous words of historian Melvin Kranzberg. As parents, I believe it's our job to enhance the good for our kids even as we try to mitigate the bad, and more than that, to remain open to learning what our children's media interests have to teach us.

Sonia Livingstone, a professor in the Department of Media and Communications at the London School of Economics, leads a research project called Parenting for a Digital Future. "Parents are panicked by the messages about the dangers of the Internet that come from the popular media," she says. "The messages come from garbled sources and reach parents in various forms—a girl at school was sexting, a girl in the paper was abused, there's stranger danger, bullying, and by the way more than two hours will damage their eyesight." When parents look for advice on media, she says, "They tend to find ten ways to say *don't,* but no ways to say *do.*"

What I've been trying to do in this book so far is to ungarble those very messages so you can make your own judgment calls. The risks and the harms are real. They must be managed. Let's assume for a minute that you're not currently facing some big waving red flags to cut back on your kids' media use, like unhealthy weight gain, poor sleep, attention, or learning or behavior problems.

It's time to brighten the screen a little bit. When do screens bring us and our children together? Have you experienced moments of joy, laughter, excitement, discovery, creation, or connection across the room or across great distances? When it comes to families and media, the potential is at least as dazzling as the dangers are dark.

I want to suggest an approach to parenting with media, not just against it. One that emphasizes these positives as a means of driving out the negatives. To return to the healthy-diet metaphor, we have some idea what excessive consumption looks like, what kinds of ingredients are toxic, and the symptoms of dangerous allergies. But what is the media equivalent of the family dinner prepared with farmer's market veggies? What about the backyard barbecue with watermelon and s'mores?

Digital media, unlike food, may not be strictly necessary to raise great kids. Warren Buckleitner, who's been involved in researching and fostering the development of high-quality educational technology since the 1980s, led with this point when we talked. "I think it's one question that should lurk in the back of every adult's mind: could you raise a happy, healthy child without any technology? The answer is probably yes. It would be hard but you could do it: they need nutrition, love, tell them some stories, and they'll be fine."

I would stipulate that there are situations where digital media and communications may be highly desirable, such as when families are separated by work, divorce, or other circumstances, or when kids need special accommodations. And many would argue that they're an essential part of a twenty-first-century education—a proposition we'll debate in chapter 6.

Furthermore, the digital environment is ubiquitous and only getting more so. If our only intervention as parents is to limit screen time, a growing group of researchers argues, we're not preparing our kids to navigate the world as it is. "I don't think we should completely sequester kids so they don't see any media at all" beyond early childhood, says Eric Rasmussen, who researches effective parental mediation of media at Texas Tech. "To understand how the world works they need to be exposed to how the world works."

BREAKING THE SILENCE

Research on *parental mediation* shows that when parents get involved with their kids' technology use, risks go way down, and positive effects go up. "I think parents vastly underestimate their influence," says Erica Austin at Washington State University, who has been researching parental mediation of media for almost thirty years. But to become great mediators, first, we have to talk openly among ourselves.

Michael Rich, the Harvard "Mediatrician," told me that expert knowledge, while admittedly imperfect, just isn't reaching parents. "The biggest gaps we have right now are between the research and consumers," he says. "There's a lot of research available and people just don't get to it or don't understand it. I would say the vast majority of people are operating with advice they got from friends or someone at the playground. It's anecdotal."

He's right, although I would take his statement a step further. I think most parents don't have good exchanges even of anecdotal information. When I see posts to the parents' email lists I'm on, or to Facebook, asking for recommendations of kids' TV shows or apps to try, there's a standard disclaimer: "We're going on a long flight." Everyone understands the necessity of hypnotizing your kids with a screen on a plane ride; it's practically a civic duty.

Normally, though, plopping your kid in front of the tube is seen as, at best, a minor indulgence for which we reflexively self-deprecate or apologize. It's a little like drinking: do it after five p.m. while cooking dinner, on weekends or holidays, in good company, and no one bats an eye, but for many hours a day, or start before noon, and you may have a problem.

The prevailing concept of "good parenting" vis-à-vis media, among upper-class, educated parents at least, is minimalism and prohibition. You can see this ethos reflected, ironically, in the parenting images we choose to share on social media. My Instagram feed is full of pictures of my kid in costumes, at the beach, at the aquarium. There are no shots of her glued to *Doc McStuffins* while I nap with the baby. Similarly, when Alicia Blum-Ross, who works with Sonia Livingstone on the Parenting for a Digital Future project, was interviewing parents who blog for an ethnographic study published in 2016, she told me, "They'll spend the first hour telling me about the benefits they get from blogging: connecting with a community, finding their voice, making money." Despite all the positives the parents experience in their own lives, there's a double standard at play: "When I switch to talking about what they do with their kids, suddenly it's like, no screens ever!" One mother told her, "I want them to have a *Famous Five* upbringing," referring to a British children's adventure book series published in the 1940s. It's heavy on boats, hiking, caving, picnics, lemonade, and other pastoral pleasures.

Setting aside the irony of basing a media-free parenting style on a fictional depiction, let's get real. What would happen if we actually talked with other parents about what's working for us and what we can do better, not to limit screen time but to help us and our kids get more out of it?

THE BEST OF TIMES

In order to craft better family practices around screens, we first need a powerful vision of positive parenting with media. Here are three examples.

Sci-fi author and journalist Cory Doctorow wrote an essay about telling his two-year-old daughter Poesy the story of "Jack and the Beanstalk," with the assistance of a Flickr search to convey general ideas of a harp, a goose and a giant, and various YouTube videos with different versions of "Fee, fi, fo, fum!" Then they acted it out, with homemade props.

"Being a writer, I yearn to share stories with my two-year-old. I can't claim to have found the answer to all this, but I think we're evolving something that's really working for us—a mix of technology, storytelling, play, and (admittedly) a little electronic babysitting that lets me get to at least *some* of my email before breakfast time," he wrote. "The laptop play we've stumbled on feels *right*. It's not passive, mesmerised, isolated TV watching. Instead, it's a shared experience that involves lots of imagination, physically running around the house (screeching with laughter, no less!), and mixing up story-worlds, the real world, and play."

We follow this example at home, blurring the lines between the screen and the living room. When I was first working on this chapter, we started reading *The Secret Garden* to four-year-old Lulu. So of course my husband, Adam, had to go on YouTube to research how to do a proper Yorkshire accent, which all three of us started practicing (it sounds to me like a drawl, kind of like John Lennon in *A Hard Day's Night*), and to look at pictures of the moor.

Dana Stevens hits similar themes in an essay in the online magazine *Slate*. She explains how sharing movies like *The Wizard of Oz* and *101 Dalmatians* with her nine-year-old daughter has informed and expanded both their play together and her own work as a film critic. "Much of our shared playtime consists of an ongoing long-form improvisation in which we walk around the house doing regular stuff while interacting as characters from movies," she writes. "Watching P. grow into a very different kind of watcher than I am—less passive and analytic, more collaborative and engaged—has been a welcome stripping away of my own viewing habits and assumptions."

Jordan Shapiro, a professor of psychology at Temple University, has become a globally cited expert on games and learning in the last several years, a blossoming of interest that he attributes, more or less, to his divorce. Suddenly, joint custody meant he was spending lots more solo time with two video-game-obsessed little boys. He started learning about the games at first as a way to connect with them. "I never play video games alone; I always sit on the couch with my boys (eight and ten years old) and we all thumb away at our gamepads together," he wrote in response to some of my thoughts about positive parenting with media. "Gaming is one way we bond with one another—one way we engage in 'family time.'"

Shapiro also sees this kind of joint involvement as something more serious: a parental duty. "As their father, I see it as my job to make sure that they don't blindly accept these digital narratives. I need to make sure they learn how to think critically about the rituals in which they engage. . . . When I play video games with my kids, I'm helping them to develop a new critical media literacy for the 21st century. They need me to help them analyze and interpret the games that we're playing together, the rituals they're engaged in on a daily basis." And to give that assist, he needs to know what they're playing and why they like it.

Finally, in June 2015 the *New Yorker* ran cover art by graphic novelist Chris Ware showing a postmodern playdate. Outside the window, a swing set stands empty in an idyllic grassy backyard on a beautiful sunny day. Inside, two girls sit back to back at separate screens that show their avatars interacting in the world of Minecraft, the video game.

But this wasn't meant to be a dystopian vision. Minecraft has more than one hundred twenty million registered users and a following among educators. Many see it as one of the purest possible instantiations of constructivism, an educational philosophy that extols the virtues of learning by doing. It's an infinite sandbox where children build their own worlds, fix things when they break, and make up the rules as they go along, and it's spawned a vast interpretive literature in the form of blogs, YouTube videos, video auteurs, and more.

Ware wrote for the *New Yorker*'s blog that his ten-year-old daughter, Clara, loves the game, and clearly, he loves watching her play. "Clara has spent hours, days, weeks of the past two years building and making navigable block worlds fuelled from the spun-off fizz of her accreting consciousness: giant ice-cream-layered auditoriums linked to narrow fifty-foot-high hallways over glass-covered lava streams, stairs that descend to underground classrooms, frozen floating wingless airplanes, and my favorite, the tasteful redwood-and-glass 'writer's retreat.' (It has a small pool.)" You can picture the artist and his daughter, hunched companionably over neighboring screens, happily sketching away.

An author telling stories to his toddler; a researcher discovering a new shared interest with his sons; a critic watching and inhabiting the world of movies with her daughter; an artist keenly observing his daughter at play.

One common theme here is creativity. Children's imaginations fall hungrily on any available fodder and build castles in the sky, or on the screen, to suit. When parents enter into that world with them—or simply supply an audience—magic can happen.

Is there a reason three of my four handy examples of positive media parenting are from fathers rather than mothers? Yes, I think so. First, there are the stereotypes of men as the geekier sex. Another piece of it may be that Western culture tends to assign fathers the role of playmate, especially one who engages in riskier activities like rough-and-tumble play, which leaves mothers as the enforcers of rules and of safety. But moms, dads, and other concerned adults all have essential roles to play as media mediators.

WHAT THE EVIDENCE SAYS

I've painted a picture of what positive digital parenting looks like: cooperative and creative play, good messages with parental reinforcement, play that moves from the screen to the 3D world and back again. Now we need to understand why this benefits kids and how to make it happen.

Evidence-based media strategies for parents go beyond setting limits on time, place, and occasion. They start off with a stronger hand in the early years and gradually step back, helping kids build their own individual strategies of healthy use.

They include, fundamentally, participating with your kid. Just as healthy eating habits start around the family dinner table, joint media engagement starting in the earliest years basically means treating an app or video like a picture book: sitting with a kid on your lap, naming objects, talking about what's happening, and asking questions. It means actively and consciously modeling the use of media for communications, learning, and creation.

They include the understanding that different kinds of content and patterns of use are appropriate for different contexts. That the stuff out there varies from extremely fun and hilarious, truly educational and culturally enriching, open-ended and imaginative, to violent, excessively commercialized, or just crummy. That our needs vary too: to create, to connect, to get things done, to answer questions, and sometimes to just check out and take a break—both adult and child. And tastes and priorities in all of the above may vary from family to family.

They include balancing screen time with nonscreen activities like, say, playing actively, cooking, crafts, or gardening. And sometimes, finding balance by extending screen time into all of the above—turning it into "screens on the side" time.

They include—and can inform—a more mindful approach to our own media use.

Later on, say the researchers at the forefront of promoting this vision, it means treating our children's media and tech interests like any other interests in their lives: supporting, encouraging, listening, and helping build bridges between current passions and future opportunities.

LEARNING FROM SCREENS

I'm speaking to you right now, fellow new parents. The earliest childhood years are when habits are formed that tend to last a lifetime.

Research shows that those considered high users at young ages, with all the dangers that can bring, are likely to remain high users when older.

Early childhood is also, not incidentally, when parents have the most control over their children's use. So it's the best time to pay attention. They're certainly paying attention to us. Studies by Heather Kirkorian and her team at the University of Wisconsin–Madison have shown that as early as twelve months, when a baby is watching TV alongside a parent, he or she is more likely to look when the parent looks.

Positive parenting with media means helping kids learn from screens, starting at a very early age. Rachel Barr, a developmental psychologist at Georgetown University's Early Learning Project, has shown that with the help of a parent sitting beside a child on the couch to point things out and direct their attention, the age of learning from media can be pushed down to as early as six months. "When a parent says, 'oh, that's a cat like our cat,' the parent is really helping them connect that screen information with the real world," says Barr. "And that really has been shown to allow some learning."

Any form of media that supports a positive interaction between a caregiver and a child can be enriching and educational, Barr says.

Let me emphasize that point again. If a form of media—a book, a song, a YouTube video of a great horned owl, a drawing app, an episode of *Bob's Burgers*—supports a positive interaction between a caregiver and a child, that's a net gain for that child. "Having a bookshelf full of books doesn't make your child smarter. Having the child engaged is what helps reading. And the same thing is likely to apply to learning from any form of media—any 2D symbol," says Barr.

Sarah Roseberry Lytle is the director of outreach and education at the Institute for Learning & Brain Sciences at the University of Washington. Their lab has a noninvasive brain imaging device that looks something like a hair dryer at a salon, enabling them to peek at the brainwaves of children too young to hold still inside a traditional MRI machine. They've been able to establish, looking at these brain patterns, that children as young as six months old are actively working to make sense of spoken language, sort of "rehearsing" the sounds they'll be using in several months. Lytle echoes Barr on what makes learning from media effective. "To the extent possible, children should be viewing with caregivers and incorporating those social interactions into the media experience around and through the screen."

Michael Levine and Lisa Guernsey pick up this theme in their 2015 book *Tap, Click, Read: Growing Readers in a World of Screens.* Levine is with the Joan Ganz Cooney Center, the research arm of the group that produces *Sesame Street* and related children's programming. Guernsey is an author and researcher at the New America Foundation with a long-standing interest in technology and early learning— her book *Screen Time* is very much worth reading. Their argument in *Tap, Click, Read* is that when parents and other adults get involved, screens can transform into an essential tool to help young kids become great readers.

This is in part because a basic building block of literacy is background knowledge. Cory Doctorow stumbled upon this principle with his daughter Poesy, using pictures and videos to help her understand the concepts of *goose* and *harp.*

Media can also give children opportunities to overtly practice specific literacy skills, like recognizing individual letters. And watching TV shows or using apps together can give parents clues about how to help their children learn.

"When my children were young we would sit together watching Sesame Street or *Mister Rogers' Neighborhood* as 'co-viewers,'" says Levine. "I would later ask my kids to point out the letters on a stop sign or say numbers like the Count." Today, he suggests, when hit with "Why? Why? Why?," parents should absolutely pull out their phones and consult Wikipedia or YouTube to satisfy curiosity together.

Joint media engagement is also a pretty powerful argument for choosing TV shows and movies that have some appeal to you as an adult. I always thought it was a little cheesy for shows like *Sesame Street* to wink at the adult audience. But if it inspires co-viewing, it's a good strategy. So is, frankly, watching something that interests you, like the basketball game, together, even with a baby—as long as you're taking time to point out the "ball" and the "yellow" and "blue" uniforms, or maybe counting up the score.

Learning goals vary by family, of course, and tech can be an avenue to pursue goals that are harder to address in your immediate environment. There are online resources to help your child learn to chant the Torah in Hebrew or the Qur'an in Arabic, for example, and a dozen or more Bible and Gospel apps for young kids. "We had a choice between two hours schlepping after school on a Monday and going to sit in a barren room, or twenty minutes on Skype with her tutor," says Beth, a mother in the New York City suburbs with a daughter getting ready for her Bat Mitzvah.

Similarly, Jessica Robles seeks out books that show girls with naturally curly African American hair because she wants her daughter to have a positive self-image. And *Doc McStuffins,* which features an African American girl as the main character, is one of the few TV shows her daughter is allowed to watch.

The joint approach to screen time can be a tough sell if you're mainly using screens to give yourself a break. It doesn't have to happen every minute the kids are plugged in, though. And as children get older, they build their attention spans and their ability to learn directly from media, and you can feel more free to leave them to it for reasonable periods of time—especially if you discuss the show, game, or image search with them afterward.

PARENT ENDORSEMENTS

When kids still need our help to unlock the iPad or search for shows on Netflix, mediating their media diet is relatively simple. When they get a little older, our role shifts.

Erica Austin is the director of the Center for Media & Health Promotion at Washington State University. She says parents influence children's perceptions of media by what they say, and just as important, by what they don't say. "You may be endorsing things you don't realize you're endorsing," she says.

Role-modeling is important; parents' use of screens is one of the biggest predictors of children's use. Your own consumption habits, Austin has found, may matter just as much as what your kids are taking in.

Reality check: in a national survey of parents of children ages eight to eighteen, they reported seven hours and forty-three minutes a day using screen media for personal purposes, often multitasking while working. And yet 78 percent of them rated themselves as good role models to their kids.

In one of Austin's studies, college students who recalled their parents laughing heartily at beer commercials were more likely to drink alcohol. In another, students whose parents often brought up things they'd seen or heard on the news were more civically engaged.

The language Austin uses to talk about mediation mirrors the extremely influential framework of parenting styles developed in the 1960s by psychologist Diana Baumrind. Baumrind takes as a starting point two essential parenting dimensions: warmth and structure. You have *authoritarian* parents, who are harsh and demanding; *permissive* parents, who are affectionate pushovers; *neglectful* parents, who score low on both dimensions; and *authoritative* parents who score highly on both dimensions. In case you didn't guess it, that last way is the way to aim for.

Dan Romer at the Annenberg School of Communication points out that authoritative mediation requires knowing what kids are watching and doing. "To be authoritative you have to be confident and know what's going on."

Eric Rasmussen, at Texas Tech, is an author of the superhero, Disney princess, and Daniel Tiger studies mentioned in chapter 2. Formerly in PR, he transitioned into media effects research in 2009 when his fourth daughter was on the way. He says his work is part of a mini-trend of looking at media effects not just as a two-way relationship—kids and screens—but as a three-way relationship—kids, parents, and screens. Parental influence may be the key to decoding what makes some kids sensitive orchids and others robust dandelions. "Parents are the biggest influence on kids in how they respond to media. Especially in the first twelve years. People are starting to realize that."

And, he says, setting rules is less important than talking and listening. "I tell people, the best thing you can do generally is talk to your kids about media. Kids need to know what you think about the media they're consuming."

For example, in Rasmussen's Daniel Tiger study, preschoolers who watched a total of ten Daniel Tiger episodes over several weeks showed improvements in empathy and perspective-taking, compared to a control group that watched a nature show. These are exactly the prosocial messages the show was designed to reinforce. But there was a big caveat. These improvements happened if *and only if* the parents of the kids who watched Daniel Tiger also indicated that they were already in the habit of often discussing the content of TV shows with their kids.

Thus far research like Austin's, Rasmussen's, and Livingstone's has been relatively buried in all the blaming, shaming, and fearmongering. Austin's and Rasmussen's bottom-line message is that parents have more influence than they may realize. We are the first and loudest broadcasters in our children's lives. That means we set the tone for how they hear other messages later on, including those coming from peers and media.

Influence, however, is more indirect than control. Just as in so many other matters, children are more likely to follow what we do rather than what we say. And the quality of our relationships with them will determine the impact of our words.

Austin argues that families that are too authoritarian in general may discourage critical thinking about media messages. Ironically, by demanding unquestioning obedience, you could be setting a kid up to "believe anything she hears." If instead you discuss issues that come up with your kid and ask for his or her input, that sets up a context where it's possible to get them thinking about the complexities of messaging in the media or on social platforms.

For example, in a discussion of the character Elsa from *Frozen,* you might bring up the fact that you like that she has powerful magic, and that it's good she learns how to admit her mistakes and solve her problems with her sister, but add that you don't have to wear lots of makeup and fancy dresses, or have blonde hair and a thin body, to be a powerful and important girl.

Other good times to speak up are when your kids encounter content that scares them, or that is otherwise inappropriate. Those can all be springboards to talk about the difference between fictional and real situations, or about special effects, or "What do you think would happen in real life if someone did that?" or about strategies to deal with big emotions.

This kind of persuasive, supportive assist in interpretation could go over much better in the short term than setting hard-and-fast rules, and it could be more effective in the long term, says Austin. "Rulemaking actually goes only so far," she says. "Rules can be flouted. You can go to a friend's house."

Rasmussen agrees. "Research shows rules don't work as well for older kids" as they approach adolescence. "Kids want that autonomy. We call this psychological reactance: kids are more prone to do the things that you're trying to prevent." At the same time, toward the end of elementary school, kids become more sophisticated in their interpretations of media, understanding advertising messages for what they are, and getting better at telling fact from fiction. So they can have more sophisticated conversations. "I think it goes from setting more rules and still talking to them, to afterward talking to them more, asking questions, and helping them understand."

Dr. David Hill at the American Academy of Pediatrics also suggests involving school-age children in making rules about media. "Ask them what they think appropriate electronic media use looks like and what sorts of consequences might be warranted for breaking the agreed-upon rules. You may have to help guide them in these discussions, but often you'll find that they have expectations that are not that different from your own."

When setting family policy becomes a two-way conversation, kids may want parents to change their behavior as well. How you feel about this may depend on how democratic your approach to parenting is. Catherine Steiner-Adair's book *The Big Disconnect* and Sherry Turkle's *Alone Together* chronicle the feelings of many children and young adults who wish their parents would put down their phones when interacting with them.

POSITIVE PARENTING AND PORN

One of the toughest mediation tests for many parents is when your kid comes across sexual content, or creates it. There is little solid scientific evidence on the potential effects on kids of the increased availability of pornography that has come with constant connectedness. Believe me,

I looked. The one fact that researchers agree on is that porn is every-where and kids are going to find it. A common estimate is that boys, especially, are looking at sexually explicit images beginning at an aver-age age of nine or ten. And the parents I know are extremely worried about it and don't really know how to talk to their kids about it.

One of Rasmussen's studies asked whether parents had discussed pornography with their middle-school and high-school–aged children—not necessarily with blanket condemnation, but honestly sharing their values. When kids whose parents had discussed porn honestly with them got to college, they were less likely to view porn themselves. And if they were in a relationship with someone who looked at porn, it was less likely to affect their self-image or self-esteem. "When you're dat-ing someone who looks at porn your self-esteem takes a hit," Rasmus-sen says, citing other research. "Except if your parents talked to you about it." Whether it's because the parents who manage to broach this uncomfortable topic generally have closer, stronger relationships with their kids, or healthier attitudes about sex, or for some other reason, the porn talk seems to have a lasting protective effect, like an inoculation.

Devorah Heitner is a media researcher, a parent educator, and the author of the 2016 book *Screenwise*. "When I started in 2012 doing these talks at schools, I would say, don't put filters on your browser and feel like your job is done. We need to mentor kids on making good decisions. However, I kept meeting parents of boys who are addicted to porn, so whether you filter or don't filter, you can't ignore this issue." Given what we know about the prevalence of screen addiction, the power of teenage hormones, and the psychological effects of extreme content, it seems plausible that a small percentage of kids can run into trouble and need filtering and blocking and other forms of restraint.

Most kids, though, will encounter porn in the ordinary course of events. Most of them need little more than our authoritative media-tion, as Rasmussen's study suggests. "Parents should talk to kids from their own values," Heitner says. That could mean speaking about the objectification of women, or religious modesty, or the sacred role of sexual pleasure within loving relationships.

Paul Malan, a Mormon, wrote a Medium post addressed to his son titled "The Naked People in Your iPod" that is a master class in this type of conversation. "The first time you saw them, by accident, you were too young to feel embarrassed," he wrote. "I answered every question you asked, and hoped you couldn't tell I was embarrassed. We've both grown up some and talked a lot about them since, hoping to make the naked people in your iPod just another thing in your world, like jealousy in school, blood in video games, and sugar in soda."

Malan distinguishes between our natural human drives and the ways in which we choose to satisfy them, which ought to be influenced by morality and culture—though, he says, "conservative religions" like his own Mormonism go too far in denigrating all sexual arousal. He also points out the difference between sex in real relationships and sex as depicted in porn, and how it's hard to tell the difference when you're too young to have the real-life context. And he asks his son to consider applying awareness in the moment to his choice to indulge in porn—to stop and ask whether he's trying to drown some negative emotion that would better be faced. This test is always worth applying when we, or our kids, reach for our phones for any reason.

He concludes, "Our conservative culture tries to make it scarier than it needs to be, but ultimately porn is just another thing in your world. I know you're going to bump into it from time to time, and I can't tell you the right way to blend your physiology, morality, and religion. It's something you get to decide for yourself. Sometimes you'll handle it well, and sometimes you'll act in ways that don't line up with who you are. When that happens, learn from the guilt, but don't buy into the shame."

I don't know how much of this talk he's actually had with his son. It's most likely to be a series of shorter, developmentally appropriate conversations over many years. But bravo.

FANS AND GEEKS

Henry Jenkins at USC Annenberg School of Communication is one of the country's preeminent new-media scholars. Jenkins is balding and bearded, and his primary mode as a scholar is one of enthusiasm. He upholds and celebrates the importance of geekdom, fandom, and even regular old social networking. "Kids who are playing games and programming Minecraft and writing fan fiction or even using Facebook are learning the ways to produce and share knowledge for the twenty-first century," Jenkins argues. "They are getting spectacularly important information."

When Jenkins's now-grown son was between four and five, they used the computer for experiments in storytelling. "We alternated nights. One night we would read a story, and the next night make up a story, type it on the computer, and draw pictures. And we sent it to the grandparents. It was a whole publishing enterprise."

Besides being a fun way to keep in touch with faraway family and practice reading and writing skills, Jenkins saw this activity as a chance to learn how his son was processing pop culture. He suggests that "parents can build a conversation around media that gives them a great insight into what's going on with their children." His son's stories would often feature characters from *Pee-wee's Playhouse* and other shows he was watching—a form of proto–fan fiction. (Fan fiction or fanfic, in case you're not a confirmed geek, is a whole alternate universe of noncommercial creative expression where people create original stories and art featuring their favorite existing fictional characters, usually in genres like fantasy and sci-fi. *Fifty Shades of Grey* is probably the biggest multimedia hit to emerge from the fanfic world; it had its start as anonymously self-published fanfic of the vampire saga *Twilight*.)

For Jenkins and his son, those bedtime stories were the start of a years-long conversation. "That created a context for us where down to the present day we talk regularly about media and the stories it tells. That's become how our family relates to each other." Today, his son is a budding screenwriter.

Something else that was happening in those storytelling sessions, anthropologist danah boyd observes, is that Jenkins's young son was learning some essential ground rules of online communication. "One of the things I wish more parents spent time doing is allowing kids to communicate with family in advance of peers," she says. We write paper thank-you notes to Grandma to practice etiquette. Now intergenerational emails, texts, and chats serve a similar purpose. "You get the trial runs in. You learn how to interact."

A friend of mine had a daughter who learned how to FaceTime her mother's best friend in California at age four. It was cute for a while. But eventually she had to learn to respect the time difference and not to bother Aunt Mo at work. Both lessons would be invaluable in the future.

THE NEW BAND PRACTICE

Jenkins wants to see more parents copy his approach: to value and take seriously what our kids are up to in their hours of screen time. Just think of media like band practice. "If we treated the online world as something like extracurriculars, we'd be ahead of where we are right now," he says. "Good parents go see a band concert not because they like to hear Sousa played off-key but because it's important to encourage the arts."

By the same token, he says, it pays to take seriously your kid's habits and interests as a viewer and participant in media. Think about it. Very few of our kids are going to be prima ballerinas or NBA stars. Every one of them is going to be living in a context where digital forms of creation, expression, and connection are even more ubiquitous than today.

Jenkins says if we take screen time seriously enough to be worried about it, we should take it seriously enough to be interested in what our kids are actually doing online—what they're getting from the shows they're watching, apps they're using, games they're playing. "Parents are told all the time that kids are just wasting time online. If nothing important is taking place there, why should they take it seriously?" So-called experts, argues Jenkins, have let parents down. "Parents are being taught to fear the Internet rather than engage with it, so they're not doing the work they should."

Start these conversations when your kids are young and they crave your attention, boyd argues. Then, when they're teenagers looking for more privacy, lines of communication will already be laid down.

At the dinner table, Jenkins suggests, we should be asking, "How was school?," "How did the game go?," and "What did you see online today?" This is vastly preferable to installing software that tracks every place our kids surf, or insisting that they friend us on Facebook, says Jenkins. He compares this kind of digital surveillance to putting an ankle bracelet on our kids or physically trailing them when they leave the house.

"How do we understand the lives of our children when they're not in our presence?" asks Jenkins. "One scenario is we stalk them and follow them with our cars. The alternative is to say, let's have conversations about our lives."

A study published in 2015 provided some support for this point of view. Based on a nationally representative online survey of teenagers and their parents, it found that parents paying attention to which sites kids visited online and talking to them about it reduced the likelihood that teens experienced online harassment. Not only that, this mediating approach was much more effective than parents trying to monitor or prohibit Internet use outright.

Sonia Livingstone, who is based in London, says that British parents are far more likely to respect their children's privacy when it comes to their devices and social media accounts, while US parents are quicker to surveil. And, she says, the British approach is better. "Research shows that if you monitor and surveil your kids, they'll have Facebook for you and Tumblr for their friends and they won't tell you about the Tumblr. And if you set up the computer so it monitors everything, then they'll go round to a friends' house."

Researcher danah boyd has a really interesting take on this issue, one that may scare straight some parents who are tempted to snoop or hover. "If you're demanding passwords, or texting your kids ten times a day, that's really bad templating," she says. "You're setting in motion the idea that this is what love is." "Love" means no secrets. "Love" means knowing where someone is all times. Translate that into the world of teen relationships and you get stalking or other forms of emotional abuse.

HANGING OUT, MESSING AROUND, AND GEEKING OUT

Mimi Ito is a cultural anthropologist at the University of California, Irvine, who's been a collaborator and co-author with Jenkins and boyd and part of the same MacArthur Foundation Digital Media & Learning research network as Livingstone. She echoes this line of thinking.

The "messaging that [parents] are getting through mainstream channels," she says, is about "policing, regulating, and limiting." Her research points in a very different direction: that the paradigm of good parenting in the online domain should not be very different from what it looks like in the real world. "We're hoping adults in kids' lives can shift toward more of a context of trust and mentorship and support and watching kids' backs."

Ito, a canny, warm Japanese Californian who goes surfing with her teenagers, watches and listens to find out what diverse groups of young people are getting out of their time online. Her seminal ethnography, published in 2010 with boyd and many other authors, was titled "Hanging Out, Messing Around, and Geeking Out: Kids Living and Learning with New Media."

Those categories have become incredibly useful shorthand across this emerging field for understanding what kids are getting up to online. Of course, they use it to socialize and connect with peers ("hanging out"), which is critical as young people grow up and start to form independent identities. And they use it to blow off steam, play, and be entertained, as all humans need.

And then there are these other, rarer categories: the amazing things that happen when kids take advantage of the infinite worlds available to them to do deep dives on their interests and teach themselves new skills ("geeking out"), and to look under the hood of technology to start tinkering and create and share the fruits of their labors ("messing around"). These can include designing apps and websites, of course, but also writing and sharing stories, drawing pictures, shooting and editing videos, animation, making and remixing music, or modifying video games.

Understanding how "geeking out" and "messing around" happen, and making space for our kids to do it, is Ito's number one priority for parents. She advocates curiosity, not fear. And her advice is to start by forgetting about blanket screen time limits, at least for kids above age seven or so.

"These media messages that are coming to parents all the time that you have to regulate screen time: No!" she says. "That's much less important than understanding what's happening with their media use.

It's a huge opportunity for learning, civic engagement, discovery of passions. The online world is what you make of it and you have to, as a parent, guide kids to the positive."

Her work follows a public health methodology with the delightful name of *positive deviance*—essentially, seek out the most successful members of an at-risk population and try to figure out what they're doing right. The hope is to amplify the positive habits that emerge spontaneously from within a community, rather than try to impose solutions from outside.

For example, one of Ito's graduate students, Melissa Brough, has been interviewing a group of largely working-class, Hispanic immigrant families in Los Angeles. Their teenagers take part in CyberPatriot, an after-school cybersecurity competition sponsored by the Air Force that requires computer programming skills. In a community with fewer resources than most, Brough singled out a group of exceptionally engaged digital citizens, happily pursuing technology interests, to find out how they did it.

Brough has discovered that these families, even when they lacked resources and education, supported their kids' interest in media and invested in laptops, phones, game systems, and high-speed Internet service at home when they could. (Other research has shown that low-income families, Hispanic families in particular, tend to invest disproportionately in digital resources for kids, and are more likely to see them as positive for learning).

The families in Brough's studies didn't necessarily know everything their kids were doing online, but they understood that it could be a valuable connection to college and careers. Just as they often relied on their kids for English translation, they solicited their help with troubleshooting computers for viruses or setting up the home Internet. One single mother of four was tolerant even when her son, at age 8, was playing with the electricity and blew a fuse. "I said 'Don't worry, son, the next time it will work out, check what you did wrong.' I didn't reprimand him, I didn't scold him . . . we learn from our mistakes.'" By high school, her son was earning money building and refurbishing computers.

In the course of my reporting career I've talked to many young people like this. Some kids just get inspired to teach themselves online. Like Martha Chumo. As a schoolgirl in Nairobi, she landed an internship that gave her access to a computer for the first time at age eighteen. "Learning to code became my obsession," she wrote. She quit her job, bought her own laptop, and plunged into free resources and communities for coders online, with names like Codeacademy, Treehouse, and GitHub. She also found a real-life community at iHub, a coworking and incubator space for Kenya's budding startup scene. She got active on Twitter, landed a job as a developer with a local Ruby on Rails shop, and taught and mentored other aspiring coders. Denied a visa to study in the United States, she raised money on a crowdfunding site and started a Dev School, an informal, intensive, boot camp–style program to get other young people started with coding. All this by the time she turned nineteen. The school has since conducted training in Kenya, South Sudan, and Somalia.

Of course, there's no magic formula for empowering kids to become like Martha Chumo. Merely having the resources available clearly isn't enough. But two of the positive parental habits Ito has picked out are *sponsoring* and *brokering* or *translation*.

When you think sponsoring, think soccer mom or dad. Driving a kid to a video game tournament. Attending a My Little Pony convention in costume, as my friend did with his nine-year-old son. Giving your five-year-old daughter an old computer and the tools and encouragement to disassemble it, as a self-taught engineer mom friend of mine did. Even supplying the snacks when friends come over to play Minecraft.

Brough says the families she interviewed tended to take this approach. "They valued their children's interests (whether tech-related or other). They validated and supported their curiosity. From the time their children were young, they took a hands-on, mess-around approach with tech. They weren't necessarily directly involved themselves, but they saw it as valuable for their children."

Brokering, or translation, takes things a step further. When our kids get excited about something they see on TV or find in an app, we help them connect that interest to other fields of study.

"It's great for kids to be diving deep into fanfic or Minecraft," says Ito. "But they also don't necessarily see the connections between what they're learning and other opportunities unless the parent brokers it." Ito recalls when her son was really into Starcraft, a large-scale board game where different races battle for control of the universe. "We had a very interesting conversation that connected the game to what he was learning in school about wars and hierarchy," she says.

Although sharing your media and technology faves can lead to some great family bonding, Ito is reassuring on one point: sponsoring and brokering don't require being a geek or mediahead yourself. "I don't think you have to be a gamer parent or spend every minute of your life doing Arduino circuit boards with your kids," says Ito.

This is a relief for me because I just don't like video games or robotics that much. Adam, my software engineer husband, is the gleeful geek in the family. My contribution to Lulu's media diet is more about discussing the stories and characters in movies and TV shows we love, and sharing how I use computers and smartphones as a tool for research and communication.

You might look for a teenage babysitter who shares your kids' love of Minecraft. Or help them find an online forum where they can share their fandom safely. Or an after-school program like a robotics or gaming club. Or encourage them to use their video editing skills for a school project.

What sponsoring and brokering really requires, says Ito, is a simple shift in perspective. "You have to see the value that you add to your kids' digital lives not primarily in terms of limiting and policing access, but in creating connections and opportunities."

Shelley Prevost, a mother of three kids ages thirteen, ten, and six, is face to face with this issue. "My oldest is by far the most technically inclined. . . . I've had to learn to honor that about him. My middle son is a baseball player. I can go to his games, I can throw a baseball with him. I have a history and context for that," she says.

"With my gamer, I don't have that. I can't go and cheer him on. I'm trying to figure out, what does it mean to be an engaged parent when I have this really techy kid?"

Sonia Livingstone suggests that you can start simply. "Look at what your child enjoys online and have a conversation about how you can develop and support that. Instead of saying, 'You've been playing that game too long,' say, 'What is so interesting about it? Show me!'"

As Prevost points out, there are no established blueprints yet for being a "media mom," no well-known, tried-and-true curricula for teaching young children how to answer questions or think critically about visual information while they are simultaneously learning to read print, listen, and speak in full sentences, or for guiding older children in pursuing friendships and interests online. We have to be good role models. We have to be curious. Above all, we have to pay attention and be part of the conversation while our kids are still listening to us.

THE POWER OF PLAY

One pathway that makes a lot of sense to me starting with younger children is to collaborate with our kids using digital media as an accessory to creative play. Angie Keiser is the mother to a little girl who uses the nickname Mayhem on social media. Back when Mayhem was 3, she really, really, loved playing dress-up. The two started making dresses for Mayhem out of paper. The dresses got increasingly elaborate—like a picture-perfect version of Cate Blanchett's robin's-egg-blue feathered gown for the 2016 Oscars. Mayhem and her mother's designs today are the stars of an Instagram account with almost half a million followers.

The time that Angie and Mayhem spend sketching, cutting, gluing, and photographing their tissue-paper creations is very much hands on. But the research they do is all on computers and phones. Some of her designs are fan-based too: Minnie Mouse, Elsa, My Little Pony. And the process of posting on social media and getting feedback from an audience certainly helps motivate them to keep the work coming.

We're not all going to go viral. But it's really fun using YouTube, Pinterest, Flickr, Instagram, and more as inspiration for home science and art projects.

"Digital devices and digital things can be used as a tool for your making," as Lisa Brahms, the director of learning and research at the

Children's Museum of Pittsburgh, puts it. The museum has a world-class space called MAKESHOP for kids and parents to work together on projects, with resident experts in woodworking, sewing, electronics, and more. It's a seamless blend of the analog and digital, and a whole lot of fun. On a hot summer day, the sunny space is packed with kids from toddlers to ten-year-olds. Two are weaving on a floor loom. A few are goofing around in front of a green screen, watching themselves on an iPad. And in the center, a group of ten or so kids are transfixed by circuit blocks. These are simple blocks of wood mounted with tiny lightbulbs, spinning wheels, and other moving parts salvaged from old VCRs and printers, that can all be brought to life by attaching alligator clips to a battery.

As I walk by with Molly Dickerson, the museum's learning resource coordinator, a blonde girl tells us, "My battery's dead." "You connected that one, what about this guy, though?" asks Molly, holding up one of the two alligator clips. Presto—the lightbulb goes on, literally and figuratively.

Screens are hardly the central focus here. Maybe a parent will pull out a phone and look up a couple of different designs as guides while cutting out a balsawood glider. Or a visiting artist will do a quick YouTube search to help explain a principle of physics behind a wood and metal Rube Goldberg device. On the flip side, when they can't get to the museum, several thousand people around the country and the world follow it on Instagram, doing their own version of the projects they see, and then posting and tagging the museum in turn.

Many people promoting this kind of play are excited about robots and sensors—bringing digital technology into 3D spaces. "Working with tangible objects, it's fundamental for young kids," affirms Marina Umaschi Bers. "There's a ton of learning that comes from manipulating physical objects." Bers is a foremost mind at the intersection of technology and early learning. She's a professor of both child and human development and computer science at Tufts University. She's also the co-developer of ScratchJr, a programming environment designed especially for kids, and a commercially available robotics kit called Kibo.

Kibo is a set of wooden blocks that can be snapped together as instructions for a robot. But you don't necessarily need a dedicated gadget for this. Bers endorses Henry Jenkins's methods of connecting the online and offline worlds through play by any convenient means: through a word processor, a copier, or the camera on a phone.

"A good antidote to excessive screen time, TV, or video games, is to bring the play off the screen and back into the child's living quarters," suggested Edith Ackermann at the Massachusetts Institute of Technology (MIT), who wrote extensively about digital literacy (we spoke several months before her death in December 2016). "Examples of this include kids' programs that encourage viewers to dance, or exercise. Another option is to have dedicated viewing times for specific programs, with occasions to reenact and discuss what's been seen, with siblings, peers, or parents."

Extending storylines from TV and movies into roleplay, like the film critic Dana Stevens described, is yet another way of bringing play off the screen that really does feel good for my family.

COMMUNICATION AND CLOSENESS

Anyone who follows debates about young people and technology is probably confused as to why I haven't yet discussed at length the work of Sherry Turkle, who teaches at MIT and wrote the books *Alone Together* and *Reclaiming Conversation*. Her core argument is that digital technologies are isolating people and undermining human connection, and that you can especially see these depredations in the declining social mores of younger people (Turkle is a baby boomer).

I saw her speak twice while I was researching this book, and I found that the points she raised were undeniably provocative and done with a sense of humor. But for me, at least, her arguments didn't stick; they sounded, to me, not completely off but anecdotal and one-sided. She overinterprets findings, such as those on the rise in narcissism, that the researchers themselves aren't ready to call causal.

"Turkle has a knee-jerk reaction that is very attractive to the press but doesn't hold water," says Justine Cassell at Carnegie Mellon. Cassell is informed by an unusually deep humanities background for an AI researcher, with degrees in comparative literature, literary theory, psychology, linguistics, and anthropology.

"Take this idea that we need face-to-face interaction and therefore kids are missing out and can't interact. But in many cases technologies like Skype are allowing face-to-face interaction in ways that parents and kids never had it before. What if you live in New York but your parents are in Nebraska?" Or you live in New York and your children's father lives in California. Or you live in Florida and your children's mother is deployed in Afghanistan. Or you work in Queens and your children are in Manila. Nearly as often as it divides us, media can bridge enormous distances.

Video chat has quickly become a part of early childhood. And there's emerging evidence that it's meaningfully different from other forms of screen time. As part of her psychology dissertation at Georgetown University, Elizabeth McClure conducted a study, referenced in chapter 3, showing that babies as young as six months old appear to respond differently to a video chat with a relative versus a prerecorded video of that same relative. When video chatting, they appeared more engaged and took part in the kind of back-and-forth interactions that are crucial precursors to speech and many types of learning. It's a good reminder that when I'm home with the kids and crave a little digital distraction, video chatting with their grandparents or aunts for fifteen minutes is a great alternative to another episode of *Peg + Cat*.

For the entire time she's been raising her eight-year-old son Caden, Lyn King-Sisco has been a military wife, moving four times while weathering her husband's deployments and temporary-duty assignments to posts like Korea, Okinawa, and Abu Dhabi. She says it's gotten a lot easier to keep in touch as technology has evolved quickly over the years. At first they would share photos via email. Around 2009, she said, "Facebook did emerge as a big additional new way of communicating with him." Even when they were in opposite time zones, her husband could check in and see Caden's trip to the botanical gardens. "He'd message and say, 'Caden's growing! These pictures make me feel like I'm really there.'"

As her son got older, she says, "He was much more aware and angry that Dad's gone. There was more acting out. What saved us, what helped us tremendously to bridge the gap, was that we could now successfully FaceTime." Despite being on opposite sides of the world, they now chat faithfully every week. "If we have a school event, birthday party, we're out at the zoo, wherever we are, we can show Dad with the phone. It makes us feel closer and bridges the separation."

The US population includes forty-two million immigrants. Digital communication has utterly changed how they relate to their families abroad. A 2012 ethnography by Mirca Madianou and Daniel Miller documents how migrant workers from the Philippines use video chat, Facebook, email, text messages, and more to remain in close contact. One of their subjects, Donna, works in a nursing home. She skimps on sleep to video chat with her entire family every day, texts one of her sons daily to remind him to take his asthma medication, plays peekaboo with the baby, and plays online games with her kids on Facebook. On weekends she'll leave the video link up to her mother's house as a sort of telepresence portal, as family members come and go, for up to eight hours. Donna even manages to be a bit of a helicopter parent from afar: she has her older kids' Facebook and email passwords and checks up on their accounts once a week.

As of 2014 just 46 percent of children in the United States lived with the traditional setup of two married parents in their first marriage. For divorced, single parents and blended families, communication technologies are becoming crucial. A family attorney I know, Diana Adams, says that *virtual visitation* rights are now commonly ordered by judges or included in custody agreements. Many states have passed laws requiring that it be considered as an option. Complying with these orders may include assisting a caretaking grandparent in downloading the correct software, or building monthly Internet costs into child support.

Jai Kissoon is the creator of Our Family Wizard, a specialized technology platform for divorced and separated co-parents. The tool combines a secure messaging channel, an information bank with information like immunization records and the kids' shoe sizes, an expense log, and a shared calendar to help smooth out the bumps that can arise with joint custody.

Kissoon's mother was a longtime family lawyer. "From the time I was ten I could remember being in her office listening to the knockdown drag-'em-out battles in her conference room," he says. Back in

2001, one of Kissoon's cousins was trying to schedule Christmas with his newly ex-wife. But they accidentally booked overlapping trips, causing an amicable relationship to sour into yelling. "He called up my mom and said, is there anything we can do to make this better, because if this is how life was going to proceed, I might as well have stayed married."

The application struggled to find its niche at first. But a few years in, a family court in Minneapolis ordered some of its most high-conflict families to try it out. "These were families who landed in court week after week for petty minutiae: I never got this, she never said that. The judge put forty of these families on the website and for two years, not one of them came back to court."

Our Family Wizard has about sixty thousand users, and it's now been court-ordered in all fifty states and seven Canadian provinces. Courts have repeatedly found it to be in the best interests of children. It also saves money and burden on the family courts, which are over-loaded in many places. Say you want your ex to take the kids this weekend in exchange for two weeks from now. Going through your lawyer with such a request could cost $500 or more. Our Family Wizard has patented a feature known as *trade swap,* where you can make the offer and even set an expiration date on it, in case you need to buy plane tickets or make other arrangements. And the whole messaging history is secure so that you can take documentation to the judge if necessary to show when and why you've both departed from the custody agreement.

Unfortunately, says Kissoon, sometimes in the course of a custody battle, parents will falsify emails to bolster their points of view, or they'll claim not to have received certain messages. Messages sent within Our Family Wizard have an additional layer of encryption, time stamps, and receipts to make that more difficult. For especially contentious relationships, one of its premium features is called *tone meter.* "It's like a spell check for your attitude," says Kissoon. "It can prevent you from saying something that's aggressive, humiliating, or that might be misconstrued by the co-parent."

I find this so interesting because most communications technologies, to put it mildly, are not explicitly designed to foster cooperation and harmony. Features like push notifications and instant chat seem to ratchet up the pressure to respond to people immediately, which isn't always conducive to thoughtful or respectful communication. But for a price, you can access a system that has been proven to lower the temperature on family conflict.

I'm also curious about how all families can take a leaf from those separated by migration, deployment, divorce, or other circumstances, and think of creative ways to use communication technology to come closer together. Lots of us are using shared Google Calendars and Google Docs, photo-sharing services, group chat, payment systems, Pinterest, and more to keep in touch and manage family business.

Peder Fjallstrom, a Swedish tech blogger and developer, wrote in February 2016 about how his family of four uses the chatroom app Slack, which is designed for work teams. They set up chat channels like "to-do list" and "vacation planning" and "random" for sharing cat GIFs. He also built an integration with an online grocery-ordering service, so they can all automatically add grocery items to the weekly order any time it occurs to them. "Where are the kids" talks to his sons' Find My iPhone apps and returns a Google Maps image of where his ten-year-olds are located at any moment. "They like it at the moment at least because it's a convenience, but in a couple of years they might not be too happy about it," he said in an interview. "We'll renegotiate then." Other integrations provide updates from Google Calendar and the kids' school. "Everything works much better than before," Fjallstrom told CBC Radio.

When my girls and I can't be together, of course we can video chat and I can also text with their caregiver. We can exchange short video and audio messages, or send emojis back and forth; read a book together; or collaborate on a drawing in Google Apps. The possibilities are expanding all the time.

"My daughter is an exchange student in Copenhagen," recounts Warren Buckleitner, the ed-tech specialist. "She's living with a family with two young girls and they love to make drawings on her Apple Watch and send them to me. So I get these little 'taptic' alerts on my wrist and see this drawing from a six-year-old little girl named Freya, and it's in real time."

FOLLOWING JOY

Researchers like Henry Jenkins, Erica Austin, Eric Rasmussen, danah boyd, and Mimi Ito have laid out a powerfully important and optimistic vision of what positive parenting with technology can look like. I'm intrigued by the contrast between the attitude of freewheeling openness and curiosity—and fun!—endemic to the Digital Media & Learning network and the Maker movement, and the stance taken by researchers like Nancy Carlsson-Paige who worry about how media is, to their view, limiting and stereotyping children's play.

Jenkins and his ilk say, yeah, engagement with media is deeply entwined with our lives and our imaginations from a very early age. We imprint on characters and act out what we see. And that brings both good and bad. But they believe in the power of young minds and imaginations, with the right support and guidance, to perform a sort of alchemy on the media they encounter.

As seductive as this vision is, I'm not a full media Pollyanna. I often feel like I have to forcibly close my laptop screen, knowing there's so much hypnotizing sludge and crap spewing at me.

But the point is, our role as mediator of media is not to smile on everything our kids may encounter, but to be a protective influence, model, share our values, and instill critical thought. And, where needed, balance. To do that, we need insight into what they're doing and why.

And there are other benefits besides fulfilling our parental duties. Like Jordan Shapiro and Dana Stevens, by paying close attention to what our kids are doing and joining in their play, we may even be able to learn, get inspired, and get a sense of the broader emerging possibilities in media in our own lives.

The food analogy holds up really well here. When families come together to share a meal, positive values can be communicated and bonds strengthened. When kids and parents get involved in creating meals together, there's even more to learn and more fun to be had—and a correspondingly greater chance of getting vegetables (an analogy for content that most helps your kid learn and grow) into those bodies.

If you're afraid of what screens might be doing to your kids, then that's all the more reason to try to figure out what a better life with screens and kids looks like. And if you enjoy screen time with your kids, like I do at the movies, then talk about it! The stakes are high. We owe it to our kids to do more than get freaked out. We have to get smart. But following joy . . . that can be a good start.

5 AN HOUR AT A TIME: HOW REAL FAMILIES NAVIGATE SCREENS

I WROTE THIS BOOK TO HELP MYSELF AND FELLOW PARENTS SORT OUT WHAT to do about digital tech. I found out as much as I could about the science, the dangers, and the opportunities. Now it's time to get down to the nitty-gritty. In this chapter you'll hear how hundreds of real families make technology rules, as well as what the experts do in their own homes. Then you'll get the ingredients to make your own healthy media plan and update it as circumstances change.

WHAT WE DO

Let me start by showing my own hand. I grew up in the 1980s in a household of two working parents who took little notice of how much time my sister and I spent with screens. We never did get a video game system or premium cable, but there was effectively unlimited network TV, a VCR, and, by the 1990s, computer games and early dial-up services too. When my little sister was in preschool, she watched the movie *Who Framed Roger Rabbit* on VHS every afternoon for pretty much an entire year.

My husband Adam's family was at the opposite end of the spectrum. His mother, who stayed at home when he and his sister were little, limited their TV time, PBS only. There were limits on computer games and Nintendo too.

Today, we're both reasonably well-adjusted adults, with careers, hobbies, friends, family togetherness time, workout routines . . . and we're both pretty much immersed in media from the time the alarm goes off in the morning until we rub our crusty eyes and go to bed. In this, we're fairly typical: 2016 Nielsen figures for adults show an average of 11 hours and 12 minutes of use per day, including 6.5 hours of TV and movies, not necessarily including work-related use. Similarly, Common Sense Media found in 2016 that parents, specifically, used almost 9 hours of media a day, 82 percent of which was personal, not work-related.

When setting rules for screen time in our own home, we had to compromise between my experience of parental permissiveness and my husband's of more strictness. We also both wanted to share our positive experiences with media and digital technology, mine as a writer, researcher, and news junkie and his as a programmer and gamer.

Before our firstborn daughter turned two we were pretty strict about not putting any videos on unless she was asleep. We got rid of our television and cable subscription years ago, so we watch movies and stream TV shows on a projector screen hooked up to a laptop or Apple TV, which takes a bit of time and setup. That means no mindless channel flipping or background TV.

When my daughter did turn two we started allowing videos on Saturdays, plane rides, car trips longer than an hour, and the occasional sick day. On Saturday, there's no real time limit, other than turning it off before dinner, and few content limits. We monitor and turn things off if she's getting scared or upset for any reason. My husband is more likely to veto shows when he doesn't like the themes, like a Barbie series full of shopping and gossip.

Using screens one day a week keeps them out of our day-to-day routine. That generally makes for a quieter, calmer household, and more focus on each other when we're home together. (Adam and I will still watch a show or a movie after the kids are in bed, with headphones if necessary.) The Saturday rule means we're not constantly fielding requests for more, more, more, which is something I hear from a lot of parents is an annoyance.

Where we can, we try to sit on the couch and watch shows or play games with her, or at least discuss what she's seen afterward. Finally, having had some tantrums related to transitioning out of video time on Saturdays, I've enlisted her help in trying to better manage that transition. Before we turn on the video we plan an activity for after it's off. And we remind her that crying or complaining when it's turned off is going to mean we say no the next time.

Our younger daughter is still tiny as of this writing, but it's a fair bet that she'll be exposed to more secondhand TV, earlier, through her sister.

The weekday ban applies specifically to passive video watching. During the week, we often look up answers to questions on our phones or do an image search together. One morning at the coffee shop before pre-K, Lulu gave me an "Eskimo kiss" and then asked me what an Eskimo was. This led to watching YouTube clips of the Iditarod and Inuit life at the Arctic Circle for about fifteen minutes. We also video chat with her grandparents about once a week.

Another nonpassive weekday exception that was popular for a while was a kids' yoga video series. I liked this because it had her on a mat, stretching, acting out twenty-minute stories with various animal characters.

In the long week between viewings, Lulu at ages two and three tended to use her imagination to return to a favorite story or characters. We encouraged this kind of play by buying book versions of the stories and plenty of costumes. At ages three and four she dressed up almost daily and requested that we participate in extended role play as her favorite characters: Mulan, Merida from *Brave,* Elsa and Anna from *Frozen,* Ariel from *The Little Mermaid,* Cinderella and Snow White, Sally from *The Nightmare Before Christmas,* Jen from *The Dark Crystal,* and Harry Potter (from the books, not the movies). We'll also play the soundtracks to movies on request, and audiobooks on car rides.

When Lulu turned four and started using an iPad at pre-K, we got one at home as well. We keep a limited number of games and apps, some of which are educational (DragonBox Numbers, The Foos, Endless Reader) and others that are just for fun (Toca Hair Salon, a drawing app). For the iPad we created a pass system: three passes, each of which is good for twenty minutes of use during the week. In practice, she hardly ever asks for the tablet any day other than Sunday.

Most of her friends are more relaxed about screens than we are. If she's on a playdate for an afternoon, we don't really sweat it; if it's a longer time, like when we share a house on vacation with other families, we try to gently encourage taking breaks from TV for other activities, and the other kids are often surprisingly willing to go along.

That's our strategy for right now. Of course it will continue to evolve as the kids get older, but as a general approach it works pretty well for our household.

THE SURVEY

For this book I created an online survey asking how people dealt with screens in their households. Then I called up, and sat down with, many families to get more details.

There were over five hundred responses in my unscientific sample set—a mix of races and ethnicities, education levels, and big city, suburban, and rural dwellers. Some broad themes emerged.

Most parents are trying to set screen rules in their houses in the following ways: by time; by occasion; by priorities; by content; by convenience, and by emotion.

By Time

The most popular way to set rules is by time. Out of 550 responses, 360 mentioned "time," 114 mentioned "hour" or "hours," and another 58 mentioned "minutes."

The single most popular rule by far among all families in my survey was "an hour a day." Assuming those families stick to this rule, they are by definition not average families.

This strategy has the advantage of simplicity. It dovetails with how researchers commonly look at screen usage—we call it *screen time,* after all.

The disadvantage? It's pretty arbitrary, which can make it hard to explain or enforce, especially with older kids. It's also lacking in subtlety or discrimination, between active and passive use, for example. And sometimes it's more of a placeholder than an actual enforceable number. Often the fine print looks more like this:

"Can watch TV up to a certain amount of time during the week (1 hour), can be more on the weekend. iPad is limited to an hour, needs to have a few hours break between various technologies"—from a dad of two living in the suburbs.

By Occasion

A second popular practice is to restrict usage to certain days of the week or times of day, or conversely to ban it at certain days or times—weekends only, "no-screen Sundays," mornings or afternoons, designated family times. This is what my family does with our Saturdays-only rule.

The most popular occasion for enforcing a no-screen rule is at the dinner table; 150 respondents mentioned "the table," "meal," or "mealtimes."

"There is definitely no tech allowed at the dinner table ever!" said a mother of three older kids.

And the word about sleep seems to be spreading—many parents mentioned banning electronics after dinner, stopping use an hour before bedtime, or not allowing them in the bedroom. "No electronics in the bedroom (except the bedside table alarm clocks)."

Limiting by occasion is a possible answer to researchers' concerns about screens crowding out other desirable activities. Pegging your rules to the day of the week or the time of day is similar to other practices recommended by parenting experts, who say daily routines are reassuring and help orient young children. If a habit like toothbrushing becomes part of the routine, it's much easier to enforce and is less likely to cause a power struggle. Setting guidelines in this way can help you think about how screen time can complement the rhythms of your household.

However, this strategy doesn't address content.

By Priorities

As a flip side to the occasions rule, many parents, especially of older children, set rules by setting priorities. "No tech until homework is done" is the classic limit. Another common priority is emphasizing outdoor play.

"Health and education come first. So, as long as they complete their daily chores, get their homework done, maintain good grades, perform well in their extracurricular activities (i.e., practice and perform well in music and sports to the best of their ability), eat and sleep well, then there is room for tech down time. It's an earned activity."—from a suburban mom of four kids.

"Limits vary depending on weather, physical activity they've already done that day, etc."—from a mother of two in the suburbs.

"Homework and any chores first," said a parent of one teenager.

A blogger who uses the handle NarrowbackSlacker popularized this approach in a post that garnered over seven hundred thousand hits. She's a freelancer who works from home with a son and daughter in their young teens, and she said she places no limits on screen time. Instead, before they can access any devices, she requires her kids to complete the items on the following list:

ABSOLUTELY NO GLOWING SCREENS UNTIL:

- You have *read real text (not comics)* for at least 25 minutes
- All your homework is done (one item may wait until morning with approval from Mom/Dad)
- You have marked the calendar with any upcoming tests or deadlines, and made an appointment to study with Mom/Dad
- You have done something creative, active, or productive for at least 45 minutes
- Your bed is made and your room is tidy
- You have done at least one chore (see chore list below)

I've heard of other families of older kids changing the Wi-Fi password daily as a means to enforce chores and homework being done.

Like setting guidelines by occasion, setting priorities encourages balance and a good rhythm for your household. However, some would argue that "creative and productive" activities, not to mention homework itself, may often include glowing screens.

By Content

Most parents who make rules by time, occasion, or priority also try to weigh in on content. For example, they may try to keep tweens off sites like Instagram or Snapchat, or reserve the right to look over their shoulders. "No friending strangers on Facebook," wrote a mother of a young teen. "Mom has all passwords," wrote another. Or they may restrict video games by rating, or TV shows by channel.

Many parents, like us, make a distinction between video viewing and iPad, smartphone, social media, or other interactive use, but it cuts both ways. Just like the experts, some parents would prefer that their kids use educational apps rather than watch TV; others are more attuned to the addictive potential of video games and less worried about movies or TV shows.

"If we sense they're getting overly snarky we cut off those shows that model that behavior for them (*Wizards of Waverly Place* and *Caillou* were big offenders on cable; YouTubers are the big offenders online)," says a small-town mom of two kids under ten.

"I encourage shows and apps I like, like the ScratchJr coding app or the stop-motion animation app that feels more creative."

"I pre-select the shows she can watch and they have positive messages and learning components, such as *Daniel Tiger* and *Sesame Street*."

"No M (mature) rated games"—from a parent of a teenager.

Other Strategies

Some families reserve screen time as a reward for desired behavior. Or they check in and check out devices as a way of enforcing time and priority limits. This is similar to what we do with our iPad passes.

"We use screen time tickets. Up to 10 per week. Each can be used for 30 minutes of screen time. Get 3 tickets free on Sunday. Earn more when you read or practice math skills."—from a parent of a seven-year-old.

One parent gives out iPad minutes as an incentive: half an hour of reading earns half an hour of iPad time.

"Technology gets 'checked in' after school, and can get 'checked out' for use after homework gets done. When tech is needed for homework (which is more and more a reality as kids get older), we use 'self control' app to block their favorite distractions."—from a mother with a house full of teens.

By Convenience

Making screen time rules is different from some other parenting decisions in one major way. When you teach your kids to use good manners or enforce a regular bedtime, it benefits you, the parents, in both the short and long term. It is very pleasant to hear "please," "thank you," and "excuse me," and to savor a glass of wine with your partner in your quiet apartment at nine p.m.

When you limit TV and video games, though, you're denying yourself precious free time. This is a big source of internal conflict for almost every parent I talk to, and for me personally. Cooking dinner at night, getting ready in the morning, plane trips, car trips, restaurants, waiting rooms . . . it's hard to hold the line when a means to occupy your kid always beckons.

"Honestly it varies based on how stressed or busy I am!!" one mom wrote.

"TV when I am cooking so I can cook. Ipad only on long road trips or at a restaurant so they don't disturb other patrons."

"Outside of a desperate to distract them setting (i.e. I'm in a meeting) generally no playing with our phones."

"Normal weeks the boy earns time via a star chart for baskets of behaviors. Vacation, parties, etc. we let it slide for our own convenience."

In general, permitting screen time by convenience is easier to explain and abide by when it's a big, obvious exception to the routine, such as travel or illness.

But at home, on a random Thursday at eleven a.m.? If you say yes this time, how will you say no next time?

"We don't have specific timelines—when Mom allows it, they use it, when Mom doesn't they can't," says a mom of two in the suburbs.

The problem with permitting screens just when it's easiest, of course, is that vague rules made at the parents' convenience are the most exhausting to enforce, engendering the maximum of conflict.

"The rule is that I am the absolute dictator and I decide on a case-by-case basis what is OK" —from the dad of a six-year-old boy.

"For my older son, we've tried so many rules, but haven't been able to make them work." —from another mother of two in the suburbs.

Here's what we're really doing when we give in in this way. In the world of behaviorist psychology, this tack is called intermittent reinforcement. It's by far the hardest kind of conditioning to extinguish.

Regular reinforcement works like this: if you give a pigeon a food pellet every time it presses a lever, it will become conditioned to press the lever. But once you stop providing the pellets, the pigeon quickly stops pressing the lever.

Intermittent reinforcement works like this: if you give a pigeon a pellet randomly, averaging, say, every four times it presses the lever, you can take the pellets away forever and it'll keep hitting the lever, trying its luck, till it literally dies of exhaustion.

I know this sounds harsh. In our lives as parents, none of us is ever going to be perfectly consistent about screen time or anything else. And I'm not suggesting that this variability is going to inflict lethal damage. We all need a break sometimes. We have all given in to our kids' whining and tantrums on occasion. And kids are resilient and can handle a bit of fuzziness in the rules.

I'm simply arguing that if going case-by-case has been your whole approach to screen time, and you feel that it's causing the kinds of problems I describe, a different strategy may work better.

I've known Justin Ruben since college. He's a political organizer formerly with MoveOn, his wife is a yoga teacher, and they have two young kids and have lived abroad in places like Guatemala. Ruben readily admits that they've fallen prey to the convenience trap, allowing the kids to binge on screens when, for example, they are packing up for another big trip.

"So screen time is this capricious thing that they don't understand, because our system of whether we give it to them is totally opaque," he says. "Like from their perspective you just ask, it's like the gods either say yes or no, and you have no idea why."

Perhaps not surprisingly, he compares his kids to addicts: "They would mainline it like heroin. They would never get tired of it. They whine when we turn it off."

By Emotion

Speaking of whining, many parents are motivated to set limits in response to the negative emotions their children exhibit after engaging with media. Again, this corresponds to what some researchers find.

"I am starting to cut back on the TV watching, since he seems to not be able to function without the TV on and that bothers me," says the mother of a seven-year-old boy.

A mother of two in a small town not only sets limits by content and time but also demands good screen etiquette. This tactic seeks to ensure that kids are able to keep their emotional attachment under control. "Use respect—stop/pause what you are doing—when someone is speaking to you. Acknowledge the person if you are unable to stop at that moment." This seems like an example worth following.

"Time's up when . . . they are glazed from looking at the screen too long," says the parent of two young school-age kids. "My kids get cranky when the screens go away, withdrawal-like symptoms. It's this state that keeps me from giving them more screen time. How do I avoid that glazed state?"

"If she is cranky, extremely emotional, or throwing a lot of fits then we limit it even more, sometimes to the point of none since it will only exaggerate her emotions more," says the small-town mother of a five-year-old daughter.

Research upholds the connection that lots of us are observing between media exposure and emotional outbursts. The clinicians I talked to spoke casually about the "explosive" response from turning off the screen, as overstimulated kids react to the yanking of that stimulus with yelling and screaming or even hitting.

Regulating in response to emotions is an intuitive, flexible approach. But to kids, it may also seem arbitrary and opaque. It also puts you in the position of either negotiating or setting a hard limit with kids in a moment where, by definition, they're not in their best mood.

Tom Warshawski, a pediatrician in Canada who is a "screen smart" crusader, has a simple suggestion to make this easier. "Use a timer," he says. "Set it for fifty-five minutes, and then give them five minutes to wind down. Otherwise there's an explosion of anger when you snap off the set."

You may be better off setting clear limits in advance and helping with the transition by offering an alternative activity or a snack. Even when Lulu was as young as two, before we commenced video time in the morning, we would talk about our planned trip to the playground for later in the day.

And if "that glazed look" is getting to be a problem . . . maybe snap off the set sooner next time.

WHAT'S EVERYBODY ELSE DOING?

When I got on the phone with parents to talk about their screen time rules, it was pretty much impossible to stop them from talking about OTHER parents' screen time rules.

"My husband's brother—they're just like Exhibit A in what I'm talking about," a Brooklyn mother of one son, whose name has been withheld to protect family Thanksgiving, told me. "We're really close and I like his brother a lot, but we don't want to vacation with them because his wife is very very very permissive. She's just completely alien to us. I want my son to be close to his cousins, but they're always plugged into the TV. They use it at dinner. At bedtime the kids don't read books."

"I have friends who even when they go to the supermarket the kids have to watch something," says Jessica Robles, a New Jersey mother of two young children. "We're more old school. Even on road trips we sing songs. I do see a difference between my daughter and her peers."

"Compare with some classmates who have their own phones, at age 8!, and email, text and Instagram. Our kids are allowed unlimited access to books and they read," wrote a parent of two school-age kids. And by the way, she comments, these other parents are being pretty irresponsible! "Mostly it seems like a passive babysitter in the morning, evening and weekends so parents can do something else. Either be involved with your kid (and parents can co-watch and co-participate, which is fine) or deal with the consequences."

Our judgments of other parents' decision making, on screen time as on anything else, occur in a broader social context of parenting decisions that are highly scrutinized, and feel highly competitive—among other reasons, because of class lines, and because of the prevailing tone of many discussions on social media.

Lynn Schofield Clark at the University of Denver is the author of *The Parent App,* an ethnographic study of parenting in the digital age, published in 2012. Her work is nuanced and compassionate. She takes care to point out that the very position of being able to limit screen time is a privileged one. It presumes that you have the means to offer your child a safe and preferable alternative, whether that be your own presence, high-quality paid care, organized activities, or toys or games.

For parents, intervening in screen time always comes with trade-offs: "Limiting screen time might result in more hours of paid childcare, more money spent on takeout food, or more chaos in the household," Clark has written. "Those don't seem like very attractive options for most families, and they're not developmentally desirable either."

The practice of prohibiting screen time "gets wrapped up in upper-middle-class norms," she told me. "The responsibility gets shifted to the individual rather than the institution and society."

We could all stand to have a little more empathy for each other. And we shouldn't be looking at this as solely a parenting issue. It's the responsibility of the public health system, including regulators, to try to ensure that the media environment is more beneficial or at least benign. And government at all levels could do a lot more, from paid family leave to childcare subsidies and after-school programs, to ensure that all children have more safe opportunities to learn and play away from screens.

Also, our perceptions of what other parents are doing may not be so accurate. I asked parents in my survey how they thought they stacked up against other parents. Not surprisingly, there was little consensus there.

Many of the families who said they were a 5, the strictest, on a scale of 1 to 5, sounded little different from the ones who said they were permissive.

"They only look at a screen when i give permission. The total amount per week is ~ 4 hrs."

"TV and LeapPad when me or kid is sick. Mostly unlimited."

"Yes to 30–60 min of screen time after school. Yes to 30–60 min of screen weekend mornings and weekend afternoon or eve."

Really, they don't sound all that different from those who rated themselves as a 2:

"He doesn't get the phone/iPad whenever he asks for it, unless we're on an airplane (and then he gets it as much as he wants)."

"No screens on weekdays until homework is done. Weekends—try to limit to 2 (or so) hours."

The few families who described themselves as a 1 or least strict noted that they were parents of teenagers and had pretty much given up trying to control their kids' usage—which is exactly what our parental mediation experts in the last chapter recommend, provided you're not seeing signs of problematic use.

"They are both teenagers involved in school and sports. The time they do spend on iPhones, game stations, etc. is all recreational and not much time for that due to other commitments."

FORBIDDEN FRUIT

The community norms issue comes out in another way: there's a sense that it's hard to draw lines because any media rule enforced at your house is going to be broken down the block.

"We don't want him to be unaware, nor for tech to be a forbidden fruit that he binges on as soon as he's away from us" —by a dad of a three-year-old.

"I know I need to put limits on screen time when they are young, but when they grow up I don't want them to end up watching TV non-stop just because they never learned how to set their own limits and always relied on me to do so."

Helping kids learn how to set their own limits is an important parenting goal in itself. This is a good argument for practicing mediation rather than simply restriction.

FAMILY CONFLICTS

It's one thing to wonder about what the parents down the block or your in-laws are doing. It's another thing to try to enforce consistent rules when there is disagreement within the family unit or across a blended family. A little over a third of my respondents said they disagreed with their partners or others they co-parent with about how much technology to use around the house and how much to permit their kids to use.

Robles says her husband is a lot more attracted to technology than she is, and it does cause conflict. "He's in IT so he's always in front of a screen. He gets home, and he's on his phone updating his Twitter feed. . . . I remember one thing I said to drive home the point: I think you've had more tweets than books you've read to your children. I was really upset. And he said, you're right." She says they both take pride in being equally involved co-parents, and her husband particularly takes pride in contradicting stereotypes about black fatherhood, but his preoccupation with tech has become a sticking point.

"My wife would just like there to be as little screen time as possible and is willing to endure huge amounts of conflict to create that type of environment. I'm allergic to even normal levels of conflict, yet I appreciate how much effort she puts into forcing the girls to connect to our family," says Karel Baloun, a father of two girls in Silicon Valley. After a year of iPhone fights with their teenage daughter, they called in a therapist/parenting coach to referee.

"Our rules are no screens in the bedroom . . . their mom has other rules," one stepmom told me, "because my ten-year-old stepdaughter talks about Minecraft gamers she watches. There was a time when we were told by her eight-year-old sister that when they wake up in the middle of the night, they play games on their phones."

SIBLING DIFFERENCES

Many families have developed different rules and policies for different kids, based on their different reactions to or interests in media, or just changing household circumstances. For example, it's usually harder, if not impossible, to hold the line on "no screens before two" with younger siblings, although one mother and stepmother in a blended family of four sons says that she does prevail on her eleven- and seventeen-year-olds not to watch screens when their toddler brothers are around. "Hard stuff!" she comments.

Generally speaking, boys tend to be far more interested in video games, while girls are more attracted to social media. Parents' rules may respond accordingly. And they may place different limits on girls because of different concerns for their safety. "No bikini shots on Instagram," is an example of a rule clearly intended for a daughter.

Alex Birnbaum has an unusual situation: a four-year-old son with cystic fibrosis who requires daily manual chest percussion, plus time in a forced-air vest attached by tubes to a compressor. Both procedures help free the boy's lungs from mucus. They get through this time with a lot of PBS Kids and Minecraft videos on the iPad. "I don't really have a problem with the screen time because it keeps him compliant with the medical treatment he needs," Birnbaum says, but it's still hard for his daughter, age seven, to understand. "It is unfair. It's a personal affront to her that [her brother] gets to sit up and play with his iPad while she has to go to bed. That's a hard time of the day for all of us."

FAMILY TOGETHERNESS

My anecdotal sample of parents have picked up on research findings that video chat differs from other forms of screen time. It's a commonly expressed belief that Skyping with Grandma doesn't count as bad screen time, even for babies.

"[We] try to not let him see screens or us using screens at all, except to Skype with grandparents maybe once a week or less," said the small-town father of an infant.

"My husband is deployed and I work from my phone so it's an important connection tool for our family," said a suburban mother of three kids under five.

"FaceTime with her grandparents in Mexico for an hour or more" is perfectly fine with a big-city mother of one daughter.

HOW DIFFERENT IS IT, REALLY?

Dealing with constant connectedness is a new rite of passage of parenting, alongside helping our children with sleeping, eating, and using the potty. Just a few years after the introduction of the iPhone, children's developing brains, their relationships, and family life are feeling the ripples.

But people are resilient and adaptable. We're not helplessly at the mercy of the screen. As the years pass, families will come up with better strategies. We'll develop and share practical wisdom to help us through these passages.

It may be helpful to know that although some pediatricians like Christakis are fatalistic about the ability to intervene in children's media exposure en masse, others are more optimistic. Targeted interventions aimed at giving parents strategies for change have sometimes shown significant results.

A 2014 study gave parents information and counseling on the harmful effects of screen time, along with alternatives for spending time together. Parents were instructed to take the TV out of their kids' bedroom and to place "no screen" signs on other screens around the house. Average screen use per household fell dramatically during the study, from ninety to twenty minutes a day. But there wasn't a long-term follow-up to see how the kids were doing.

Tom Warshawski, the anti-obesity pediatrician in Canada, did a large-scale school-based intervention called Screen Smart with 340 kids in second through seventh grades. His Screen Smart materials promote the formula 5-2-1-0, for five servings of fruits and vegetables a day, no more than two hours of screens, one hour of physical activity, and zero sugary beverages.

In one of Warshawski's tests, participants showed a one-hour-per-week reduction in television watching after several weeks, compared to a randomized control group. "Not quite as dramatic as you want," he concedes, "but hopefully if you follow over time it continues to improve." Or, equally, as with many intervention studies, the effects could disappear completely.

In his practice, Warshawski coaches parents facing problems with too much media to gradually cut back. "Cut the hours in half over three to five weeks," he tells them. "You're the parent. If everyone else was smoking cigarettes, would you let your kids smoke too?"

WHAT THE EXPERTS DO

Many of the experts I interviewed for this book are also parents. So naturally, when appropriate, I asked them how they made screen time rules at home. None of them held themselves up as paragons. It was interesting to see how the priorities they focused on in their own research corresponded to the priorities they set at home.

House Rules for the Sleep Researcher: Lauren Hale at Stonybrook is mother to a one-year-old and a four-and-a-half-year-old. She strictly enforces the rules of no screens in the hour before bed, no screens in the bedroom, and no screens as part of the bedtime routine.

"My four-year-old knows the reason. He told my mom recently, who was watching something on her iPad, 'You don't want to look at a screen before bed because it tells your brain to stay awake.'"

House Rules for the Junk Food Advertising Researcher: Kathryn Montgomery at American University, whose research focuses on holding the media industry accountable, notes that she was a working mother. She herself grew up doing homework with the TV on, and she didn't enforce very many rules for her child. "You go to these conferences and you think, oh my God, I'm doing everything wrong: I let them play video games, watch stuff that's inappropriate." But she resists believing that her kid suffered any terrible consequences. "There's too much of a guilt trip put on parents all the time. We're supposed to be protecting kids 24/7. We're always being blamed for everything."

House Rules for the Anti-Obesity Doctor: Tom Warshawski and his wife split their pediatrics practice when their son and daughter, now teens, were growing up so that one of them could always be home. "We limited TV to an hour on weekdays after all other homework was done," he says. "We said categorically no video games—my daughter didn't care, but my son thought it was extremely oppressive and unfair. Then he resigned himself. Ultimately, both of them have thanked us."

House Rules for the Media and Violence Researcher: Doug Gentile at the University of Iowa has a daughter in high school and one in college. He says when they were younger, he "pretty much followed AAP guidelines: one hour a day in elementary school, two hours as they got older. But I'm much more strict on content than I am on time."

Not surprisingly, he doesn't rely on ratings; he would watch something himself before allowing his girls to see it. They were big fans of the Harry Potter books; they would wait for each movie to come out on video and then watch it in short bits, fast-forwarding through the scary parts.

But, he says, being the strict dad did once backfire in a funny way. He's a huge *Star Wars* fan. "I was thirteen when the original movie came out. I waited ten years, ever since she was born, to share this pivotal, important movie with my older daughter, and then she says, 'No. All they do is fight all the way through it.'

"'Oh, please?'

"'No, Dad.'

"She had learned the lesson—if the movie is just about people fighting it's not going to make her feel happy. She's not going to enjoy it."

House Rules for the Anti-Screen Crusader: Victoria Dunckley tells her patients' families to place strict limits on video game use, on the order of fifteen minutes every other day. She's less concerned about old-fashioned TV, especially if it's slow-paced programming viewed from across the room so less blue light gets into the eyes.

House Rules for the Autism Researcher: Karen Heffler, the mother of an adult son who is autistic, says she didn't make screen rules when her son was young, which she now regrets. "I'm a physician and my hours were pretty long. I suspect that he was exposed to a lot of screens, but I don't know for sure."

House Rules for the Autism Advocate: Shannon Rosa has two neurotypical daughters. She takes away her seventeen-year-old's phone at night, and the eleven-year-old gets the iPad only when she's done with work and chores. Her autistic son, she says, is much better at self-regulating. "He has it for ten minutes, and then he knows when he needs to put it away."

House Rules for the Pediatrician: Jenny Radesky, lead author of the 2016 American Academy of Pediatrics guidelines on screen time, and her husband have two young boys, ages five and almost two, and demanding careers. What are the media rules in her house?

"It's a little tricky . . . " she starts out. "We both grew up watching tons of TV and playing video games. We have a big flatscreen TV. I have a smartphone. We're not a tech-averse household."

Her bottom-line answer? About an hour a day . . . just like the predominant response in my unscientific sample. More on snow days, or "If we need to catch up on work, [the older boy] will watch a lot of Rescue Bots."

House Rules for the Parental Mediation Expert: Eric Rasmussen at Texas Tech has four daughters ranging in age from six to fifteen. His research is on the importance of parents in determining media effects on children. And his stance seems fairly laissez-faire. "With the fifteen-year-old we don't monitor as much what she does on the tablet or the phone," he says. "With the other kids, they need to ask: can I do this, can I play on the tablet, can I watch these videos on YouTube. As they grow, gradually we have less rules. Our kids come to know what to expect from us as far as what's allowed and what's not." In his house, "We trust PBS," and Disney and Nickelodeon for entertainment. Violent and sexual content are off-limits.

A RECIPE FOR SUCCESS

The evidence is too new and patchy to rely on expert advice alone. Parents need to make screen rules ourselves. Actually, that's what the experts are doing too. Base them on what works for your kid and what feels good for you. They're certainly going to change over time and that's okay. When your family is at transition points, such as adding a new sibling, moving, or a separation, are also good times to look at the rules and see what needs updating.

Some parents I've spoken with find it helpful and important to restrict more early on, so that home can become a refuge from the technology kids will encounter later. Others are more concerned with scaffolding their kids' use, introducing them to technologies and helping them learn how to set limits. There can be benefits to both approaches.

Throughout this book I've been returning to the metaphor of healthy diet as a way of talking about the role of screens in family life. The total level of intake, or screen time, is a fundamental metric to think about, but it's not the only one. We also want to think about avoiding, or consuming in moderation, certain potentially harmful ingredients and promoting positive, healthy consumption habits. Ultimately, the hope is that we're turning screen time, like mealtime, into a time of togetherness, and engaging kids in creative habits.

Most experts suggest that simple, unilateral limits on time and content work better for infants, toddlers, and young children. But even when they're very young, your responsibility doesn't stop there: it's also important to help them interpret what they see, both for learning and to mediate the messages they're getting.

By the time a child is eight or nine years old, you should bring him or her into the process of setting screen policies, including negotiating priorities and family screen-free time. And authoritative mediation becomes even more important.

Time

Dimitri Christakis and other members of the American Academy of Pediatrics say no more than thirty minutes of screen time a day for infants under age two and up to two hours for older children. Other researchers, like Nancy Carlsson-Paige, argue that it's better to cultivate the ability in young children to play and occupy themselves without screens. Conversely, researchers who focus on the power of parental mediation argue that setting limits by time in older school-aged children, above age eight or nine, is unnecessary, as long as you maintain awareness of how they're spending that time and no specific problems or issues have arisen.

Occasion/Priorities

Keep screens out of the bedroom and turn them off an hour before bedtime, sleep researchers say. Also, there's a wide consensus that family mealtime should be screen-free as a rule. And obesity doctors like Tom Warshawski focus on making an hour of outdoor time or other physical activity a priority.

Parent Involvement

Whether your kid is six months old or sixteen years, some of their screen time should happen with you. For toddlers that means sitting on the couch alongside them and treating a TV show like a picture book. As they get older it means discussing the messages of various shows or games, talking about what happened to them online that day, and helping them find opportunities to create using media or with "screens on the side."

Connecting Goals

Some initial studies show that even for infants, video chat can be more like face-to-face communication than it is like watching TV or playing a video game. One best-practice use of digital devices is communication: Skyping with Grandma, tapping out emojis to Mom at work, drawing a picture or making a short video to email to a friend. Sometimes I'll post a picture of my older daughter on social media, with her permission, and read her the nice comments. As children get older and start using social media independently to connect with peers and strangers, your role as a parent will shift to modeling and encouraging positive forms and habits of connection.

SPECIAL ISSUES

If your child faces any of these special concerns, here are some thoughts on how to address them through screen policies.

Health/Weight

Besides limiting total time to two hours a day and making physical activity a priority/prerequisite, you may want to try to limit exposure to junk food advertising and marketing. Consider prohibiting snacking while watching. Try favoring games as an alternative to video watching. Also look into physically active video game systems like the Wii and Kinect, and activity-based videos, such as yoga, or dance-themed TV shows like *The Wiggles*.

Sleep Issues

Besides keeping screens out of the bedroom and turning them off before bed, also consider whether you're letting tablet or TV time substitute for a nap that your kid still needs. You may have to shift TV time to the morning and keep the afternoons screen-free. Or experiment if you suspect certain kinds of content get your child too revved up.

Attention Issues

There are some correlations between excessive exposure to lots of frenetic action (e.g., Powerpuff Girls cartoons, racing games) and attention disorders. For younger kids you might want to enforce choices of slower-paced shows. For older kids, you might want to install an app like Freedom to limit multitasking when they're doing their homework. There are also certain games like NeuroRacer that promise to help children develop attentional control.

Behavior Issues/Emotional Regulation/Aggression

In some kids, screen time can be a trigger for explosive and aggressive behavior. You may be able to get around this in the short term by setting a timer and giving a five-minute warning. Learning to manage this trigger can be an important part of kids' growing up. Help kids strategize through the transition away from screens with the expectation that if they complain or cry, the answer will be "no" next time.

If aggression is a problem in your house, limit specific shows, sites, or games that correlate with this behavior—as a general rule, violent content on the screen is associated with violent actions, as well as anxiety and desensitization. In extreme cases, psychiatrist Victoria Dunckley would suggest getting rid of video games and limiting screen time to slow-paced television shows, with the screen physically far away from the viewer.

Anxiety/Depression/Narcissism

Social media use, particularly at night, is associated with anxiety, depression, and narcissism in adolescents. So are long bouts of video game playing. Limiting these or even doing a "screen detox" may be considered along with other forms of treatment.

Addiction/Compulsion/Problematic Levels of Use

Addiction is not defined solely by time spent at the computer or on the phone. It's defined as a lack of interest in other activities, a "pruning away" of offline connections, and practical problems coping at school or at home. If you run through the checklist in chapter 2 and see some red flags, talk with your child and consider calling in a therapist as well.

6 SCREENS AT SCHOOL

WHEN MY OLDER DAUGHTER, LULU, WAS IN PRE-K, SHE INFORMED US THAT her favorite activity during "choice time" was the iPad station. Even as we were limiting screen time at home, she was pinching, tapping, and swiping away at school. The only thing she definitely learned in this fashion was the nursery rhyme "Little Boy Blue," set to what, in her rendition, sounded like a vaguely Eastern European dirge.

For the last decade my beat as a journalist has been education, specifically educational innovation, which often involves new technologies. One of my big motivations to write this book was to make sense of the incredible disconnect between two conversations: one about screens in school and the second about kids and screens everywhere else.

As we've been exploring for several chapters now, the "kids and screens" conversation at this moment feels dominated by anxiety. Whether we're hearing about adverse effects on early brain development, attachment disorders, attention problems and emotional regulation, sexting, cyberbullying, addiction, anxiety, depression, or narcissism, the dominant message is that it's the job of all responsible parents to walk back and shut down kids' technology use.

A big part of what I've been trying to do here is to add nuance and balance that message, using healthy eating as an analogy to talk about what healthy media experiences look like. But the conversation about kids and screens *at school* seems to be taking place on an entirely different planet.

If you listen to tech industry leaders like Mark Zuckerberg or Bill Gates, you'll hear about the near-messianic potential of technology to educate the masses. Low-cost mobile devices and free content will deliver basic learning resources for all. New applications of artificial intelligence will accelerate learning beyond anything previously seen, by providing customized content at the perfect pace for each student—a magical "robot tutor in the sky," in the colorful words of one entrepreneur. Meanwhile, as digital literacy takes its rightful place alongside reading, writing and math, every child will become a coder, unleashing a generation of geniuses empowered to design and engineer us a utopian future.

If you can't tell, a lot of this is hype. In some cases, dangerous hype. But there are still good arguments for incorporating technology into your children's education, and best practices for doing so.

These practices can be seen as an extension of the mores of positive parenting with media. Innovative educators and innovative parents share the goals of fostering creativity, connection, geeking out, messing around, and helping kids achieve their personal goals and visions while gaining important skills in the bargain.

There are amazing learning resources and communities online. There are fascinating models for engaging teaching and independent learning in any subject using technology. You can start exploring digital literacy with your kids as young as age three or four. I'll give you the best available research-based guidelines for sorting out the good, the bad, and the mediocre.

But although this chapter is called "Screens at School," I have a caution. Truly excellent digital learning experiences facilitated by your kids' teachers at school are likely to be the exception, not the rule. Just like any other great teaching, sadly.

Parents should play that sponsoring and brokering role in our kids' digital education. Often this happens through informal learning opportunities like mentors, tutors, after-school programs, and summer camps. I see many parents leveraging digital resources to enhance and supplement what schools offer. There are also some worst practices to watch out for with computers in the classroom and for homework, particularly for the parents of highly sensitive orchid children.

WHAT MAKES COMPUTERS EDUCATIONAL?

I was surprised to learn that the history of personal computing in general is utterly entwined with the history of educational technologies intended for children.

In the early 1960s, a South African mathematician named Seymour Papert came to MIT. Cognitive scientist Marvin Minsky had invited Papert to become co-director of his new artificial intelligence lab. Papert was not your stereotypical antisocial math geek. His passion was "thinking about thinking." He had previously spent several years in Geneva working with Jean Piaget, perhaps the most famous developmental psychologist in history.

At a time when computers were the size of a room and cost hundreds of thousands of dollars, Papert was one of the first to argue that every child should have one. In 1967 his team introduced LOGO, the first programming language intended for children. By putting together simple commands, represented visually, children could instruct a robot turtle or an animated turtle on a screen to draw pictures, say, or play a song.

Around that time a PhD candidate named Alan Kay visited Papert's lab. Inspired, he shortly thereafter sketched something called the Dynabook, considered one of the earliest prototypes of both tablet and laptop computers. The design decisions Papert had made to make computing accessible to children helped inspire the personal computing revolution.

Papert dubbed his theory of learning *constructionism*, echoing the name of Piaget's most famous theory, known as *constructivism*. Piaget was interested in children's processes of observing and forming theories about the world. He is credited with the idea that children move through more or less predictable stages of abstract reasoning as they grow, and that they learn more from actively encountering the world than they do from being explicitly taught by grown-ups.

Programming computers and using them as creative tools, argued Papert, gave children an opportunity to construct their own understanding of abstract concepts. The computer was a virtual space, a kind of Math-land where kids could acquire math the same way they pick up French by visiting France.

In later decades, as personal computing advanced, Papert's argument for technology in the classroom got simpler. In 2000, he was living in Maine, where he became involved with the first state initiative to provide a laptop for every student.

"Every seventh grader should have a laptop computer because everybody should have a laptop computer," he said around that time at a speech at Bates College. "And why? Again the short answer is 'Well, I have one.'" After audience laughter died down, he continued, "I couldn't get to do a quarter of the things I do without it and everybody I know with very, very few exceptions engaged in any sort of intellectual creative work—writers, artists, historians, mathematicians—they have and use these things, so it seems obvious that it's the prime instrument for our days for intellectual work. Now you might not think that the work of kids is intellectual . . . If you don't think that, that's why we're in such trouble. It is and ought to be. And so, . . . Why would it occur to anybody to deprive them of this intellectual tool?"

Children have important intellectual work to do. They need tools. This vision of educational technology is simple, progressive, and empowering. The idea of one-to-one educational computing—a device for every student—has now become commonplace.

And Papert, who died in 2016 at age 88, directly inspired a long list of present-day educational trends, like the children's programming languages Scratch and ScratchJr, the One Laptop per Child project, the Maker movement, and the programmable robotic LEGO known as Mindstorms after one of his books.

But as ed tech has become more popular and powerful, Papert's progressive vision has not taken over mainstream education in the United States or anywhere else. Instead, in many cases screen time in the classroom looks very similar to what it was in my daughter's first year of public school in Brooklyn—a fairly passive, isolated, and conventional activity, controlled and directed both by teachers and by the people who create the software.

Let's take a closer look at why that is.

THE GOOD, THE BAD, AND THE MEDIOCRE

Most parents these days encounter tech that makes educational claims well before kids start formal schooling. Since the iPad debuted in 2010, a hundred thousand different "educational" apps have appeared. The plurality [i.e., more than any other age group but not an absolute majority] of these are directed at preschoolers. "It's a torrential downpour flooding the market every single day," says Kathy Hirsh-Pasek, a developmental psychologist with decades of experience in the science of learning. "There's false advertising, just as there is in the 'educational' toy business. How's a parent to know what's worthwhile?"

Hirsh-Pasek can tell you. She's the lead author of a widely cited 2015 paper that provides a set of guidelines, based on learning research, for separating the few good apps and videos from the many bad and overwhelming number of mediocre ones. With some exceptions, what's most common in this first wave of apps, she says, "are simply digital worksheets, games, and puzzles that have been reproduced in an e-format."

According to Hirsh-Pasek and her collaborators, educational technology offerings, whether videos or interactive apps, work best when designed for participants to do the following:

1. Be actively involved ("minds-on") vs. passively watching or mindlessly responding
2. Be engaged with the learning materials vs. distracted by irrelevant bells and whistles
3. Have meaningful experiences that relate to their lives, vs. shallow and rote learning without context
4. Socially interact with others in high-quality ways using new material

Let's unpack these four principles a bit.

1. Active involvement: Some thoughtful action is taken on the learner's part. For example, in one study, when adults were tasked with learning how to tie a nautical knot via video, they

performed better when they were allowed to pause and rewind the video than when they were permitted only to watch it. In a kid's app this could mean hunting for a shape within a hidden-pictures scene, or tilting the screen to move an animated ball through a maze.

2. Engagement: You have to be careful on this score. Moment-by-moment engagement in a TV show or app is often procured through bright colors, loud music, quick changes of scene, and "reward" effects. These can distract from the learning goal. For example, a 2013 study by Hirsh-Pasek and others found that when an ebook had animation in random parts of the picture—say grass waving in the background—three-year-olds had a harder time following the story. On the other hand, if Babar the Elephant is waving and saying hello, it might be easier for kids to tell that he's the main character.

   In order for a learning game or app to consistently hold a child's attention, it has to be age-appropriate. Even better if it's suited to a child's particular interest, such as animals or music. Stories and compelling characters are a tried-and-true path to engagement.

   Research has shown that children as young as eighteen months can form parasocial relationships with beloved characters encountered in videos and elaborated through play, and that they can learn a given task in, say, math, better when presented by Elmo vs. a random red bear.

3. Meaningful experiences: It's been shown, Hirsh-Pasek writes, that children have an easier time recalling educational content when it's tied into a narrative of some kind. Even better if a task relates back to some other experience in a child's life. Hirsh-Pasek uses the example of an app that asks children to take photos of "something square" or "a group of three things," requiring them to take a new look at objects in their surroundings.

4. Social interaction: As we saw in chapters 2 and 4, research shows that children learn best when another person is listening, asking questions, encouraging them, and providing feedback.

Hirsh-Pasek recognizes, however, that "sometimes you need to do dishes or laundry," and that the whole point of educational apps for most parents, and, realistically, in many classrooms as well, is to keep the kids independently occupied.

"You could not have one of these four features and still be a darn good app," she argues, and "the one that's the most dispensable is social interaction. But if you're going to optimize learning, there's no question that the best way to optimize is to be with your kids."

Warren Buckleitner has been devoted to rating and reviewing educational technology since his master's thesis back in 1984. He publishes the *Children's Technology Review,* which has an online database of twelve thousand reviews of digital educational products (for paid subscribers only), and also holds an annual conference devoted to research on the topic. Echoing Hirsh-Pasek, Buckleitner says that in the world of kids' educational media, "There's a lot of mediocre products, a few are truly excellent, and likewise a few that are really poor quality."

The questions Buckleitner says that parents should ask when checking out an educational app are:

- What do children walk away from the experience(s) with that they didn't have when they first came to the experience(s)? That is, what is the new content or concept here?
- How does the experience empower (or disempower) a child? (In Hirsh-Pasek's terms, requiring active engagement and supplying meaning are empowering; drumming concepts into someone's head through repetition is disempowering.)
- Does this experience leverage the potential of technology in a way that traditional, nondigital, or nonlinear experiences cannot? (Is it basically a digitized worksheet or set of flash cards?)
- How does this product compare with similar products?

The bad apps are usually a result of "bad pedagogy that's been digitized," he says, and he's not afraid to name names. A $1.99 app called Leo and Pals 2D Shapes, for example, is designed for preschoolers, yet it requires reading to use the main menu. Both the animation and the audio are amateurish. The animal characters distract from the educational content: instead of, say, finding a triangle in Leo's mane, you simply see a blue triangle, replaced by an unrelated image of Leo, a sequence likely to challenge the attention span of a two- or three-year old. And the app provides feedback in the form of frowny and smiley faces, of which Buckleitner says, "Developmentally, that's a bad thing to do."

Darren Steadman, developer of Leo and Pals, responds that he built his app in part based on recommendations from the Children's Television Workshop, and that it is in daily use at educational establishments in the United States and the UK. "No app is perfect but we feel that we have learnt a lot from the first app we created and we are always happy to receive feedback (good or bad) that will allow us to make better apps in the future."

Aside from *Children's Technology Review,* which sports a delightful 1990s-era interface, Common Sense Media has more than two thousand free ratings and reviews of educational apps, videos, and websites.

In finding more quality ways for your kids to spend time with devices, sometimes apps and content not explicitly designated "educational" are the best bet for satisfying Hirsh-Pasek's and Buckleitner's guidelines, to say nothing of Papert's. The camera and its filters, a paintbox app, a voice recorder, a word processor, voice-based search, and digital musical instruments can all be active, engaging, meaningful, and empowering ways to learn using technology.

COMPUTERS IN CLASSROOMS

Screens are at school to stay. The Programme for International Student Assessment (PISA) found that the average ratio of students to computers in the United States was two to one by 2012. The adoption of the Common Core State Standards in more than forty states, starting in 2011, came with new state tests administered online, which further accelerated the need to buy computers and install additional bandwidth. In 2016 alone, US K–12 districts bought 12.6 million devices like laptops and tablets, an 18 percent increase over the year before. When you add in the mobile devices that many US children start owning at a typical age of ten, the true number of screens at most schools is probably one for each student, or even higher.

The downer is what's actually being done with all that processing power. Just as the world of general consumer educational apps is distinguished by a few good, some bad, and a whole lot of mediocre; by digitized versions of paper worksheets; and by not-so-hot pedagogy brought to the pixilated screen, the same can be said, by and large, for apps and technologies used in classrooms, and also for the way they are incorporated alongside the rest of what goes on in school.

I'm inside classrooms around the country usually a couple of times a month. When it comes to how technology is actually being deployed, the most common trends and scenarios I and other researchers encounter can be summarized as follows: the Paperless Classroom, Rotation Stations, and Distraction Derbies.

The Paperless Classroom

Google's free suite of apps for education (GAFE) may be the most popular software tools used in schools today, with seventy million users as of 2017, and also among the least disruptive to the status quo. What the "G Suite" and other learning management systems do, fundamentally, is bring basic classroom functions like the calendar, grade book, assignments, syllabus, notes home, and behavior tallies online, where they are accessible anywhere and searchable.

There are some pedagogical advantages here. Text-based discussions may give shy students more time to think over their answers. Grading essays over Google Docs, where you can flip instantly back and forth between different versions, may give students more insight into the revision process. When a group presentation is created in Google Slides, teachers can see exactly how many edits each person made and assign a collaboration grade accordingly. Some of these systems offer parents a lot of insight into the learning process, with daily texts, photos, or even peeks at the grade book, which can be helpful or not so helpful depending on what parents do with that information.

Even if the G Suite or similar learning management systems are only used to support traditional teaching, you would think anything that takes bureaucratic tasks off a teacher's plate ought to be a net gain for learning. The problem is that digital tools, both software and hardware, age quickly compared to their analog precursors. And they're subject to fads: the classroom market share of Apple products, for example, fell dramatically from 40 percent in 2013 at the height of the iPad craze to 17 percent in the first quarter of 2016 as schools realized they'd rather students have keyboards.

The constant need for upgrades—and even more so, for professional development to bring teachers up to speed with new systems—bogs things down. Internet speed is a problem at too many public schools as well. So the net benefit of the paperless classroom in terms of efficiency is hard to calculate at this point, not that it's stopping school districts from signing up and spending the money.

Rotation Stations

Almost as common as digital recordkeeping in schools is the use of computers and software to help deliver traditional educational subjects. This is commonly seen in a rotation model: students spending time each day or each week at a classroom computer station, in a computer lab or the library, doing solo practice, quizzes, and tests, with occasional support by a teacher. The teacher may also take advantage of that time to give more individual attention to a smaller group of students. Tech-based lessons may also take the form of "pullouts" for kids identified as needing extra help or enrichment. Or technology teachers may "push in" to classrooms with a laptop or tablet cart and offer instruction in topics like coding.

All of the major dead-tree textbook publishers now produce learning software, along with some newer kids on the block. The majority concentrate on math and English language arts, then social studies, science, and other subjects. Some of the most popular names in the biz are i-Ready, 360 Degree Math, ST Math, Lexia, DreamBox, and Khan Academy.

Today's educational software, with its "gamified" features like gold stars and leaderboards, offers a relatively painless way for students to memorize content like letter sounds or multiplication tables. But that's just the beginning of the claims made by these products' manufacturers.

The biggest selling point with these programs is the idea that students will be able to move through material at their own pace. In a large 2014 survey of twenty thousand American teachers, three quarters said that the students in their classes spanned four or more grade levels in reading ability. And yet in a traditional public school classroom, what's covered in a given day depends more on the date on the calendar than it does the individual mastery level of twenty-five or thirty diverse students in a class. Within a program like DreamBox or i-Ready, students start by taking a diagnostic quiz and don't move on until they've given enough right answers to multiple-choice questions to prove that they've mastered each piece of material.

But ed-tech developers promise more than going at each student's own pace. At their best, these tools give students many more choices in how material is presented than is possible within a traditional lesson. Text, video, interactive displays and exercises, hints, and endless practice problems are all available.

For example, DreamBox lets students explore math through virtual "manipulatives"—that is, animated, interactive versions of the abacuses, blocks, puzzles, compasses, clocks, and other tools that students often don't get enough access to in a traditional paper-and-chalkboard math classroom, because there just isn't enough time or space.

Tim Hudson, the company's vice president of learning, argues that DreamBox's online versions of these activities are smarter and therefore better. In a typical first-grade math exercise, he says, students might be asked to line up thirty-seven wooden beads. The DreamBox system assigns a higher score to a student who shows good number sense by choosing three groups of ten, a five, and two singles, compared to the student who laboriously counts from one to thirty-seven. If the exercise was done in the real world, both students would arrive at the same correct answer. The teacher wouldn't know the difference unless she happened to be watching at the time. And the students wouldn't get that feedback. (On the other hand, young children, especially, are likely to learn something from touching real wooden beads that they don't get from a digital display.)

All of the software companies I've mentioned can produce research studies showing that they can improve and accelerate student learning.

Large meta-analyses of similar programs have shown that in some situations they can work as well as a live private tutor.

But a comprehensive 2015 report by PISA undermined some of these claims. PISA is a standardized test given to fifteen-year-olds around the world. The report found that among thirty-eight developed countries, the *less* they used computers for schoolwork, the *higher* they scored in math. In reading, a minimal amount of computer access had a positive impact, but the students who scored the highest accessed computers less than once a *month* for practice drills or other school-related purposes. Even when they tested the tenth-graders on tasks that actually required a computer—their fluency and retention when reading a text online, their ability to navigate and stay on task without distractions when browsing the web for information—those who reported using computers the most frequently had the lowest scores of all.

Sending a message by email is definitely faster than posting a letter. Booking a flight online is inarguably easier than going through a travel agent. But a process as complex as learning doesn't seem so susceptible to efficiency through automation, at least in these early days.

Many ed-tech salespeople today are moderating their rhetoric to focus on assisting rather than replacing teachers. "We're focused on supporting great teaching and learning," Jessie Woolley-Wilson, the CEO of DreamBox, told me. "There were times when some people had the belief that blended [learning using software] was going to replace live instruction." Not so, she argues. "The best blended implementation happens . . . in partnership with teachers. . . . That's the real win."

To decode a bit, that means that when students do homework in a "rotation station" program like DreamBox or i-Ready, a teacher, theoretically, walks into the classroom the next morning already understanding the progress each student has already made on each concept being covered that day. If the teacher only has five minutes to spend one-on-one, he or she can spend those five minutes going over the exact problem a student needs help with. And, not for nothing, the teacher can spend next to no time grading multiple-choice questions by hand.

Brian Greenberg runs a foundation called Silicon Schools. They invest in many Silicon Valley–area charters considered cutting edge when it comes to the use of technology, including Summit Schools,

Khan Academy, and Alpha Schools. At these "rotation station" schools, students spend part of the day working on laptops with personalized "playlists" of online practice problems and activities, and part of the day in small-group tutoring and more hands-on group work. Students are generally grouped by ability and interest, not by age.

The vision here is of highly skilled teaching augmented by tech. "What would happen if kids sat through as few lessons as possible that weren't right for them or that they weren't ready for, and teachers spent less time in tasks that could be replaced by technology and shifted to tasks that only a skilled teacher could do—goal-setting, feedback, deep Socratic conversation?" Greenberg asked. "I think there's a huge amount to be gained."

Technology is no magic potion that turns Cameron Diaz in *Bad Teacher* into Michelle Pfeiffer in *Dangerous Minds*. These innovators suggest that learning technology doesn't work best as an add-on to a traditional class. It needs to be integrated thoughtfully, with plenty of support from instructors who can communicate the benefits. And sadly, too many teachers do not have that training.

Distraction Derbies

Even as school systems are seeing only modest gains from incorporating tech tools into their processes and routines, there are also costs. Neil Selwyn is a professor of education at Monash University in Australia, where he did a three-year ethnographic study of technology use at three different high schools. He deliberately chose schools that were far from the bleeding edge when it came to the use of technology. One had Dell laptops for every student, a second had an iPad program where students could either bring their own or lease one from the school, and the third had a "bring your own device" program, meaning students could use any model of laptop, tablet, or mobile phone they wanted.

A key finding was that "schools as a site are just not well set up for technology." Charging was a constant problem, as was Internet speed, as were chronically outdated devices that got bogged down with malware, viruses, and spilled soda, requiring students and teachers to constantly troubleshoot. I see these mundane problems at nearly every school I visit.

Another issue should be familiar to any parent. When students have access to all the world's information and entertainment at their fingertips, teachers fight an uphill battle for their attention. The first five minutes of each class, Selwyn reported, was generally devoted to "firefighting," with the constant refrain, "Lids down, earbuds out, phones on table."

In tech-enabled classrooms, students' work habits start to resemble those of modern-day office workers, for better and for worse. On the upside, computers give students the option to work independently, allowing for more personalized learning, just as advertised. On the downside, Selwyn observed, some teachers allowed students to listen to music all day, and it was pretty common to have schoolwork open in one window and a social network or chat windows open at the same time.

Selwyn doesn't necessarily see this as a disaster. Everyone needs to zone out sometimes, especially in the highly regimented and standardized atmosphere of school. "You or I would have looked out the window. These kids are listening to Jay-Z or Grimes. Fair enough."

But some kids may not be able to cope well with the ever-present distraction. It could exacerbate ADHD or other issues. Victoria Dunckley, the anti-screens psychiatrist from chapter 3, says that until a few years ago, she could simply write notes excusing her most sensitive patients from using computers at school. The advent of one-to-one iPad programs, she said, changed all that. "I tried to talk to a school and say, just stop that, and I got a lot bigger pushback. I'm like, this child has autism. We need to just help him develop. Who cares about the Common Core?"

The adoption of computers for schoolwork and homework also makes it much harder, as we found early in our family, for parents to negotiate overall screen time limits and boundaries at home. How do you ground a kid who needs her computer to do homework?

Devorah Heitner, author of the book *Screenwise* and a parent educator, has a practical suggestion. "Get the grade level expectations for homework from your kid's teacher. If it's ninety minutes a night and your child is taking four hours, there's something wrong and you want to look at that. Maybe your kid is snowing you, playing games or doing something else, or they truly don't recognize the toll that distraction is taking." You could try using a productivity app like Freedom or turning off the Wi-Fi after a certain time at night, but as always, it makes sense to try to get buy-in from your school-aged kid on any plan you make—and share your own struggles and strategies too, says Heitner. None of us is immune to distraction.

Sonia Livingstone published a book in 2016, *The Class: Living and Learning in the Digital Age,* that took a close look at the technology habits of middle schoolers in London. What Selwyn and Livingstone both found, and what I find in many of the schools I visit as well, is an awkward blend of the worst of both worlds: the old crashing into the new. Tech mandates come from above and change yearly; purchasing orders for devices and software are written at the district office. Tech often adds to teachers' workload through chores like increased email volume or monitoring students in online forums after school. The teachers who seemingly effortlessly communicate their enthusiasm for tech to students, are exceptions to the rule. "I don't hear the same excitement that there was ten years ago," says Livingstone. "It's only around the really geeky enthusiastic teachers that things are happening." Heitner sees the same issue in the schools she works with. "A lot of schools are sold on the benefits of a one-to-one program, for example. They're not necessarily doing enough professional development for teachers, who don't all have an equal level of confidence and competence."

THE CHEETOS ISSUE

Even as ed-tech developers are working to create new applications, and schools and universities are grappling with how best to use them, some argue that a "hidden curriculum" is being delivered: marketing messages from technology companies. Brett Frischmann, an intellectual-property expert at Cardozo Law School, and author of the book *Being Human in the 21st Century: How Social and Technological Tools Are Reshaping Humanity* (Cambridge University Press, 2017), points out, "When McDonald's or Cheetos brings their crappy food into the schools, it's not about making money, it's about shaping children's preferences. That's the same thing Apple and Google are trying to do [with education apps, iPads, and Chromebooks]. They're . . . building lifelong customers," he argues. "Why in second grade do students need Chromebooks to do math? Maybe there are some gains, and that's what people emphasize. The thing that no one talks about is how you're conditioning kids to always interface through a screen."

Commercial vendors, like textbook publishers, have always done business with public schools. Still, the growth of educational technology has meant an increasingly prominent role for corporate interests, from large tech and entertainment companies to small startups. This shift is epitomized by the journey of Pearson Education. Founded as a British construction company and later growing into a huge conglomerate, Pearson has gradually sold off its noneducation businesses in the last several years to become the largest education business in the world, providing standardized tests, software, and educational materials and even operating fully privatized schools both bricks-and-mortar and online.

ONE LAPTOP, ONE LESS TEACHER?

The intersection of technology and the profit motive has already had grave results for students. Today, almost two hundred thousand children and teenagers attend for-profit, fully online K–12 charter schools in the United States. Their results are generally so abysmal that even the charter school lobby has called for many to be shut down.

Meanwhile, all over Africa and Asia, chains of for-profit schools like Bridge International Academies provide just several weeks of training to teachers, who quite literally read scripted lessons directly off tablet computers—an interaction about as skilled as the one you have with the person behind the counter at a rental car company. Pearson, the Gates Foundation, and Mark Zuckerberg have all supported this model, and the nation of Liberia, incredibly, outsourced its entire public school system to Bridge Academies beginning in 2016.

Betsy DeVos, the education secretary named by President Donald Trump, is a major advocate of both online schools and privatization. In Michigan, where she concentrated her philanthropy and lobbying, 80 percent of bricks-and-mortar charter schools are run for profit, the highest percentage in the country.

DATA DRIVEN

Hand in hand with concerns about privatization come concerns about privacy. The ed-tech industry keeps gathering more information on students and making it easier for teachers to record and share it.

The increased volume of student data is at risk from hackers, accidental leaks, and marketers. Multiple breaches have already been documented: in February 2016, the University of Central Florida admitted the theft of sixty-three thousand social security numbers and names of students and alumni. Most current agreements between schools and their vendors for data storage don't even require parents to be informed when student data is exposed.

Besides the data they collect for record keeping, school-provided computers are turning some schools into little Big Brothers. One such security program I reported on for NPR, called GoGuardian, has triggered several interventions where a school IT director calls parents because a student is searching terms related to suicide—in his or her own home, at night. Elana Zeide, a research fellow at NYU's Information Law Institute and an expert on student privacy and data, told me she worries about the hidden message: "Are we conditioning children to accept constant monitoring as the normal state of affairs in everyday life?"

A glaring ethical and legal question to be resolved is the future of the real-life permanent record. A modern-day student data file now contains a wealth of personal information that could be life-changing if misused. Currently the law recognizes no right to seal or alter these records. This raises the specter that your child's suspension in third grade could be used to deny him a job fifteen years later. Or that someone could be nudged out of university because big data predict she is overwhelmingly likely to drop out.

"If someone makes an 'adverse decision' about you based on your credit report, they have to inform you," Joel Reidenberg, a privacy expert at Fordham University School of Law, told me. Yet no such right to know—let alone a right to appeal—exists for student records.

Some states including New York and California are appointing student privacy czars, and several pieces of legislation are in circulation.

If you're concerned about this issue and want to learn more, a good place to start is the Electronic Privacy Information Center's student privacy project.

SHARING SCREENS

I've painted a pretty dismal picture of screens in school thus far. After several years on this beat, it actually surprises even me what a dyspeptic view I've been taking. But the fact is that media in schools is often applied in unimaginative ways, adding sludge to educational processes, opening up schools to the intrusion of commercial interests. Privacy is a growing and real concern. And the impact on learning—the point of the whole thing, one would think—is mixed at best.

On the one hand, says Livingstone, tech is "good for things that schools are struggling with," so-called twenty-first-century skills like multimedia communication, collaborative projects, and interest-driven learning, and of course engineering and other skills related to technology itself. On the other hand, she says, "it's also not quite established for schools what the benefits are yet. We're asking them to change teacher training curriculum, management, investment, funding, and in return, there are some evaluations that show a result of better learning and more equality, but plenty of studies that don't. So that's not the most appealing message: change everything and we think it might work. We wouldn't roll out new drugs on that basis."

I agree with Livingstone that there's a real resonance between the use of technology and the cultivation of ways of learning that kids need to experience, today more than ever. I've personally witnessed some pretty miraculous encounters between tech tools and curious kids. In 2009, at a migrant-worker camp in Baja California, Mexico, with Stanford professor Paul Kim, I saw a group of indigenous children who don't get the chance to regularly attend school band up in groups of two or three to figure out the controls on a handheld educational device called TeacherMate. Within minutes they were reading along with stories in Spanish and playing math games, all without direct instruction.

At the World Maker Faire in Queens in 2014, which is one of the best places to see a vision like Papert's come to life, I talked to Huan

Zhang, captain of the Titanium Tigers, an all-girl high school robotics team. In their rookie year, they made it to regional competition with a programmable contraption that rolls around picking up and stacking blocks. "Class is so mandated," the seventeen-year-old told me. "I suffocate myself with studying, studying, studying. With this, I put in my own effort. It's like my child, seeing it come to life."

And in the fall of 2015, at a public school in Los Angeles called the Incubator School founded by teacher Sujata Bhatt, I spoke to a group of sixth-graders using the video game platform Minecraft to construct a historically accurate environment for a specific Neolithic people, based on real-life artifacts discovered at an archaeological site in Pakistan. Some focused on the background research, others on troubleshooting the technology. "I really like this history project," Ahad Lakhani, a well-spoken sixth-grader with glasses, told me. "If I went to any other school I wouldn't play Minecraft for a grade. And I feel like this teaches us to collaborate. This is graded as a group and it's also graded individually, so you really have to choose well and work with your group. And everything can't be your way. That's what I've learned."

Creative teachers across the country and the world are harnessing kids' fascination with digital media to set the stage for awesome learning experiences, both in school and after school. Passion-driven learning, collaboration, geeking out—it's all there. Often these experiences combine individual research, group collaboration, and creative presentation—all in ways that "leverage the potential of technology in a way that traditional, nondigital experiences cannot," in Buckleitner's words.

What also makes schools like Bhatt's exciting is the sight of teachers and students working side by side to fully take on the challenge of imagining what education in the twenty-first century should look like. "We want to offer rigor, creativity, and freedom," Bhatt told me.

To generalize greatly, if you want your kid to be in a classroom or after-school program like this, one thing to look for is a bunch of students sharing a single screen at least some of the time. That means they're probably working together toward a goal and engaging with each other rather than being distracted by off-topic conversations, games, or music.

Maer Ben-Yisrael is technology director at Ecole Bilingue de Berkeley—a PK–8 independent French bilingual school. "Every school year, some fourth- to eighth-grade parent will inevitably seek my guidance about their student's use of technology," he says. He encourages parents to see themselves as partners with the school, keeping in mind that different uses of technology are appropriate at different times.

"I always recommend two things:

1. Encourage and give space for the student's *constructive, creative, and collaborative* use of technology (or introduce new avenues for such). There are really easy entry points at their fingertips: Scratch, Minecraft, moviemaking on iPads. . . . Kids can transfer these skills to academic work as well as personal endeavors.

2. Give them some fixed amount of time for pure media *consumption,* be it videos or playing games, and be present for it. This acts as a pressure release valve. Motivated kids will *always* find a way to screw around, but my experience with one-to-one device programs in grades six through eight is that kids *need* to be able to explore their device and the world it allows them to tap into. When you give them time and space to do it, they are more likely to respect the rules of the road at home and in class."

COMPUTER SCIENCE FOR ALL

"In the coming years . . . every student [will receive] the hands-on computer science and math classes that make them job-ready on Day 1." That promise came from our former commander-in-chief, President Barack Obama, in his final State of the Union address in 2016.

This idea is on a roll. The biggest public school systems in the country, New York City and Los Angeles Unified, have both announced that they're moving toward exposing all students to computer science.

The economic argument for this is that more and more jobs will require at least a basic conversance with coding. The cultural argument is that as our society becomes increasingly dominated by digital technologies, people who lack the keys to build their own technological solutions to problems—who today are disproportionately women and minorities—will be increasingly disempowered as citizens and as individuals. And the educational argument is that digital literacy is indeed a basic literacy—that coding requires skills crucial for regular reading, writing, and arithmetic, such as sequencing (putting ideas in a given order), and syntax (matching abstract symbols with ideas).

Regardless of how you feel about the merits of each argument, there's a long way to go. The Computer Science Teachers Association estimates that only about one tenth of the high schools in the United States—to say nothing of middle and elementary schools—offer a computer science course today. "The pipeline [for computer science teachers] is the biggest issue. There isn't a pipeline," Leigh Ann Sudol-DeLyser with CSNYC, a nonprofit helping implement New York's Computer Science for All initiative, told me. The problem is clear: people with tech skills can make a lot more money working in private industry than they can as teachers.

But the field has a lot of momentum, and there are new resources every day. A nonprofit called Code.org, founded in 2013 with broad support from the software industry, has had tens of millions of students take part in its Hour of Code project, an annual mass online day of game-based coding lessons in public schools, and has helped prepare thirty-one thousand teachers to teach computer science as well.

Entrepreneurs and educators are also getting involved in coding for early learners. My daughter enjoys a game called The Foos that teaches the ABCs of coding to pre-readers. Creator Grant Hosford was inspired when his older daughter signed up for a robot-building class in first grade. She was the only girl, and the youngest by a couple of years.

"If we were teaching coding like reading and math, we would break it down into bite-size chunks, make it more fun with songs and stories, and give students two decades to reach mastery," Hosford told me. "With coding we throw you in the deep end in high school or college and are surprised when most kids drown."

Mitchel Resnick, a longtime colleague and friend of Seymour Papert's, has been at the forefront of computer science and early education for decades. He heads up the Lifelong Kindergarten group, which develops new technologies for creativity at MIT's Media Lab. His team developed Scratch, a visual programming language designed for kids that depicts commands as blocks that can be snapped together, like

LEGO, into complex chains of instructions. A version called ScratchJr, intended for those as young as age five, has been downloaded over 1.5 million times from the Apple App Store and has partnerships featuring kids' characters from PBS and Cartoon Network.

Initial play with ScratchJr often means instructing cartoon characters to dance, sing, and act out lines of dialogue. "Coding is not just a set of technical skills," Resnick told me. "It's a new way of expressing yourself. It's similar to learning to write—a way for kids to organize, express, and share ideas."

Marina Umaschi Bers is another former Papert collaborator. She has published small research studies showing that programming improved young children's skills in other areas. For example, when asked to describe the process of brushing their teeth, children gave just three or four steps. After going through a robotics and programming curriculum, they were able to break down the process into twenty or more steps.

"If you get better at sequencing, it has a measurable positive effect on reading comprehension," Bers says. "A parent can have their kid engage in coding with the knowledge that a lot of kids won't become programmers, but there is this broad-based benefit."

WHAT COMES NEXT

The problems in our schools start with a lack of equity, access, funding, and respect and support for teachers. This is all beyond the scope of what tech can fix. But if I'm a bit jaundiced about the status quo of screens at school, I'm still optimistic about the next chapter. As teachers and parents get more savvy about what great learning with technology looks like, there's a chance of more of the good catching on, the bad being stomped out, and the mediocre fading to the background. As for my own daughters, I know it'll take only one great teacher or mentor to get them excited about what technology can do: maybe at school, maybe at summer camp, maybe in middle school robotics club. As Alfred Thompson, a former Microsoft engineer turned high school computer science teacher in Vermont and a member of the board of the Computer Science Teachers Association, told me, "At least once a semester I hear some kid yell, 'Wow! This is like magic!'"

PART II

Our Own Devices: Parents and Screens

7

THE MOM WITH HER PHONE AT THE PLAYGROUND

IT WAS JUNE 2014, A SPARKLING SUNDAY MORNING. I WAS AT THE PLAY-ground with Lulu, then two and a half. I had also just started a new job and I was eager to prove myself. I got involved in a complicated discussion with my boss over email about how to follow up on a breaking news story, glancing up only occasionally at my daughter happily toddling about on the play structure by herself.

In other words, that day, I was the "Mom on the iPhone," the title character of a scalding, scolding 2012 blog post about the evils of looking at your phone at the playground.

As the writer put it:

> Now you are pushing your baby in the swing. She loves it! Cooing and smiling with every push. You don't see her though, do you? Your head is bent, your eyes on your phone as you absently push her swing.
>
> Talk to her. Tell her about the clouds, Mommy. The Creator who made them. Tickle her tummy when she comes near you and enjoy that baby belly laugh that leaves far too quickly.
>
> Put your eyes back on your prize. . . . Your kids.

That post accrued ten million hits. Clearly, she hit a nerve. Mine, for sure. Who was this woman? I wondered. According to her blog, she was a Christian stay-at-home mother of four young children, a disciplinarian whose motto was "slow obedience is NO obedience." But the most telling thing she wrote, to me at least, was in January 2015. She briefly closed the doors on her blog, citing her own preoccupation with technology. In her signoff post she wrote: "Each time [my son] Paxton takes my face in his hands and turns it away from the screen, 'Look at ME, Momma' is one time closer to the time he stops asking all together."

So, it seems like the original mom on her iPhone may really have been talking to herself.

Listen, the years of parenting are short, as the saying goes. But the days . . . the days can be endless. And sometimes you really need to check your email.

While I set out to write the book about kids and screens, I quickly realized that a vital part of the equation was missing. This chapter and the next will unpack the issues that are arising around parents' use of technology. Millennial parents, in particular, spend more time online than any generation before them. That has to affect how we parent.

As my friend Jennifer Bleyer, a writer, editor, and mother of three, wondered in an unapologetic response to that blog post on the parenting website Babble, "Is my habit of punctuating long stretches of undivided attention by communicating with others really *that* bad?"

Good question.

Just as with diets, research shows that kids tend to follow parents' lead when it comes to screen time habits. It is harder to foster your kids' healthy relationship with food if your own relationship is compulsive, furtive, or guilt-ridden. It stands to reason that the same would be true with screens.

The same problems that go along with excessive screen use for younger people—poor sleep, bad eating habits, anxiety, depression—can also affect adults, and by extension, the quality of your parenting and other relationships. However, without pooh-poohing those very real risks, if the research on kids is limited, the present-day research on how parents' everyday, mainstream use of screens may be affecting children, independent of other confounding factors, is almost nonexistent. When you pull aside the curtain, the act of deploring parents' use of media is often based less on evidence and more on an ideological stance that judges mothers for not being fully available to their children at all times and that scapegoats working-class families in particular.

I'm focusing on mothers in this chapter because they are the primary targets of much of this recrimination. Historical theories of child development and attachment, too, put mothers at the center again and again. Dads, that doesn't mean you shouldn't reexamine your habits too. With that cultural baggage in mind, this chapter takes a critical look at the research and debate on the use of digital media, particularly handheld devices, and its influence on family dynamics.

FAST FOOD

You met Dr. Jenny Radesky in chapter 2. She first got interested in the intersection of parenting and digital media while working in an affluent Seattle community.

"I worked in primary care in this large practice that serves a lot of Microsoft families. The iPad had just come out and all these families had smartphones. I thought it was fascinating the way it was changing the dynamic in the clinic room," she told me. She said she actually welcomed it when parents marched in armed with information; less so when they were blatantly Googling for a second opinion even while she was sitting across from them giving the first one. What fascinated her above all was how technology was diverting, channeling, and sometimes thwarting our parenting instincts.

Radesky has published some of the limited research on tech-distracted parenting. She got worldwide media coverage for a small observational study she published in early 2014.

She and her assistants sat in a fast-food restaurant and took notes. Out of fifty-five adults seen eating with children under ten, forty were observed using their smartphones. With Mom, Dad, or sitter heads down in their phones, children made more, and escalating, "bids" for attention, whether positive (singing, making faces) or negative (hitting your sister). When caregivers were sucked into those screens, they responded to the children more slowly, harshly, and otherwise inappropriately.

"Caregivers absorbed in devices frequently ignored the child's behavior for a while and then reacted with a scolding tone of voice, gave
repeated instructions in a somewhat robotic manner (eg, without looking at the child or relevant to child behavior), seemed insensitive to
the child's expressed needs, or used physical responses (eg, one female
adult kicked a child's foot under the table; another female caregiver
pushed a young boy's hands away when he was trying to repeatedly lift
her face up from looking at a tablet screen)."

Again with the pleading little hands on the face.

So, what is the purpose of this study? Besides breaking your heart
into a million pieces?

"I'm interested in how phones shape interaction," Radesky tells me.
"Is this a possible window into changing the dynamic of a family? Especially around family times we know are important to a child's social
and emotional well-being?"

A Happy Meal with Mom buried in a phone is a far cry from the
idealized family dinner. But it's almost as common these days. Is this
really shifting the balance in a bad direction for otherwise healthy,
well-functioning families?

Well, we don't really have any good large-scale data on that yet.
We do know that parents who watch more TV have kids who watch
more TV, which can contribute to adverse effects on those kids. But
there's little proof that a parent's ordinary use of a mobile device is
hurting or otherwise affecting his or her kids either immediately or
down the road.

As we covered in chapter 2, again the dose really seems to make
the poison here. It's impossible to tell by observing a family for just a
few moments whether that trip to the fast-food restaurant might have
been a caregiver's only break in a fourteen-hour day, or whether she
was responding to a demanding boss or checking in on a sick relative.

Nor do we know whether in the past those caregivers might have
occupied themselves with, say, a book, a magazine, or the TV set in the
restaurant instead of focusing on the kids in their charge.

What we can definitively say is that the practice of publicly blaming, shaming, and policing mothers—by the scientific community, the
media, and society at large—is well established and far predates the

advent of any digital technology. When we talk about moms on their phones at the playground, or anywhere else, that history will certainly come to bear. The panic about moms with iPhones, in this way, resembles the moral panic about girls, screens, and sex.

Still, we have to give a fair hearing to the question of whether parents really are going around too much of the time "in a somewhat robotic manner"—with half an eye and half a brain.

OVER OUR HEADS

Certainly real dangers can arise with the hyperavailability of technologies designed to capture and hold our attention and to offer the constant opportunity to connect with people other than the ones in front of you.

In June 2015, three siblings drowned in Irving, Texas. Their mother, Patricia Allen, was at the pool with them and their two younger siblings. A witness initially stated that Allen had been distracted by texting on her cell phone just before Anthony, eleven; August, ten; and Trishawn, nine, slipped under the water.

A tragic story. Is it repeated often enough to rise to the level of a public health threat? Well, one study with an intriguing design suggests that parents distracted by technology are indeed allowing real harm to come to their children. Between 2007, when the iPhone was introduced, and 2010, nationwide, nonfatal injuries to children under age five rose 12 percent, after falling for much of the prior decade, according to the Centers for Disease Control and Prevention magazine's reading of emergency room records.

When the iPhone was first introduced, it could only be used on AT&T's 3G network, which meant that it expanded unevenly into otherwise similar communities. This created a perfect natural experiment to investigate whether there's a causal relationship between the rise in injuries and the spread of smartphones.

In a paper published in 2014, Craig Palsson, an economist at Yale, posited that he'd found just such a connection. Palsson took a look at hospital injury reports collected by the Consumer Product Safety Commission. These reports described where children were, what they were doing at the time of the accident, and whom they were with.

The results are pretty dismaying. In counties that fell under the iPhone coverage area, the rise in serious injuries was larger the younger the children were. It topped out at a 10 percent increase for infants under age one, compared with areas that did not have iPhone access. Interestingly, injuries increased only in cases when children were under parental supervision—coaches, teachers, and daycare workers, presumably, abstain or are restricted from thumbing away on their phones while watching our children for pay.

Palsson suggests that smartphones "increase the opportunity cost of supervising children," by tempting parents to access either work or entertainment instead. Spoken like a true economist. Personally, a cost-benefit analysis is the opposite of what I'm doing when I pull out my phone at the playground. Instead, I'm too often responding to that *ping!* with all the mindfulness of Pavlov's dog.

A final note on risks: we have solid evidence that by far the riskiest time that parents may be using phones is behind the wheel of a car. Car crashes are the leading cause of death for school-aged children, and cell phones are currently estimated to be involved in one in four of all fatal crashes. Traffic deaths have been trending upward since 2014, after declining for decades, and some identify handheld devices as the culprit. Meanwhile, in a 2014 survey, 90 percent of parents said they were distracted by smartphones, CD players, or the onboard navigation system while driving with children in the car. And those are just the ones who admitted it.

THE STILL FACE STUDY

Tech distraction poses real risks to our children. Yet most of the hand-wringing about moms at the playground is not about a small, if measurable, increase in physical risk to kids, but about a hard-to-quantify emotional risk to the health of our families and our developing children. And here too there are real concerns to explore (albeit buried under a whole lot of judgment).

There is a video of a psychological experiment. I challenge you to watch it without getting a lump in your throat. An infant is strapped into a seat. His mother leans toward him, smiling, widening her eyes, playing peekaboo and this-little-piggy. He squeals, laughs, responding to her coos in the kind of baby conversation crucial to the development of speech and healthy attachment. Then Mom turns away for a moment. When she turns back to him, her face is set in a blank expression that doesn't change or react.

Just like the children in Dr. Radesky's fast-food study, the baby makes a series of bids for his mother's attention. He smiles and then giggles. He tries again and again, squealing, arching his back, clapping his hands, reaching for her, pointing—pulling out his whole baby bag of tricks. Her face is like stone. He looks confused then, starts biting his fist uncertainly, and twists around to peek at the observer. Researchers have found that stress hormones are skyrocketing in his little body, and his pulse is racing.

Finally he slumps in his seat and starts to wail, red-faced, and his mother breaks her expression and comforts him. It's only been a few minutes, with no injury or discomfort, no yelling or scolding. A four-month-old baby seems to remember this brief experience up to two weeks later; if you re-create the situation, the child freaks out much more quickly.

Edward Tronick at the University of Massachusetts Boston has been conducting these "still face" experiments since the 1970s. He uses them as a laboratory model of the effects of neglect and maternal depression, especially postpartum depression, which affects about one in ten women. He's found that repeatedly denying children opportunities to connect in this way can cause severe distress. But even when chronically neglected, children can heal and thrive when restored to consistent, responsive loving care.

When I saw the "still face" video I flashed immediately on my own moments gazing impassively into the black mirror of my phone in my children's presence. I imagined Lulu trying a new trick on the playground, looking around for my approval, slumping in despair.

Our increased absorption in screens brings trade-offs that we can feel in all our relationships. When people are physically separated, screens can connect them, but when we are physically together, screens can reduce closeness by competing for both parents' and children's attention. This is the same crowding-out issue we talked about in earlier chapters.

The opposite of joint media engagement, which requires conscious action on the part of parents, this is more like "joint media detachment." And it may be far more common.

Research by Dr. Dimitri Christakis has shown in controlled experiments that when television is audible in a home, even in the background, there's a 90 percent drop in the number of words per hour that adults address to babies and young children. He speculates that this reduction in conversation could be a prime mechanism for observed effects of heavy screen use in children, such as language delay.

SMARTPHONES AND SLOT MACHINES

An association between more screens and less-than-optimal family relationships or child development doesn't mean that the first causes the second. It could be that parents with social anxiety or depression, who feel preoccupied by work, or who feel economic pressure and stress turn more heavily to screens rather than engage with their children, who end up less securely attached for all these confounding reasons.

We know that lower-income, less-educated parents are more likely to keep the television on during the day and to subscribe to parenting styles that emphasize compliance over engaging very young children in conversation. And some studies of immigrant families have found that they prefer to expose their kids to English via media, rather than speak or read to them in the language used at home—yet another factor that could affect the relationship between heavy media use and child development.

So it's a complicated picture. But the influence of tech is still worth looking at. Television, including "background" TV, can distract people from each other and reduce face-to-face conversation, as discussed. A landline phone gives a parent the ability to conduct a conversation with who's not present, ignoring a child who is. But smartphones offer both at the same time, anywhere you go. And they're built to capture our attention in a way that TV, with its blaring commercials and car crashes, can only dream of.

"Push" notifications on smartphones offer the intermittent reinforcement of an actually meaningful or enjoyable message coming in every so often. A small 2014 study showed people getting an average of 63.5 notifications a day, or one every fifteen minutes while awake. Those who received more notifications reported more negative emotions.

Natasha Dow Schüll's 2012 book *Addiction by Design: Machine Gambling in Las Vegas* is based on fifteen years of field research into the world of computerized slot machines. She describes how computer programmers working for gambling companies create hypnotic rhythms of rewards and near-misses designed to maximize *time on device*. Makers of consumer technologies, she and others argue, are doing much the same thing in the same ways for the same reasons. "The currency of the Internet is time spent," argues Tristan Harris, a former design ethicist at Google, in similar terms. "That leads to a race to the bottom of the brain stem. We need to change to a new currency."

GUILT VS. GOOD ENOUGH

The anxiety is fresh because these technologies are so new. Are we parents with our dinging phones at the playground, at the fast-food restaurant, at the pool, inadvertently imposing a form of the still face experiment on our kids? Is it happening generally at a dosage that's likely to cause harm?

I don't pose these questions in a leading way, to trigger automatic judgment or recrimination. Let's think about this dynamic in a broader context.

Within the triangle of mother, child, and mobile device swirl complex, invisible forces. Multiple filters can be imposed on the same image, Instagram-style.

There is the view of digital distraction as a public-health risk when engaged in activities like driving or supervising children at risky play. We may need stronger rules, enforcement, and better cultural practices to raise awareness and curb this risk.

Then there is the concern raised by psychologists like Catherine Steiner-Adair, critics like Sherry Turkle, and pediatricians like Jenny Radesky that digital distraction among parents is sapping the quality and quantity of parent-child interaction required in order for babies and young children to grow and thrive.

But this is more complicated. Our children do need critical amounts of our loving responsiveness and focus. They don't, however, require our full attention to their needs at each moment. In fact, excessive scrutiny in itself can be harmful. We can hurt our children's development if we don't give them the space to thrive, explore, and make mistakes on their own, or to learn that they can work through difficult feelings without constantly having to be rescued or told what to feel.

The British pediatrician and psychoanalytic psychologist Donald Winnicott, often cited as a foundational authority on mother-child bonding, referred, memorably, to "the good-enough mother."

A baby, he says, begins as physically part of the mother. As a newborn, he or she is entirely dependent on maternal care. As the child becomes more capable, he or she comes more into independent existence. The mother slowly backs off. She "starts off with an almost complete adaptation to her infant's needs, and as time proceeds she adapts less and less completely, gradually, according to the infant's growing ability to deal with her failure."

But the contemporary image of an ideal mother seems somehow to be one who never "fails" in this way, who never backs off at all. This myth is captured by social scientists using the terms *intensive mothering* and *concerted cultivation*.

Sociologist Sharon Hays, in her 1996 book *The Cultural Contradictions of Motherhood,* coined the term *intensive motherhood.* Another paper defines the term as "a child-centered, expert-guided, emotionally absorbing, labor intensive ideology in which mothers are primarily responsible for the nurture and development of the sacred child and in which children's needs take precedence over the individual needs of their mothers." And sociologist Annette Lareau focused on the related idea of concerted cultivation as a parenting strategy of the upwardly mobile middle class: parents who hyperschedule their children's time with extracurriculars, who get involved in their education and help with homework, who talk to them all the time and solicit their opinions.

In this culture at this moment in time, we seem to idealize a parent who is constantly physically present and highly emotionally connected: paying maximum attention all the time; teaching, guiding, and narrating the child's experience; consulting experts; providing all sorts of enrichment experiences; and putting in hard emotional effort to raise happy, loving children. And the weight of this idealized role falls more heavily on mothers, who are still considered the primary parents by default.

But it wasn't always or everywhere this way. David Lancy's *The Anthropology of Childhood: Cherubs, Chattel, Changelings,* in common use as a textbook, gives the lie to so much of what we consider "universal" about children, childhood, parenthood, and even mother love and attachment. The fact that we raise our children in groups may be an evolutionary driver for the constant work that women do to knit social networks together, such as why I remember to buy a wedding gift for my husband's aunt's stepdaughter. This kind of emotional labor, these days, often happens with the help of email, Facebook, and text.

If you've had a kid in the last ten years you've probably heard of *attachment parenting.* Attachment parents champion a combination of practices that can include breastfeeding extending into the toddler years; sharing a bed; carrying your baby or toddler for hours a day in a carrier or sling, both outside and inside the house; responding quickly to infants' needs without imposing a schedule; and practicing positive discipline without time-outs or raised voices, heaven forbid corporal punishment.

The term *attachment parenting* is supposed to refer to *attachment theory,* as described by Winnicott and others. The notion is that this closeness will establish a healthy, secure attachment in the early years. But you could be forgiven for assuming that it refers to being physically in reach of your child at all times. The organization Attachment Parenting International calls these practices "our biological imperative . . . 'instinctual.'"

Lancy is a lot more specific. In his reading, attachment parenting practices are largely modeled on those of the !Kung, a group of foragers (formerly known as Bushmen) in the Kalahari Desert in Africa who are, he writes, "the most thoroughly studied foraging society in the world." They are known for never letting their infants cry.

However, he points out that the !Kung are atypical even among foraging societies, which are atypical among most world societies—for example, in the length of time that children are allowed to play without being made to do anything useful.

So with our Ergobaby carriers and *Baby on Board* signs, we have the rarest kind of parenting arrangement: a cherub society. In this way, privileged Americans have more in common with the forest-dwelling African people formerly known as pygmies than with, say, English Puritans.

But Lancy argues that we are outliers even among the outliers. Americans and Europeans, he argues, constitute a neontocracy—where the baby is king and parents are serfs. "Children in the neontocracy are cosseted and enriched to a degree unprecedented in human culture," he writes.

The prevalent danger to children in a society like this one, he argues, isn't cold, or hunger. It's a smothering form of parental love. Parents, especially mothers, feel social pressure to hover too closely and hold too tight.

I want to underline that Lancy's characterization applies most accurately to the middle and upper classes (a point that Hays and Lareau also make about intensive mothering and concerted cultivation). By the latest figures, just over half of American children are growing up at or near the poverty line. This includes 60 percent of black, Hispanic, and Native American children, and 60 percent of children with a single mother. Most American children, then, are neither excessively cosseted nor overly enriched.

Still, for the group of Americans who tend to buy parenting books and think of parenting as an activity that requires adopting a certain "style," the neontocracy rules. And attachment parenting, intensive mothering, and concerted cultivation all appear to conflict with mothers having a personal life or being in the workplace, at least while their children are young.

In fact, Hays's use of the term *ideology* is specific to this point. If intensive mothering were simply taken for granted as a cultural norm, it wouldn't have to be so fiercely defended. But it's not. It's a set of beliefs that arose specifically in tension with the entry of women into the paid workforce. In this reading, women who don't work outside the home, who are increasingly likely to be educated and wealthy, have championed intensive mothering as "the most important job in the world" in a bid to defend their social status. Most mothers, who do work for pay, then feel pressed to pick up a "second shift" of intensive mothering when they come home, because that is the standard set by their at-home cohorts.

Lancy, a guy in his sixties, retired from the University of Utah, is more feminist than many self-declared feminists I know. He calls the mommy wars "ridiculous." "The argument over daycare, for example, is based on this huge myth, this huge fallacy that the normal, natural way children are raised is by the full-time care and attention of their mothers. If you look at anthropology and history, nothing could be further from the truth." By contrast, "In a majority of the world's diverse societies," reads Lancy's book, "women continue as workers throughout pregnancy and resume working shortly after the child is born." And the same is true today.

The image of an ideal mother right now is someone who is always connected and available, both physically and mentally. And that's the same image we currently have of the ideal worker. US workers spend more time at work and take fewer vacation days than those in any other rich country. Salaried professionals actually put in more hours than lower-paid hourly-wage workers. But the latter group is tormented by unpredictable schedules, often assigned by computer, that change week to week.

We are the only developed country with no guaranteed paid maternity leave, the only one with no guaranteed paid sick leave, the only one with no mandated vacation days, and one of nine countries with no paternity leave. Thanks in part to mobile technologies, two thirds of workers tell Gallup pollsters that time spent on work outside regular working hours has increased significantly in the last decade. Labor regulators are considering cracking down on this practice, both in the US and in France.

"Our best—and very time-consuming—ideas about how to raise a child have arrived on the scene at a very awkward moment," observes

contemporary philosopher Alain de Botton, who writes about the
"pleasures and sorrows of work." "Our best ideas about how to run an
economy and our best ideas about how to raise families are completely
at odds."

FRAGMENTED CARE

Economic forces are pulling parents away from their children even as
cultural forces are pushing us to hover over them at all times. Working mothers in particular are often using technology to cope with the
demands that we be two places—be two people—at once all the time.

I can't think of a better illustration of the perversity of this ideology of intensive mothering and how it is used against women than a
psychology paper that appeared in January 2016. "Put the cellphone
away! Fragmented baby care can affect brain development" was the
headline of the press release put out by the University of California,
Irvine. I was so excited to find this paper because it was the first study
I'd come across that purported to show long-term emotional effects
from maternal distraction by technology.

Then I found out it was about rats. The paper was about changes
found in adolescent rats' behavior as the result of a stressful upbringing. They grew up with less preference for sweet foods and playing
with peers—the equivalent of rat depression.

No matter, I thought. Sure, it's less applicable than it would be if
done in humans, but maybe they cleverly simulated digital distraction
in the rat mothers, the way Dimitri Christakis did in his mouse-in-the-
casino study.

Nope. The stress was actually induced in this study by giving the
baby rats and their mothers limited access to nesting and bedding materials. In other words, by poverty. So a much fairer headline to this press
release would be, "Growing up in poverty harms babies' brains long
term," which an abundance of research in humans has demonstrated.

But somehow, the researchers chose to focus on the fact that the
mothers' behaviors became erratic and unpredictable in this deprived
environment. They extrapolated to gratuitously shame mothers for
using technology. "Our work builds on many studies showing that

maternal care is important for future emotional health. Importantly, it shows that it is not *how much* maternal care that influences adolescent behavior but the avoidance of fragmented and unpredictable care that is crucial. We might wish to turn off the mobile phone when caring for baby and be predictable and consistent," said lead author Tallie Z. Baram. Except there's no evidence here linking ordinary mobile phone use by ordinary mothers in ordinary circumstances to "fragmented and unpredictable care."

And while we're on the subject, remember Patricia Allen, the mother of the three children who drowned? There's more to her story too. The witness's statement that Allen was texting on her cell phone at the time of the accident—the statement that became a national headline—was later officially retracted. It also turned out that the pool in a rundown apartment complex where she brought her children to swim had been cited several times for broken safety equipment and for the murkiness of the water. Child Protective Services in Dallas had already taken away her two surviving younger children and arrested her in the drowning of the three older ones. She sued to try to get her children back and for damages.

Allen is African American. News accounts describe her as a certified nurses' aide, a job that pays about $27,000 a year in Dallas. That would put her below the poverty line with five children. Other reports said that she had had trouble finding steady work.

Who or what is the primary culprit for children growing up with "fragmented and unpredictable" care? Is it cell phones? Or is it a social structure that leaves too many families like Allen's to struggle?

SYMPTOMS OF MOTHERHOOD

Without forgetting this context, we still have to reckon with screens' influence on parental attention. Because working parents are stressed, too many families are in poverty, and social and economic structures interfere with work-life balance, it doesn't mean that parents don't also tend to have a fraught relationship with their smartphones. I think we do. I know I do. And if you look down the list of harms associated with excessive media use, there's plenty of overlap with various mental difficulties endemic to new motherhood: sleep disturbances, anxiety, and depression, to name a few.

Postnatal insomnia is a recognized symptom that can occur on its own or as a sign of postpartum depression. It's a harsh irony. Being awakened at unpredictable intervals can shatter sleep patterns. Even when the baby is sleeping, the requirement of maximum vigilance is hard to turn off. Insomnia and smartphone addiction, of course, are mutually reinforcing. Sleeping with a phone, a monitor, or a baby next to your bed is a bad idea if you want peaceful rest.

Then there's the contemporary condition of chronic distraction. I remember the first time my husband and I got out of the house to see a movie as new parents. Lulu was about three months old, sleeping at home with her grandmother. The theater was just a few blocks from our apartment. As the lights went down I automatically reached for my phone to turn it off . . . and stopped. I couldn't afford to miss a text message from the person who had my daughter. Ever again. For the next few decades, just in case something might happen, I had to be reachable. So the cell phone signal becomes an extended umbilical tether when you are away from your children, and that, maybe, helps reinforce parents' reliance on the device.

In some sense, once you have a kid, you are never not multitasking. There's "whatever I am doing right now" in the foreground and "is the kid okay?" in the background. Your heart is walking around outside your body—of course you're going to be distracted all the time.

An emerging thread of research suggests that mothers multitask more than single women and more than fathers. They do so both at home and at work. At home we do more of the chores, particularly more of the mental tasks of managing and organizing calendars, schedules, and to-do lists. At work we are highly productive employees. And all the time we report being more tired and needing more sleep. To be in mama bear mode, constantly scanning the horizon for opportunities and threats, also makes us more prone to depression and anxiety. And those conditions too can drive us right back to our phones.

It may seem ironic that technology touted as improving efficiency often ends up as one more thing making mothers feel chronically overwhelmed and failing at all of their jobs. But in fact that's a pattern that dates back to colonial times. Sociologist Ruth Schwartz Cohen published the book *More Work for Mother: The Ironies of Household Technology from the Open Hearth to the Microwave* in 1983. Through meticulous historical research, she unravels an apparent mystery: after generations of labor-saving devices, why do women spend no less time on household chores in modern suburbs than they did centuries ago?

It seemed that in a gradually industrializing yet still patriarchal society, every innovation tended to require more cash from outside the household, less household labor for men, and more for women. For example, when women cooked over an open fire it was men's job to split kindling and keep the fire going. When cast-iron stoves appeared in the nineteenth century, men were freed from those chores. Suddenly families needed money to buy fuel, which meant more working outside the home. And women spent huge amounts of time cleaning ash out of their stoves and polishing them to keep them from rusting. Similarly, as new household appliances appeared, expectations rose in tandem. From rarely washed wool garments to ironed linen sheets and napkins; from hoecake baked in the ashes of the fire to white-flour breads and airy cakes. As fathers and mothers stopped spending hours tending the garden, mothers instead spent those hours driving to the supermarket. And so on.

The mobile phone is another innovation that hasn't brought us extra time. Instead it's lengthened our working days and extended our parenting responsibilities at the same time. I once was asked to appear on a panel at a conference and one of my co-panelists was running late. She finally arrived and explained that her son had been texting her from homeroom for help with his French homework.

"Less work for Mother" will never come about because of technological advances alone. It will happen because of a frank renegotiation of household tasks between opposite-sex partners, and also more social supports from government and employers.

THE WAY WE NEVER WERE

In the past few decades many observers have chronicled a shift in messaging about the proper roles of women, epitomized in the transition from the term *housewife* to the phrase *stay-at-home mom.* Housekeeping rules have relaxed a little, and there are a lot more takeout meals than before, but women are now supposed to be tending to their family's well-being all the time (and the children, not the husband, are now the most important members).

Many of the bloggers, cultural critics, and even researchers, who have hit such a nerve about digital distraction among parents, seem to pose a falsely idealized past when mothers were paying much more attention to their kids.

"Parents are less present," Victor Strasburger, leading screen researcher, father, and pediatrician, and author of a book titled *The Death of Childhood,* told me. "Parents don't spend that much time with kids. Media are occupying kids more than they are." He wasn't the only male child development expert to tell me basically the same thing.

But, I gently pointed out, this just isn't true. The opposite, in fact. Time-use studies since the 1960s show that parents actually spend more time with their children than they used to. In 1965, mothers reported 10.2 hours a week spent on childcare and fathers a whopping 2.4 hours. In 2011 mothers, while tripling the time spent on paid work, spent 13.5 hours on childcare. Fathers, while working slightly fewer hours, got all the way up to 7.3 hours, more than half as much as mothers.

Family sizes are smaller than they were during the baby boom. The individual attention given to each child, therefore, may have grown even more than that.

Think about that iPhone-on-the-playground study again. True, childhood injuries may have risen slightly in the past decade. But that's after plummeting since the 1970s, when the neontocracy really took off. Today, compared to when the boomers and Gen Xers were out there playing, playground surfaces are safer. Monkey bars are lower. Seesaws and merry-go-rounds are all but gone. And constant close parental supervision, even of older children, is the new norm.

The notion of the phone pulling us away from our children can thus be turned upside down. If I hadn't been on my phone at the playground that Sunday, I might not have been at the playground at all. I might have had to go in to the office to have that timely conversation, which I followed up at naptime by filing a story.

Or, if it were 1965, my kid might have been at the playground by herself or in the not-so-vigilant watch of an older sibling or neighbor, and I would have been home cleaning and cooking, without it ever occurring to anyone that parental supervision was needed in such a situation. "Be home by dark, kids."

In fact, Palsson, the economist who authored the smartphone injuries study, echoes this observation. He compares access to smartphones to an "income effect."

"With cheaper access to entertainment and work, parents might spend more time with their kids. For example, a mother might not need to be in the office because she can email from the zoo, or a father might be more willing to go to the playground because he has a new ebook." In other words, there's a trade-off: the phone may lower your vigilance when kids are in risky situations, but it also increases the chances that you'll take them outside in the first place.

So, what about quality time? Are family bonds weakening because of the constant overlap of demands from work and home? Are our children truly suffering because we'd apparently rather talk to absolutely anyone else other than them?

Again, you have to ask, compared to what? And when?

OF WOMAN BORN

"It began when I had picked up a book or began trying to write a letter, or even found myself on the telephone with someone toward whom my voice betrayed eagerness, a rush of sympathetic energy. The child (or children) might be absorbed in busyness, in his own dreamworld; but as soon as he felt me gliding into a world which did not include him, he would come to pull at my hand, ask for help, punch at the typewriter keys. And I would feel his wants at such a moment as fraudulent, as an attempt moreover to defraud me for living even for fifteen minutes as myself."

The poet and critic Adrienne Rich published *Of Woman Born* in 1976. It's an exploration of her experience as the mother of three sons. She depicts the intensely private and fulfilling experience of maternal love, with its range of sorrows and joys, which nevertheless takes place within a social and historical context, as all our most intimate relationships do. In her case, the context is an outwardly traditional marriage, a 1950s nuclear family, in an academic subculture just as patriarchal as the wider society. Betty Friedan's territory, and Simone de Beauvoir's.

This book is unapologetic and unambivalent even as it takes on complexity. Rich clearly loves her children. The book was written when the spadework of early motherhood was already done and her sons were grown men whom she was proud of and respected. She left that traditional-looking marriage and came out as a lesbian. But that move, radical for its time, in no way invalidates the palpable sense of security and authority she projects as a mother.

Rich fearlessly examines her changeable state of mind in those early years of motherhood, as she struggles intensely to mediate between her children's needs and her own needs to think, create, read, write, work. "I could love so much better, I told myself, after even a quarter-hour of selfishness, of peace, of detachment from my children." Selfishness, she calls it, but isn't it really just "having a self"? Rich argues that this conflict is, in reality, manufactured and artificial, just like the processed foods that filled store shelves in the postwar era. She intuits something "fraudulent" in these small boys' constant petitioning for her time:

" . . . this circle, this magnetic field in which we lived, was not a natural phenomenon."

The metaphor is striking. The magnetic field she speaks of is that generated by a nuclear family reduced to its very nucleus—just a mother with just her children, isolated for long hours, father away at work.

The question of what's "a natural phenomenon" is always complicated when it comes to human beings. But the nuclear family is certainly an anomaly in time and space. It's not at all ahistorical or strange for mothers to contribute to and be part of society beyond their roles as caregivers—that's as common as milk, as Lancy points out. What's unusual about this country and this time is the fanatical, pared-down asceticism, this insistence on the intensity and primacy of constant connection between mother and child.

And it also seems thoroughly natural for any person to want an escape from that intensity. Rich had a book or a phone call or a typewriter to provide that escape. Today we all have all three all the time.

"MY JOB IS ALWAYS"

The families I surveyed for this book claimed to be struggling with distracted parenting every day. Very few—fifteen out of over five hundred—said they "strictly" limited their own tech use around their kids.

One of my respondents, a mother of a two-year-old, rated herself a 3, slightly more controlled than average, on a scale of 1 to 5 in terms of limiting tech use. She wrote: "When I'm caring for my daughter I only look at my phone or computer if I receive or need to make a call, send a message, or look something up." Quite a long list.

"I wish I was better about limiting my own technology use around them," wrote a small-town mother of two. "But I'm a freelance writer and my job is always. Plus, they're home one day a week, and I have to answer client emails and sometimes take calls."

"I wish we had better rules," echoed a big-city mother of a baby. "I try not to use my phone in front of my son, but my husband is terrible about it. I find myself checking the phone underneath the kitchen table. It feels very disrespectful to my son and also like a clear double standard."

"Ugh, I use my phone in front of her constantly. I wish I didn't," wrote another mother of a baby.

"I sometimes listen to podcasts (with one earbud in) while interacting with them," said a parent of two.

"I'd like to put my phone away when I am with my kids, but I have a hard time—for no reason whatsoever," wrote another. "Then I feel guilty for being distracted."

"I wish," "I wish," "I wish," "I feel guilty." These parents are portraying themselves as powerless over their own use of devices. Guilt is offered up as a token to purchase indulgence for what we are choosing, moment by moment, to do.

I hear that kind of language as a fig leaf for something we can't quite admit to ourselves and others. As parents we want to be there for our kids, of course. We don't want to miss a giggle, a question, a moment of their brief time of growing up. Yet, at the same time, we also crave space from the exhausting emotional and physical labor of attending to their constant demands. And if we can't get physical space, we'll take a moment of mental distraction as a meager substitute. Maybe we're re-belling inwardly against the ideology of intensive motherhood. Maybe it's too heavy a yoke to shoulder for hour upon hour of the day.

We want the chance to learn about the world around us, to accomplish things and communicate with others. We quite often need to be in two places at once. And with the phone at the playground, we can be—at the price of feeling torn, or at least saying we're torn.

There's an undeniable hypocrisy to this, that kids will surely pick up on, as danah boyd points out: "You don't want your kid checking their phone at dinner? You can't either. You don't want them sleeping with the phone? You don't either."

No one is immune from this prostration, it seems. I asked Dr. Jenny Radesky, the author of the fast-food restaurant study with the "robotic" parents and the pleading little hands on the mother's face, how she deals with digital distraction when at home with her two young children.

"My husband's really good," she says. "His stuff is always just on the kitchen table and he hardly checks it unless it rings. But if I'm on call I have my pager on. If something is an emergency that's how I can be found." When she's not on call, the dinnertime-to-bedtime hours of five to seven p.m. are "sacred," she says . . . unless there's something about a patient she needs to follow up on.

I am no one to point fingers, but I don't know whether to laugh or cry. This isn't easy for anyone. We need an intervention. A better way of thinking about what we are doing and what we wish we were doing. Because our kids are watching us and learning from our habits every day.

THE INTERVENER

I'm a C-minus attachment parent, but I am a big enthusiast of another parenting philosophy, known rather prosaically as Resources for Infant Educarers or RIE.

RIE is the brainchild of Magda Gerber, a Hungarian-born, Sorbonne-educated child therapist and infant specialist who died in 2007. As expressed in her book *Dear Parent: Caring for Infants with Respect,* RIE doesn't base itself on an imperfect reconstruction of the practices of some faraway, exoticized culture. It takes what science tells us about children's development and blends it with contemporary Western ideals about individualism.

With RIE, beginning in infancy, during caregiving rituals you really focus on your baby. You approach her gently and speak to her respectfully, explaining in plain English what's about to happen, giving her a chance to react. You talk, sing, and connect during diaper changes, feedings, baths, and bedtime.

The rest of the time, as long as your baby's not clearly asking for attention, you leave her to explore in a safe, enclosed space with very simple objects—a hand mirror, a cloth napkin. Basically, you let her chill out and get on with the business of being a baby. It's sort of the opposite of attachment parenting, intensive mothering, or concerted cultivation.

"I took my daughter to an RIE class when she was three months old," says Janet Lansbury, an RIE educator, author, and podcaster for more than two decades in Hollywood, California. "Every waking minute I'd been entertaining her. I was totally exhausted and spent and felt like a failure. And they said, just lay her down on this blanket and observe her. For two hours she lay there awake, peaceful, on her mat, sucked her thumb, looked toward some light, and that's when I saw my child for the first time and realized there's a whole person here with her own thoughts and ideas."

A lot of RIE's tenets—like allowing plenty of "tummy time," enabling children to develop at their own pace, speaking to babies and narrating what's going on in the environment—are supported by the best developmental science. But in the end the feelings communicated by RIE are stronger than the research behind it. It's a philosophy of how to be relaxed and respectful around your child. It assumes that you enjoy being together, but you also both have other important things to do. It helps you find a rhythm of loving and playful engagement punctuated with comfortable silences. And this approach offers a couple of strong answers to the question of what to do about screen time and distraction, both for parents and children.

"It baffles me that the experts give warnings and criticisms, but nobody offers parents viable alternatives to using TV as a babysitter," Lansbury says. The tantalizing alternative she offers is this: when you regularly allow your infant to interact with open-ended playthings in a safe space without interruptions, when you resist the temptation to buy some minutes to yourself with things that make noise or flashing lights, he will grow into a toddler who can amuse himself for forty-five minutes with a rubber ball. (There are videos on Lansbury's blog to document this incredible feat for skeptics.)

Educators in the progressive Montessori method advocate something similar. "The environment itself will teach the child . . . without the intervention of a parent or teacher, who should remain a quiet observer of all that happens," Maria Montessori wrote.

Montessori books advise parents to occupy themselves with some clear-cut household task—sweeping, cooking—and offer the child a chance either to help, with their own kid-size tools, or to go about their own business of playing and exploring, again with open-ended toys. My friend Marina's mother is a Montessori teacher who advised them to instruct their sitter to leave their three-year-old to her own devices (not online devices) for thirty to forty-five minutes a day, gradually lengthening her stamina and ability to play on her own.

Left alone, in judicious doses, that toddler or preschooler will in turn grow into a kid who can pay better attention in class, use her imagination in play, and be patient with friends. Meanwhile, you will be left with plenty of free moments *in the course of watching your kids* to get back to your boss, text your partner, do the dishes, or check in with a friend.

I honestly can't think of a better deal than that.

"This is something you can cultivate from birth. But we aren't really told about this in other approaches," says Lansbury. "We're told we're supposed to stimulate them this way and that way."

This takes time, patience, and self-awareness to do right. The cornerstone of the RIE approach is the "respectful" attention you give your child when you are doing things together, or when your child expresses that she needs you. By focusing on her at the right times, you leave yourself and your child the space to focus on other things at other times. In other words, replace fitful task-switching and distraction with mindful alternation of attention.

This is something I've tried much more regularly from birth with my younger daughter, in part out of necessity since we now have two children to attend to. And by whatever luck of the draw, this baby has an incredible attention span. I have a video on my phone of her at age four and a half months, on her tummy, pawing at a pile of Mylar and clear plastic as it unleashes delicious crumpling sounds and reflects different colors of light across her face. For over twenty minutes.

YOU AND YOUR PHONE

Just because there is little empirical support for the idea that my frequent use of smartphones at the park is causing my daughters irreparable emotional harm, it doesn't mean I don't fret about it. I am not here to tell adults what to do about their own technology use in their own homes and lives. Everybody has a different set of conditions to deal with. And, just as with our kids, the leeway of healthy patterns of use is probably wide. There's a lot more reason to be vigilant if you're a working parent like me who sees your kids for three hours on a weekday, for example, vs. a full-time caregiver who is eyeball-to-eyeball with them fourteen hours a day. But I have some suggestions if you worry about this the way I do.

- For God's sake, put your phone away when you're driving. And at the swimming pool as well.
- Try not charging your phone in your bedroom at night.
- Try turning off screens for an hour before bed.
- Try not checking your phone first thing in the morning.
- Try turning off notifications on your phone for all but the most essential apps. This has made a huge difference for me.
- Do Not Disturb mode on the iPhone allows you to be contacted only by a few key emergency contacts—say, at the movies.
- Try uninstalling Facebook or whatever applications you find most addictive.
- Create a landing zone near the door of your home and plug in the phone there when you walk in.

"Demonstrate your own mindfulness in front of your children by putting down your phone during meals or whenever they need your attention," says Dr. David Hill at the AAP.

Dr. Jenny Radesky has started talking to fellow pediatricians about how to communicate with parents about their own media use. "It's important to recognize your own relationship, and why it's hard to stop sometimes. Understand what makes you particularly stressed or changes your emotional regulation. Is it Facebook? Work email? If you know you get amped up around certain types of tech use, then keep that away from your family time," she suggests. Instead, focus on positive uses, like "my husband's away on a business trip and I get a text with a picture and I share it with my kids. I'm not saying family times have to be completely tech-free if we know how to filter it."

And a related suggestion from boyd: whenever you pick up your phone in front of your kids, narrate to them what it is you're doing to create some accountability and transparency. "Let's see what the weather is going to be like." "I'm going to text Dad to ask him to pick up more macaroni and cheese." By age three or four, kids can participate with you by adding emojis to a text message or using voice search to ask a question.

One of the parents in my survey, a mother with a houseful of teenagers, follows this practice. "I share with my kid what I am doing on technology when they observe me on the computer," she says. She connects this to how kids might have learned by watching their parents in earlier generations.

"Most of 'how those things work' learning for kids was, in the past, to observe them happening as they happened (watching Mom read the morning paper, seeing Dad type up his resume, etc. . . .). Now that the nuances of them are less visible and distinct, it is important to share honestly with kids what you are doing on a screen and talk about what it is that you are doing, and why. Working on your résumé looks the same as playing video games as paying your bills as chatting with a friend as reading the news . . . this practice also keeps me a bit in check for my own computer use. If I am embarrassed to tell my kids what I am doing on the computer when they observe me, perhaps I am not monitoring my own time/tech usage as well as I should either. ;-)"

8 MODERN FAMILIES: PARENTS AND SCREENS

WHEN I REACHED LESA BRACKBILL ON HER CELL PHONE, SHE WAS WAITing in line at the post office, where her daughter Tori had her own PO box. She regularly got packages from well-wishers all over the world.

The Brackbills are devout Christians who prayed for two years for a child. Tori was born in July 2014. Around age five months, she began showing symptoms of what turned out to be Krabbe disease, a rare, inherited illness that destroys the myelin sheath of neurons in the brain and throughout the body. When I spoke with Lesa in the winter of 2015, Tori couldn't walk or talk and was unlikely to live past age two. She passed away at age twenty months, in March 2016.

In previous eras parents like the Brackbills might have staggered through this ordeal with the help of family, friends, and their church. They'd be unlikely to ever meet another family in the same situation, since Krabbe strikes only one in every hundred thousand children.

These days, though, there was a novel place to turn: social media.

PARENT-TO-PARENT ONLINE

The more I progressed in researching this book, the more I realized that it was impossible to talk about children's screen habits without addressing what parents are doing. We are creating the family context and making choices, conscious and unconscious, that affect our children every day.

American adults spend plenty of time online. Parents, especially new parents, spend even more. It starts even before we become parents: a 2013 market research study found that pregnancy-related apps outpaced general fitness apps in downloads. Once the babies arrive, new mothers in America post 2.5 as many status updates, 3.5 times as many photos, and 4.2 times as many videos as nonparents, Facebook reported in 2016. And posts about babies get 47 percent more Likes and other reactions than general posts. A 2016 survey by a UK-based nonprofit suggested that parents will share an average of one thousand pictures of their kids online by the time the kids are five years old.

Aside from sharing (and occasionally oversharing), many of us are trying to answer questions. In a Pew poll released in the winter of 2015, 43 percent of mothers reported relying on parenting books, magazines, and websites for advice; 28 percent specifically said they looked at online message boards, email discussion lists, or social media for feedback. College-educated mothers and mothers of young children were more likely to do so. In my own, unscientific survey of five hundred families, 90 percent said they turned to some form of online resource for parenting information, with "Internet research" being the most commonly cited, very broad source.

It's not hard to see why social media has become such a draw for so many of us. Parenting is both incredibly intimate and inherently communal. You need support, solace, advice, and affirmation, and you need it at all hours of the night, especially in the early years. But parents today are less likely to have family nearby and more likely to be working long hours even as we adjust to sleepless nights. We are short on socializing time and isolated from face-to-face friendship. The "mom on her iPhone at the playground" is often doing just what her counterpart was doing generations ago: exchanging news with neighbors, asking relatives for advice, keeping up with friends.

However, just as managing our kids' screen time presents novel challenges and opportunities, so does managing our own. The connections offered by digital media are hardly ever neutral. They can be a lifeline, and they can also make life extremely unpleasant or even dangerous. They can affirm your choices or leave you roiling with self-doubt. They can expose your family's privacy to marketers, hackers, or trolls, and they can open you up to rich friendships and wonderful new experiences.

While I was working on this book, the spread of misinformation and online harassment crossed a line from seemingly minor annoyances into matters of major public concern. I have a secret agenda with this chapter. It's my hope that as parents, the guardians of the next generation, we can use our moral authority to push successfully for more positive ways of engaging online.

This chapter will present a range of case studies as well as ideas for getting the most out of the parenting communities you choose to engage with online. The process starts with being conscious about that choice.

LIKES AND BLESSINGS

Lesa Brackbill has kept a blog for a dozen years, since college. "Looking back, the posts were so silly, just whatever was on my mind," she said. But when her baby daughter started showing terrifying, strange symptoms, screaming uncontrollably for hours, she began to update the blog with the latest medical news. It was a way to streamline the exhausting process of calling around to concerned friends and relatives to keep everyone in the loop.

"It's like a game of telephone—people getting things mixed up," she says. "This way everyone could read it at the same time." Also, it was easier sometimes to post about what was happening than to talk about it. "It became so difficult to verbalize a lot of the situation, especially once we found out that she was dying. It wasn't something I could say out loud [at first], but I could type it."

Lesa posted updates regularly on Facebook as well as on her blog. She included photos of Tori, a saucer-eyed bundle propped up in a stroller with oxygen tubes coming out of her nose. The posts were shared widely. "I started getting hundreds of friend requests from people I'd never met, and it took me a while to realize I should set up a page," she says. The public Facebook page, Tori's Triumph, eventually collected about thirteen thousand Likes. "The day of her diagnosis, over thirty thousand people read my blog post from all over the world," Lesa notes. She's quick to add that "that's not why we do this," meaning a desire for publicity for its own sake, much less material gain. And indeed, the Brackbills' social media presence remained free of any advertising or appeals for donations.

Instead the blog and Facebook page were filled with prayers, inspirational quotes, and updates on Tori's Bucket List, family outings from catching fireflies, and visiting Build-A-Bear, Disney World, and the Grand Canyon. All the trappings of a happy childhood, packed into a few short months.

Most of us curate and spin our online lives in one way or another. The offline, day-to-day realities of caring for a terminally ill child, Lesa told me, were many shades darker than the smiling photos on Tori's blog. Partly this may have been Lesa responding to her audience. "We keep hearing from people that they're inspired by the hope and the positivity," she noted.

Lesa spent eighteen hours a day tending to Tori while her husband, Brennan, worked full time to support them. They took turns on the night shift; Tori's breathing tubes had to be suctioned frequently, so she didn't sleep soundly.

Lesa updated the blog, Twitter, and Facebook several times a week. She was often doing it with one hand, on her phone, while holding her sleeping daughter in the other arm. "Because I'm incredibly sleep-deprived, it has affected my ability to be articulate," she says. "I can communicate more clearly when I'm writing on the blog than often in person." And she could do it without leaving her home or, she says, "sacrificing quality time with my daughter."

The biggest reward of getting on social media, she says, was connecting with other families dealing with the same diagnosis, who had a private Facebook group of a few hundred members. "We never would have found them if it weren't for Facebook," she says. "They welcomed us in and said, we're really sorry you have to be here, but it's a good place to be. I don't know what our lives would be like had we not found that group." In the summer of 2015, the Brackbills packed Tori and all their medical equipment in the car and drove four and a half hours to attend a conference of families with children who had Krabbe disease, coming from as far away as New Zealand.

Social media has become an essential resource in this way for all kinds of groups. Robust, member-led online communities for families with LGBTQ parents and/or children, transracial adoptees, and children with autism, ADHD, and allergies, to name a few, offer support, information, and a platform for advocacy.

The blog and Facebook page were Lesa's project. In a lot of ways they became her life. Brennan, her husband, was supportive, though he rarely posts himself.

It's been hard for some family members to understand why Lesa wants to chronicle their lives so openly and in such detail. The pushback, she said, came mainly from the older generation. "Some of our family members didn't really like at first that that was how we were choosing to share information," she says. But Lesa and Brennan presented a united front. "It was the first time as a married couple that we were like, this is how we're doing this." As the months went by, the family accepted that this was an important emotional outlet and source of support for Lesa.

I wondered what, exactly, motivated Tori's "fans," overwhelmingly women, who post on the blog and website, who sent messages and letters and gifts of stuffed giraffes, Tori's mascot. They said they were praying for Tori. They even narrated their dreams about her and her recovery. After she passed away they continued to post messages like "I never met her in life but I hope to meet her in Heaven. She was such a sweetie. I wish you all of God's Blessings in your journey forward."

Sometimes the search for this kind of vicarious emotional experience on the Internet can veer toward the exploitative or creepy. Instagram, the photo-sharing service, has had to deal with the advent of *adoption role-play*, which consists of people copying images of babies and passing them off as their own, with fake identities and backstories.

The business and tech magazine *Fast Company* reported on the phenomenon in 2014: "On some accounts the play takes on a more malicious tone, as with the account @adoption_rp, where roleplaying often features an obsession with breastfeeding and being 'nakey.'"

On the other side of the screen, sometimes people pretend to be in Lesa's situation for personal gain and other, even murkier motives. Either the children in question or their illnesses may be completely imaginary. But in the most sinister possible case, a woman named Lacey Spears was sentenced to twenty years in prison in 2015 for second-degree murder for poisoning her son, Garnett Spears, with salt. Spears had blogged and posted on Facebook about her son's years of mysterious chronic illnesses. Prosecutors argued that she induced those illnesses, ultimately torturing her son to death, in a syndrome known as *Munchausen by proxy*.

In the face of egregious cases like these, I find it reassuring that enough basic trust still exists online that people like the Brackbills are able to reach out and connect with each other. The social cohesion may be stronger when people are united within subcultures, like the Brackbills' Christian community.

Lesa says of her thousands of readers and followers, no one has overstepped any boundaries or been negative. The worst it got, she says, is when some commenters questioned the wisdom of taking Tori out in the hot sun of an Orlando theme park when she's sleeping in every picture.

Samantha Raynor lives several states away and has never met the Brackbills face to face, but she became an avid supporter and follower. One of her own children, a daughter just a few months older than Tori, has a rare disorder called hemihyperplasia, which causes the right side of her body to grow uncontrollably and puts her at increased risk for tumors. It's dangerous and difficult but not immediately life-threatening. "It's nothing like Krabbe," says Raynor.

Once she discovered Tori's Facebook page, "it really put life in perspective and helped us. They're a true inspiration for anyone." Raynor was moved, as she says, to "pay it forward." She called in a favor from some zookeeper friends and helped arrange a private giraffe visit for the Brackbills at the Philadelphia Zoo.

"It's been so neat and we feel so supported by strangers we may never meet, but who love us and love our daughter and care for us," Brackbill says. "For all the bad in social media, this has taught us that good can come from it." She kept blogging after Tori was gone. She has a cause: making a test for Krabbe a routine part of newborn screenings in every state. If the disease is caught before symptoms appear, it can be cured.

CONTEXT COLLAPSE

Rebecca Schuman also writes honestly and openly about her motherhood experience on the Internet. Her experience, though, has been different from the Brackbills'. "It was very terrifying and wounding," she says. "I had to go on hiatus from my job." And ironically, she says, while dealing with the fallout, "I was a pretty bad parent in the two weeks after."

Schuman is a St. Louis–based author and contributor to the online magazine *Slate*. Her turn as the self-described "worst woman on the Internet" came in August 2015, when she published an essay titled "How wrong am I to flip off my sleeping infant? A philosophical inquiry."

An acerbic ex-academic, Schuman wants you to know, as she wrote in the opening of her essay, that her daughter, who she had relatively late in life, is "precious to me beyond any imaginable previous personal attachment. She has deepened and broadened and redefined my life and my humanity. I love her with a manic ferocity. Ad nauseam."

But like a lot of babies, she didn't nap very well. "My daughter is a sweet little creature, and she's a handful," Schuman tells me. "She just sometimes won't go down if she's tired." One day, she says, "It took three hours to put her down and she woke up after ten minutes." She posted a picture on Facebook of herself flipping the bird to her finally sleeping baby. Then she started posting these selfies regularly, as a way of mockingly celebrating putting her daughter to sleep.

One of her *Slate* editors, who had seen the Facebook posts, encouraged her to write about them for the site. "She thought it was shocking, but funny." So, apparently, did most of Schuman's friends on Facebook and her seven thousand Twitter followers. So Schuman published a flip—pun intended—essay. Displaying her academic bona fides, she cites Kant, Aristotle, John Stuart Mill, and Wittgenstein to the effect that, since her daughter doesn't know about the flipping of the bird and couldn't possibly understand it, she's probably going to keep doing it—even though it does make her feel a little guilty.

Schuman's admittedly crude gesture is in keeping with a lot of contemporary parenting humor. Comedian Louis C.K. has done wildly popular routines about flipping off his young daughters and about what "assholes" they are. One of his bits onstage: "I'm a dad." [Applause] "Why are you clapping? I could be the shittiest father in the universe."

Many parenting blogs and Instagram and Twitter accounts position themselves as subversive zones of real talk, with names like Scary Mommy, Asshole Parents, and STFU (Shut the Fuck Up) Parents. *Go the Fuck to Sleep*, a "bedtime story" that no one would actually read to a child, was a massive best seller and media sensation.

This kind of humor can be cathartic. Like all transgressive or insider talk, it works best within trusted circles of friends. This extends to selective online communities where people understand the ground rules. The problem is that a conversation like this can easily be misinterpreted by people who don't get it, who don't assume good intentions. And in the online world, any statement can easily reach that unexpected or unintended audience. This is a phenomenon that scholars of social media, including danah boyd and Alice Marwick, have dubbed "context collapse."

In Jon Ronson's 2015 book *So You've Been Publicly Shamed,* he tells the stories of people who posted tasteless, ill-advised, sometimes racist statements to a tiny circle of followers, only to have their words go viral and summon a tsunami of recrimination. Some of these people lost their jobs and had to go into virtual hiding.

A more worrying breed of digital mob lies in wait for women, in particular, who dare to say anything at all. The context, in this case, is the patriarchy; the collapse is of any semblance of civility behind a screen of anonymity. The unacceptable reality is that if you are a woman who writes online about, say, video games, fat acceptance, abortion, politics, sex, relationships, or any number of other topics—or if you just use a dating app—at any moment you may trigger a stream of graphic rape and death threats from strangers.

Lindy West is a feminist writer who draws on her experience as a confident, happily married, "fat as hell" woman (her phrase). Among her trolls, a total stranger impersonated her dead father on Twitter. She tracked the man down and recorded their conversation for the radio show *This American Life*; after listening, with incredible patience, she actually got an apology out of him. After the 2016 election, West nonetheless announced that she had quit Twitter, calling it "unusable for anyone but trolls, robots and dictators."

Online harassers can damage one's peace of mind and mental health. More rarely they commit material harms as well. One practice is to *doxx* a target, hunting down her address and other personal details and posting them for anyone to see. The term *swatting*, or making fraudulent 911 calls that send heavily armed police to someone's door, has also entered the lexicon of online harassment.

All this is to say that mothers, especially, take a real risk when they post online. There is a thin scrim separating us all from a terrifying underworld. Social networks don't have transparent or easily workable procedures in place to protect people from abusers. These companies enjoy immunity under US law from the consequences of defamatory and offensive speech posted by their users. Law enforcement is often ill-informed about risks on social media and reluctant to get involved in cases of "merely" verbal abuse. Katherine Clark, a Democratic congressperson from Massachusetts, has become the top advocate in federal government for better protection against online harassment. "We're not going to be able to prevent it all," Clark told *Elle* magazine, "but there has to be resources and training that gives people a reasonable level of protection and safety." She's been introducing bills to fund research on these offenses and to properly train law enforcement. And her office has also been working directly with networks like Twitter, Facebook, and Reddit to improve their harassment reporting policies and enforcement. Of course, for her trouble Clark's been trolled, doxxed, and even swatted herself.

For Schuman, the context well and truly collapsed when *Slate* posted her essay on Facebook. "I started getting this torrent of poorly-spelled, curse-filled, death-threat-filled vitriol on my personal and professional Facebook [pages]," she says. It turned out that a woman named Katie McGuire, who tweets and posts as GOPKatie, had taken Schuman's post, including the photos, and repackaged it for her right-wing audience on the blog thefederalistpapers.org, with the headline "What This Mom Does in Pictures on Facebook with Her Baby Is Sick." "It was total clickbait," Schuman said. "It was like the opposite of Upworthy," the site that repackages uplifting or socially positive stories. "It was Downworthy."

Schuman felt blindsided. She had seen her piece as part of a broader conversation. To her it didn't seem out of proportion, in its tone and openness, to other things she'd written—say, about a miscarriage. McGuire's post, which *Slate* was able to have taken down for copyright violations, cast Schuman as an avatar of cultural decadence. In the words of another right-wing blog that picked up the story, "A slimy, despicable, trashy, self-indulgent and mentally deranged liberal."

Members of the general public went further. "I was getting three messages every hour threatening violence. I had to shut down my personal Facebook [page], change my name, make myself unsearchable, and go in manually on Facebook to get rid of the death threats." Facebook, she says, was no help at all in helping her stifle the torrent of abuse. "[The trolls] say my baby should die to teach me a lesson and Facebook is like, it's fine."

Just a month before, Schuman had predicted her own predicament. She published a piece, also on *Slate*, with the subhead "What if my bad parenting choices go viral?" It centered on an incident that briefly made the rounds online: a pancake order in a diner in Maine was delayed for forty-five minutes; a toddler was acting up; the owner of the diner yelled at the family; both sides then inexplicably took the dispute to Yelp and then to Facebook and thence to blogs and news outlets that might have been thought to have better things to write about (the *Washington Post,* say.)

"Utterly mundane child-related shenanigans now become national news on a regular basis," Schuman wrote then.

True. But why?

VIRAL PARENTING

I talked to Jonah Berger, a professor at Wharton Business School and the author of *Contagious: Why Things Catch On,* about why there's so much parent-related viral content—call it mombait. First of all, he tells me, any content that triggers strong emotion, whether positive or negative, is inherently more spreadable. That certainly applies to stories involving cute, vulnerable babies and children.

Second, whenever there are conflicts, people will be highly motivated to stump for their cause and against the opposition. "I think parenting is a little bit like the Yankees and Red Sox," he says. "It feels like there's a right and a wrong." There's a high ambient level of anxiety in the contemporary parenting world. Part of it is because we've lost a certain amount of social cohesion and hierarchy that may have encouraged previous generations of parents to defer to the authority of elders, clergy, or doctors. At the same time, the current dominant parenting ideologies of intensive motherhood and concerted cultivation dictate that you do lots of research to reach dozens of independent parenting decisions, every one of which is potentially high stakes. Your buying and reading this book is an example of that diligent fact-finding.

Then, having invested so much time and effort in reaching our own conclusions about an issue like sleep training, says Berger, "We want to think that we're right." That makes parents more likely to proselytize for their own choices, and to object to anything divergent. This tendency has dangers, and not just in the sense of threats to peace of mind for mothers like Rebecca Schuman.

The most egregious example of parenting-related social media gone wrong is probably the modern antivaccination movement. A single study published in a prominent British medical journal, *The Lancet,* in 1998 purported to show a link between the measles, mumps, and rubella (MMR) vaccine and autism spectrum disorders. The paper was officially retracted in 2010 and the author professionally censured. But conspiracy theories about the dangers of vaccination have proliferated ever since. Vaccination rates have dropped dramatically in a handful of states, including California, Washington, Colorado, Connecticut, Kentucky, and Arizona. Cases of measles, considered eliminated in the year 2000, have rebounded. In small children, the disease can be fatal or produce permanent hearing loss.

No industry profits when parents keep children home from the doctor. The antivax movement has been led by parents, often affluent, educated parents, even celebrities like Jenny McCarthy and Robert F. Kennedy Jr., who take to social media to directly inform others of what they believe to be a serious public-health threat. The president, who has a strong affinity for conspiracy theories, has played host to Kennedy and his views.

Renée DiResta lives in the San Francisco Bay Area. When her first child was almost a year old, too young to be fully vaccinated, the media reported that someone infected with measles had ridden the BART metro system, potentially exposing thousands of other people to the disease.

"I found it really disturbing because I take public transit, and measles kills," DiResta said. She started looking up vaccination rates in her local preschools, which are published online in California. Two of the schools in her neighborhood had rates below 40 percent, presumably because affluent, educated parents were opting out. "I was horrified."

As the mother of a high-needs infant whose parents lived across the country, DiResta relied on online parenting communities for support and advice. But from her work in the tech industry, she also understood the pitfalls of this kind of communication. There's what she calls "an asymmetry of passion," an idea also captured by the famous Yeats line "the best lack all conviction, while the worst are full of passionate intensity."

If you are an average parent who complies with your pediatrician's directives and accepts the medical consensus on the benefits of vaccines, DiResta explains, there's not a lot of motivation to tell other people about it. But if you are suffering personally because of a child with an unexplainable autism diagnosis or have become convinced of a cover-up that goes to the highest levels of the Centers for Disease Control, there's all the reason in the world to speak out. And the more parents tend to listen to each other on social media rather than traditional experts, the more likely that they're hearing from the hard-core conspiracy theorists rather than any voice of reason.

As DiResta argued in a 2016 piece for *Fast Company,* the networks themselves have glitches built into them that "boost the signals" of conspiracies. If you search for vaccination-related groups on Facebook, the antivaxers will pop up first because there's more of them. If you click on one antivax article, Google's algorithms will tend to show you more and more in the name of personalization. They don't apply any filter for "medically acceptable evidence" or "nonsense." In 2015 Google announced that it was taking steps to address this issue by drawing on a database called Knowledge Graph to emphasize information from vetted medical authorities when people search health-related terms.

Still, conspiracy theories, in Berger's word, are highly contagious. "A 2016 study looked at the relative percentages of pro-vaccine vs. anti-vaccine content on Pinterest and Instagram, places where moms gather," DiResta wrote. "75 % of the immunization-related pinned content was opposed to vaccines. This was a dramatic shift from studies of social networks in the early 2000s, when the percentage of negative content was estimated at around 25 %."

DiResta and a group of other parents founded an organization called Vaccinate California to try to provide a counterweight of ordinary mothers speaking out online on behalf of common sense. Working in concert with public health groups, they lobbied for and passed a law that made vaccines mandatory in California, eliminating a previous exemption for parents' "personal beliefs." For her trouble, DiResta was doxxed, and she continues to be targeted for harassment by conspiracy theorists online.

"There is a lot of very virulent and nasty opposition out there," she acknowledges. But she also says, "I think the net benefit of what we've accomplished outweighs the inconveniences." Her message to parents is not to be afraid of speaking out on behalf of reason and common sense. For our kids' sake and for our own, we must do our part to (safely) shout down the echo chamber.

DATA GOLD MINE

It's important to ask who is benefiting from the circulation of all this
outrage and uplift. Sharing our parenting experiences online creates
personal positives and negatives. It also creates a trail of data that is
valuable to others. The owners of social networks, and the companies
that buy advertising on these networks, profit from the time and attention of parents. Yet they seem slow to address either the problems of
harassment or the spread of dangerous misinformation.

The parent-targeted Internet is large, powerful, and lucrative. Marketers recognize that in the twenty-first century, the transition into
parenthood may be the signal transition of adult life. In the winter
2015 Pew poll cited earlier, 94 percent of parents said that parenthood
was "very" or "extremely" important to their identities.

When adopting a new identity, we are vulnerable. We're forming
new habits and loyalties. When I was several months pregnant for the
first time, I met up with an old friend and her fourteen-week-old infant. I remember my petite friend wrestling the stroller out of the car,
struggling with the huge diaper bag, trying to get her baby to smile for
me, and being truly embarrassed when she started fussing instead.

The awkwardness, the desire to make a good impression, imagining scrutiny from an audience that wasn't really there—all of a sudden I realized that my friend and I had been there before, in the tenth
grade.

Pregnancy and early motherhood feel very much like a second pu-
berty. The gawky physical transformations, of course, are there, with
a body overwhelmed with hormones and emotions. Just as much so,
there is the feeling of trying on the new role. The transformed relationships that come with it. The desperation for reassurance and validation.

Researcher danah boyd, mentioned earlier, studies social networks.
She argues that they function as arenas for the development and testing of new identities. That's why teenagers love them. It's also why
they are often adopted by historically marginalized groups and subcultures, from the raver, geek, goth, and anime scenes to gays and African
Americans. New parents, too, need safe spaces to figure out who we

are. When 1990s teenagers hung out at the mall, there was a clear connection between consumer culture and identity formation. The cool kids wore those jeans and drank that soda. Social networks, like malls, are commercial spaces. But when people hang out online the currency is different. Your data is the product. The game is simply to keep you engaged and thus exposed to advertising.

"From a consumer perspective moms are the holy grail," says Morra Aarons-Mele, a digital marketer who has been helping brands reach mothers since 1999. "Every marketer is obsessed with Millennial moms online."

According to the *Financial Times,* for marketers, the identity of a single pregnant woman can be worth as much as the age, sex, and location of up to two hundred people. This is why companies like Target have built data-mining algorithms that scan patterns of purchasing decisions to detect when someone is pregnant. In the case of a teenage girl in Minnesota, reported by the *New York Times Magazine,* the store started sending advertising circulars for maternity clothing and nursery furniture to her home, blowing her cover before she had broken the news to her parents. Microsoft researchers say that they can predict pregnancy down to the gestational week by web searches alone.

My friend Janet Vertesi is a sociologist of technology at Princeton University. Her research takes on fascinating topics like the culture that built up around the sharing of images of the Mars rover, and the inner organizational secrets of NASA. As a personal and professional experiment, in 2014, Vertesi tried to hide her pregnancy from Big Data. At the time she was studying how closely people guarded their personal information on the Internet, and what options they have for doing so.

The Internet is an increasingly essential communication medium linking us together. It functions as if it were a public utility, like the national highway system or the electrical grid. And that's more or less how we treat it: in the background, taken for granted. But the sites and platforms we use are not public like the highway system. They are built and maintained by private entities for their own purposes. And collecting your data for marketing is one central purpose.

"In the world of contemporary Internet companies, personal data reigns supreme," Vertesi wrote in a paper she published on the topic. Like the cables, wires, and pipes hiding behind the walls of your living room, there's an entire hidden infrastructure set up to capture this data as you move around the web: "bots, cookies, trackers, canvases, and other data sniffers intent on recording user clicks, likes, and purchases."

In order to reveal the workings of this infrastructure, she set out to evade it. What would it cost her as an individual to withhold from marketers the oh-so-valuable information that she was becoming a parent?

It wasn't easy. Instead of Chrome or Safari, Vertesi accessed the Internet using Tor, a browser that routes web traffic through foreign countries and is seen as a haven for terrorism and other illegal activities. Only she used it to look up baby names. She made all her baby-related purchases in cash, forgoing both convenience and loyalty discounts. Shopping online, she used gift cards, bought with cash, and had purchases delivered to a storage locker rather than her house. She banned her family and friends from any pregnancy references on social media and unfriended her uncle when he mentioned it in a Facebook message. She had to explain to him that even though personal Facebook messages are "private" from other users, the site itself reserves the right to access the text of a message and use it to better target advertising. The same contradictory model of "privacy" applies to emails or even the Google Doc where I typed this chapter: safe, perhaps, from the eyes of other people, but never from the network itself. Basically, Vertesi had to act like both a spy and a criminal in order to avoid sharing the contents of her uterus with Big Data.

A few weeks before giving birth, Vertesi gave a talk about the project at a small Internet culture conference. And—of course—it promptly went viral. There was coverage on Time.com, Forbes, ThinkProgress, NPR, Jezebel, Salon, Huffington Post, Mashable, and more. TV shows were calling, trying to book her as a guest, while she was at home recuperating from childbirth. She described the experience of inadvertent exposure as overwhelming and has stopped giving interviews on the topic.

PRIVATE PARTS

Vertesi's experiment raises the question: How should parents be thinking about privacy online? Both our own and our children's? Most of us aren't going to the extremes that Vertesi did. And in fact, she did it partly to show how impractical it would be in present circumstances.

As we discussed in chapter 6, the legal and ethical issues are very much in flux here. The trade-offs you choose to make between convenience and privacy depend on the concerns that are uppermost in your mind.

If it's spammers who really get your goat, you may choose to set up a secondary email address for all marketing-related communications, use fewer apps, and regularly delete cookies from your browser.

If you bristle at the thought of government surveillance, you'll have to steer clear of social media. Same if you want to shield yourself from harassment. Or at least maintain separate or pseudonymous accounts on platforms that allow it (Facebook, for one, insists on real names). Some of my more politically active friends have taken to encrypted messaging platforms such as Signal.

If you fear identity theft, one recourse would be to put a fraud alert or a freeze on your credit report and use a password manager such as LastPass or Dashlane to generate secure and unique passwords for your various online accounts.

If you have experienced domestic abuse or stalking, it may warrant the use of all of the above. The Safety Net Project at the National Network to End Domestic Violence is a good resource.

Personally, because I am a member of the media, my real name and image are pretty much out there. I try to change my passwords frequently and unsubscribe from unnecessary email lists. And I've been known to conduct certain searches in Google Chrome's incognito mode so they won't show up in my browser history. (No, I won't tell you which ones.)

Posting about my daughters is a different matter. I am essentially laying the groundwork of their digital identity, and I have little way of controlling how the information might persist across time and in different contexts. Some parent privacy advocates argue that you should never post a picture of your kids' faces; with facial recognition improving all the time, it may soon be possible to identify and track a three-year-old twenty years later. Others create accounts in their children's names across social networks in order to maintain control of the "intellectual property" that is their identity. Still other digital ethicists argue that there should be a right to erase or seal the digital identities of children under eighteen—with no word on how that would, practically, be accomplished.

European authorities generally uphold stricter privacy limits than we do in the United States, including what is known as the "right to be forgotten." A 2014 European Union ruling gives citizens the right to petition commercial websites and search engines like Google to take down information that may be inaccurate or irrelevant.

French and German police have publicly warned parents against posting embarrassing photos. In France, the violation of another's privacy online—including a family member—can carry a penalty of a year in prison and up to a $43,000 fine.

And yet we go back to that average one thousand images shared online by the time a child turns five. I'm sure I'm guilty of at least twice that. Are we all privacy sinners?

Alicia Blum-Ross, who with Sonia Livingstone manages the Parenting for a Digital Future research project at the London School of Economics, has interviewed parents about their sharing practices. She takes a provocative position against shaming parents like me for posting pictures of their kids. Considering that these issues are so deeply in flux, she says, "You shouldn't be going around telling parents that they can't do things that they find useful or comforting or practically helpful," she says, in the name of some "imagined future right to privacy" on the part of our children.

I won't post my daughters' full names or birthdays or our home address. Right now, the older one's only Google hit is her great-grandmother's obituary. I'm less cautious about photos, although I know many people who prefer to share photos by text or email or with a small number of people over a sharing service like Google Photos, rather than on social networks (in which case, the images are still visible to Google's or the cell phone provider's internal trackers, just not to the public). I never post pictures of other people's kids online without asking because families have different rules. And I don't post naked pictures or photos that I otherwise think of as embarrassing.

As my daughter gets older, I'll increasingly need to ask her before posting anything about her on social media. A University of Michigan study in 2016 asked 249 parent-child pairs about social media rules. The children, ages ten to seventeen, wanted their parents to ask first before posting about them on social media; the parents were far less aware of this as an issue.

I won't insist on being my daughter's "friend" on platforms, but I will ask to look over her shoulder occasionally. And I will caution her to pause before sharing anything and imagine that her teacher and grandparents will be reading it. Her online identity will gradually become hers to manage.

I had a pretty dispiriting conversation about online privacy with a self-described family privacy expert, Lynette Owens. She's the CEO of a security software company and the founder of the nonprofit Internet Safety for Kids and Families (ISKF). She's also on the board of the Family Online Safety Institute, one of the major organizations in the business of helping parents be safe online. ISKF sends volunteers to talk to parent-teacher organizations around the country about keeping kids safe and savvy online.

Some of their basic tips: Turn off location awareness on kids' devices. Keep Instagram and Snapchat accounts set to private by default. Never share home addresses. Turn off in-app purchases on tablets and phones. Keep different passwords for different services.

However, midway through our conversation I asked her, "So I'm listening to what you're saying and basically, everybody's on these sites. If you shut down functions like geolocation you won't be able to use them as well. The privacy terms are really hard to understand. They change constantly. They're really hard to control. And even if your kids don't post, their friends will post about them. Do we just throw up our hands?"

"You know, in some way, I guess that's what we do," she answered. It's not exactly satisfying.

THE THIEF OF JOY

In words sometimes attributed to Theodore Roosevelt, "comparison is the thief of joy." The search for identity and connection we're carrying out online is compromised by a bias within the platforms we're using that's optimized to hook us in and keep us wanting more—not soothe wounded feelings, not answer questions, not lead us into a conversation with a real human being, but raise anxieties and stoke anger. Social media thrives on the battles of early parenthood: physical, emotional, mental, social, financial. In doing so, it amplifies them.

The average parent won't rely on the Internet as an emotional lifeline the way the Brackbills do. And most of us, hopefully, won't take our turns as the "worst mom on the Internet" the way Rebecca Schuman did. But there are subtler emotional pitfalls of being a parent on social media.

In a 2016 review of the research on parenting and social media, Deborah Lupton at the University of Canberra in Australia observes, "some elements of the performance of parenting have become more open to the view (and potential judgement) of others."

When I think about the "public performance of parenthood," I actually think of some pretty private moments.

"Mama, sit in my room and go tap-tap-tap." A bedtime ritual for the screen age. At age three or four, after the veggies are eaten, a spoonful of ice cream, bathtime, her toys picked up, the sticker placed on the good-behavior sticker chart, and three books are read. Lulu's in her *Frozen* nightgown, with her pink bunny. Both night lights are on. To ease the separation and help her drift off, Adam or I will sometimes— okay, usually—sit quietly in her room with our laptops on.

What am I looking at, between running errands on Amazon and FreshDirect, answering work emails, and browsing Netflix?

Yoga moms who breastfeed their two-year-olds while doing handstands on the beach in Hawaii.

Fashion moms who pose their kids in tiny Tory Burch flats and blazers.

Penny-pinching crunchy moms who cut up rags for "family cloth" instead of buying toilet paper (yes, that's a real thing).

Baker moms who stencil and stack pearlized fondant into Moana's mountaintop.

Gluten-free, nut-free, and paleo diet moms.

Homeschooling moms who hide Bible verses under the kids' cereal bowls.

Simplicity moms whose kids play happily for hours with a basket of pine cones and beach pebbles, bento box moms who make lunches in the shape of Angry Birds, #fitspo (a portmanteau for fitness-inspiration) moms with four kids under three who pose with chiseled abs and the inspiring slogan *What's Your Excuse?*, lifestyle moms who pack up the husband and tot in a custom-outfitted Airstream trailer hung with hand-sewn vintage lace curtains, drive along Route 1 in California, picnic on the rocky coast of Big Sur with organic strawberries they've just picked, and end up restoring a nineteenth-century farmhouse in Oregon with rare heirloom roosters scratching in the yard.

They are all calm. They are all beautiful. They exist only during the golden hour. I squint as I hunch over the blue light of the screen. My thighs are spreading and I'm growing crow's-feet by the minute. The cult of intensive mothering finds its ur-expression through mommy blogging and social media, and none of us can measure up.

If we're not punishing ourselves, we may be throwing stones. Hunky actor Ryan Reynolds got thousands of negative comments when he posted a Father's Day picture of himself carrying his six-month-old daughter positioned incorrectly in a baby carrier. One of the articles calling him out also noted: "Kim Kardashian is constantly called a bad parent and criticized for photos she shares of North . . . remember when Prince William did not secure newborn Prince George properly in his seat (that was major!)? Brad Pitt has said he gives his kids Coca Cola to get them going in the morning, but there's not a lot wrong he can do in the public's eyes! Oh gosh, but remember Britney Spears driving with her baby on her lap?!"

Ten or fifteen years ago we were worried about the unattainable images put forward by celebrity parents. Now they're just as susceptible as anyone else to social media shaming. But at least Brad Pitt and Kim Kardashian have money and fame as compensation for the haters. When you're surrounded by an ever-expanding galaxy of seemingly ordinary women who are nonetheless managing to craft and put forth images of perfection, the question becomes, again, *What's Your Excuse?*

I only read this stuff at night. My IQ drops as drowsiness creeps up. At nine p.m. I might be writing, editing, browsing the *New Yorker*, but by eleven thirty only Pinterest, Instagram, or the Huffington Post Parents section will do. Scroll, scroll, click, click.

The Huffington Post is one of the top-trafficked sites on the Internet. And Huffington Post Parents is consistently one of the top-performing sections on that site, especially for mobile visits—all those one-handed mothers, holding infants or warming up food in the microwave with the other hand. In a *New York Times Magazine* piece titled "Arianna Huffington's Improbable, Insatiable Content Machine," the author, David Segal, noted, "some of the most successful posts target moms who are checking their Facebook feeds late at night, apparently yearning to be told that they shouldn't be on Facebook at that hour." "You know, posts about, 'Stop procrastinating and go to sleep,' 'Disconnect your devices,'" said Ethan Fedida, the site's senior social media editor. "They go crazy for it." Yup, nailed me.

What's your poison? Superiority, inadequacy, or a queasy mixture of both? Lesa Brackbill or Rebecca Schuman? The blogger who will make you cry with her admission that she never appears in any family photographs because she's ashamed of the fifty extra pounds of baby weight, or the pioneer woman who somehow runs an entire ranch; raises four self-reliant, hardworking, blond kids; has killer brownies and nachos recipes; milks the cows and brings home the bacon; and looks glamorous doing it?

MOMBAIT

Mombait, in small doses, may be harmless entertainment. But in many studies, greater use of social media, especially Facebook, has been linked to symptoms of depression. The specific social behavior that seems to mediate that connection, according to 2015 studies at both the University of Houston and the University of Missouri, is the act of comparing oneself to others.

It's easy to forget on my late-night voyages that parenting media, whether social or not, is still media. It's never just moms chatting over clotheslines in the backyard. It's a juggernaut of publishers and advertisers and entrepreneurs who are scheming, every day, to figure out how to grab our eyeballs. There are gazillions of dollars at stake here: the 70 percent of the economy that is based on consumer spending, 70 to 85 percent of which is controlled by women. And they're playing every emotional note on the keyboard to get us to click, repeatedly, and to buy.

Mommy blogging (a derisive term that many reject) is a cottage industry that's grown to massive proportions. By some estimates there are over fourteen million mothers writing up to a third of all blogs (whether or not they always write about parenting per se).

Mom bloggers, Instagrammers, YouTubers, and Snapchatters, at their best, are like latter-day versions of Lucille Ball or Erma Bombeck. They mine fictionalized, often satirical versions of their home lives for money and fame. But in the age of social media the maker has a lot less control over the product. The cameras didn't follow Ball home to get all the details of her divorce from Desi Arnaz after twenty years of marriage. Bombeck, a newspaper columnist and TV personality, didn't use her children's or husband's real names or images.

Also as seen in the early years of television, the prominence of advertising in the mommy blogging and now the podcasting world can be jarring. Entries turn from heartfelt accounts of postpartum depression to offering readers a discount on window treatments.

As far back as 2008, Walmart recruited a group of mom bloggers to provide feedback on programs, products, stores, and services and to help build a "money-saving community." In 2009, General Mills created its own network of more than nine hundred bloggers, of whom 80 percent were moms. The group receives products for review, coupons, and giveaways. Most other big consumer brands do this kind of outreach too, and firms like Morra Aarons-Mele's specialize in matchmaking between bloggers and brands.

In 2015 *Fast Company* profiled Susan Petersen, a stay-at-home mom based in Provo, Utah, who became a successful entrepreneur through product placement on blogs. According to Petersen, "the trust that readers have in these bloggers' product recommendations comes out of a deeper emotional connection with these writers and a shared experience of motherhood."

"'There are some very lonely aspects of being a mother,'" Petersen told the writer. It's the perfect time to sell to us.

More recently, along with the rest of the Internet, mother-directed media has been transitioning from blogs to more visually oriented platforms like Instagram, Pinterest, and Snapchat. "I think attention spans have gotten shorter, so I don't think blogs are quite as popular with Millennial moms," says Kristen Howerton, who epitomizes this change. She started blogging at Rage Against the Minivan in 2007 when she was in the process of adopting her fourth child—she has a multiracial family, with two biological children and two adopted from Haiti. The blog became a full-time source of income in 2010, and she still posts frequently, covering serious topics related to racism and international adoption alongside lighter lifestyle posts.

But some of her energy these days goes to maintaining the Instagram account assholeparents, which consists of submissions of photos of crying children with captions describing non-sins like "I told her she couldn't have a cookie. . . . Because it was bedtime." "I don't think advertisers have really caught up" to the change, Howerton observes. "They're willing to spend money on sponsored posts even though, in all honesty, they'd probably get more eyeballs on Instagram."

While the mommy blogger world has its limitations, the movement of our collective eyeballs away from the galaxies of independently written and published blogs toward these image-driven, corporate media platforms represents a certain loss. In the course of those long nights online, I've read some seriously good writing that helped me, touched me, taught me, and made me feel better about parenting. This is harder to get from a filtered snapshot and a thicket of hashtags.

SANE TIME OUT

One place I wandered into early on in my motherhood journey, and wanted to hang out in, was the blog Ask Moxie, an incredibly warm, reassuring, calm place to get parenting advice. This is true not only of the posts and the site's minimalist design, but of the comments, which are respectful, support a wide range of views, and also have correct spelling and grammar. Moxie's most popular pages are guides to infant sleep and her explications of the theory of "sleep regressions" that happen at certain ages for developmental reasons. Moxie has blogged movingly and helpfully about her own experiences of co-parenting after divorce and about tough conversations with her sons on issues like consent and racism. But she also returns often to the mantra "you are the best parent for your child," which is something that we just can't hear enough.

When I get Moxie, aka Magda Pecsenye, on the phone, I realize I'm starstruck. It's a little like talking to Oprah. I am hoping for a straight-to-the-heart shot of wisdom and benevolence. And I get it.

"When I first started writing Ask Moxie in 2005, I had a three-and-a-half-year-old and a six-month-old," she says. "I was extraordinarily frustrated with the extreme polarization of anything parenting-related online."

Like Berger, she makes the point that this polarization sells. "It's either Dr. Sears, dangle your baby off your body from a linen strap, or Dr. Spock, tie your baby to a chair and only look at it every four hours."

Ask Moxie refuses to endorse either side. The posts are about finding your own way to the approach that's best for you. "I just genuinely don't care what people do. I want people to be happy with their own decision. My goal was to make one little place on the Internet where people could be honest and provide support without having to all do the same thing."

I quickly realize that what makes this site so extraordinary is that Pecsenye has never made a living from it directly. She works as a management consultant and also provides parenting coaching by phone. (Janet Lansbury, the RIE expert, has a similar model, and her blog is also a pretty relaxing place to visit.)

Pecsenye credits her own mother with the inspiration for Ask Moxie's low-temperature, no-nonsense tone. "Part of the reason I was able to foster this community is that I was not particularly conflicted about not being happy every minute as a mother. My mother

expressed frustrations with the process of being a mother every moment of my life. I hadn't expected that every moment was going to be
sunshine, and I also didn't feel like I had to hide that. And that was in
contrast to a lot of people I've met online who felt like they had been
sold a bill of goods."

She'd tapped into the dissatisfaction, even anguish, of a generation
of highly educated, accomplished women with extremely high expectations for themselves and others. "They had been extraordinary at
their jobs and they felt they'd be extraordinary as mothers. But with
motherhood there aren't any metrics you can hit so you can feel you're
doing it right.

"They'd never had any idea that there was anything but either success or failure. When I started writing about the fact that I didn't like
it, and there were no right answers and you could just suck it up, people were like, 'Me too!'"

Ask Moxie has her own thoughts on the value and historic place of
mombait. "If we were all still living in villages, you wouldn't need to
be on the Internet finding people to talk to. But that's not how we live.
We've set up this society where there's one and maybe two people with
a child. If you're at home with that kid all day, it's like OMG, how do
you survive?"

This isn't a new problem, she points out. "Are we luckier because
we have the Internet now, or were we luckier back when Betty Friedan
wrote *The Feminist Mystique* and women were popping pills?" The two
aren't mutually exclusive, of course, with references to "Mommy's sippy
cup" and "wine o'clock" having entered the mommy blogger lexicon.

As with all other parenting issues, Moxie sees a middle path with
the use of social media. "It is what you make of it," she says. "If you
know what you're doing and you focus on actual real relationships
with people, it's fantastic. If you're using it as broadcast-only, trying to
accumulate likes and hearts, it's going to destroy you." To her point,
a study published by Pace University in 2015 suggested a connection
between depressive symptoms and the number of strangers one followed on Instagram, again because of the danger of negative social
comparison.

Ask Moxie showed me that there are places for parents online where supportive dialogue and solid information hold sway. They're not an accident; they come about generally through the concerted effort of site operators as well as monitors, often volunteers, who enforce community norms.

Global Natives is an example of a sizable parenting community that has tried to improve how people interact. Founded in 2009, it has about 250,000 active members from all over the world. The primary purpose is to organize cultural and educational exchanges, particularly for teens. As opposed to traditional exchange programs that go through schools or nonprofits, Global Natives helps families pair up for direct exchanges. These are cheaper than a formal program, and because families establish a rapport beforehand, relationships can extend for years. Families with younger kids use the site too, to arrange home-visit holiday exchanges around the world.

In 2015, founder Nina Prodinger went through cancer treatment. The experience got her and her co-founders started on a conversation about what the community could achieve by going "deeper into people's real lives, their troubles and their hopes," explains Michael Wu, a psychologist who undertook a study of the experiment that resulted. The community invited its members, in no uncertain terms, to voluntarily "cut the crap." Stop lying by omission, false modesty, whitewashing. Stop making derogatory statements about others directly or by implication. Avoid politics or religion until you know people well.

On the positive side, members agreed to "use simple language," "talk straight," "embrace diversity," and describe both their families' assets and drawbacks, giving the information they would hope others would share with them.

About twelve thousand members agreed to the terms for over a year. Wu surveyed a large number of them afterward. "Ninety-one percent of all participants stated that they were going to stick with the philosophy, that they intended to stick with it in all their online activities— from daily emails to business networks and other social media—and that finally they felt that online honesty had significantly improved their lives," he reported.

FINDING POSITIVE PARENTING SPACES

In general, I've had the most positive experiences with online spaces that are noncommercial, are somewhat private, and have some connection to real-world relationships. Today, I post at least weekly to two parenting email discussion groups—one for my neighborhood with thousands of members, the other a carefully curated list set up by a fellow working mom of thirty working mothers, many of whom have become real-life friends. This is the twenty-first-century back fence, where I can get practical help, hand-me-down clothes, inspiration, and emotional support whenever and wherever I need it. As a bonus, the things I write in emails don't show up on a Google search and are less easily targeted by advertising that follows me around the web.

When I'm on Facebook, I focus on conversations with people I actually know. I go there to ask a question or offer information, and I'm pretty experienced by now in avoiding the types of conversations that are destined to flame out. Check in with yourself, your breathing and heart rate, the next time you're on social media and you'll have a pretty good indicator of whether you'll regret that post someday.

Pull your virtual circles closer. Start an email list yourself if you don't find one you like. Get just a dozen parents talking and you'll have a powerful source of support and information.

9 THE FUTURE OF DIGITAL PARENTING

I'M DELIVERING A SIX-FOOT-TALL ELMO A ROUNDHOUSE KICK IN THE GUTS. His stomach slices into angular shards as my foot intersects with it. But he doesn't visibly emote in response. Next, I step over to his friend Grover . . . closer . . . closer . . . and finally place my head directly inside his looming black void of a mouth.

This bizarre scenario was no dream. It happened on a visit to the Stanford University Virtual Human Interaction Lab. After decades in the realm of sci-fi, 3D immersive visual and audio environments took a step closer to becoming part of our everyday world in 2014. That's when Facebook announced the purchase of a startup called Oculus Rift for $2 billion. It's also when Facebook's CEO, Mark Zuckerberg, came to this lab to meet with Jeremy Bailenson. Bailenson, a professor in Stanford's Department of Communications and a consultant to many major technology companies, created this lab to design and test virtual experiences that could teach us to be better people. Hence the current, experimental collaboration with Sesame Street: a glimpse of the media world that children born in 2020 may take for granted.

This chapter will place the ideas I've already set forth in the context of the tech world coming just over the horizon. We'll also meet some entrepreneurs, many of them parents themselves, who are fighting fire with fire: innovating with technology to respond to challenges like distraction and to try to enhance family connection.

MEDIA 2020

Virtual reality (VR), augmented reality (AR), mixed reality (MR), artificial intelligence (AI), and the Internet of Things (IoT) are a group of acronyms that will increasingly shape our experience of the near future.

VR currently refers to putting on a headset that replaces your entire field of vision. Turn your head in all directions, move around—you will experience the illusion of inhabiting a visual and auditory environment with no frame and no edges. The HTC Vive and the Oculus Rift are dedicated headsets for this purpose; Samsung and Google have cheaper versions that use a smartphone as the screen.

AR means the use of location awareness, sensors, machine vision, and machine listening to add a layer of information and interaction to the world around you. The first iteration of a so-called head-up AR display, Google Glass, proved to be a little ahead of its time. But mobile apps are providing a more low-key, less socially intrusive augmentation of reality already. If you install the Zillow real estate app you can experience a kind of X-ray vision by browsing virtual tours and floor plans of the houses you pass as you walk down the street. Or in a more sinister mode, you can snap a picture of someone and use Facebook's or Google's face recognition tools to try to identify them.

MR, as the name suggests, is a mix of the augmented and the virtual. The world got an introduction to the concept in the summer of 2016 with the viral mobile game Pokémon Go, which became the top-downloaded paid application on iPhones and Androids only days after being released. Millions of people began roaming their physical cities on scavenger hunts for animated monsters.

AI is a term that's been so stretched that it's in danger of losing its meaning. At the simplest level, it's the use of computer technology to accomplish tasks of a complexity that we would previously have associated with humans, such as speech recognition. Amazon now sells a home appliance called the Echo that you can use to speak to its virtual assistant, Alexa, and bid it to play music, check the weather, turn down the air conditioning, or order a pizza.

And IoT is a term for wireless transmission and sensors embedded into everyday objects. The best-known pop-culture embodiment of this idea, a refrigerator that automatically reorders milk when it runs out, isn't too widespread yet. But IoT technologies today enable people to control the lights, security system, and climate in their homes with their phones, for example, even when they're not at home. There's also a whole category of IoT technologies marketed directly to anxious parents, like the Owlet, a "smart sock" that monitors an infant's pulse.

Now, how do the ideas we've been exploring so far about digital parenting stand up against the coming generation of technology? There's at least one big outstanding question. The current concept of *screen time* exists in opposition to a concept of *screenless time. Online* imagines that there is such a thing as *offline.* Those are exactly the boundaries that may melt with the next generation of technology. As Victor Strasburger told me, already it seems that "studying media is like studying the air we breathe," and that's about to get even more true.

If a four-year-old child is accompanied through her day by an MR, AI Elmo, an imaginary friend made visible, is this screen time? What about the AI-enabled plastic doll now on the market named My Friend Cayla—is it a doll or a computer game? What about a nine-year-old who plays outside with peace of mind supplied by a virtual tether, an alarm that sounds on his mother's phone when he leaves his block? As these technologies get more immersive and more ubiquitous, prohibition-based parenting gets more difficult. The framework of positive parenting with media becomes even more necessary.

Maintaining the family home as a sacred space free of digital connection, even for short blocks of time, may get one step more inconvenient. It's harder to have a fully unplugged family dinner when the microwave is chiming in on the conversation. But we can still put forth the idea of balance as an important value.

Being aware of the content our kids are encountering is going to be as important as ever. We need to engage jointly for the purpose of authoritative mediation. This may actually become easier as more applications move back into shared physical space.

And this new media world offers vast new expressive and creative capabilities. The imaginations of tomorrow's great artists and designers are awakening in children today. Sponsoring, brokering, and otherwise encouraging their media pursuits will be even more important.

VR

The dawn of VR as an expressive medium is occasioning some soul searching. Just as nineteenth-century audiences supposedly panicked at the sight of the Lumière brothers' 1895 film of a train pulling into a station, our twenty-first-century perceptual systems are still somewhat naïve to the overpowering effects of 3D immersion. In my tour group at the Stanford lab, I saw the VR headset make full-grown adults nauseous, cause them to scream in fear and refuse to take a step across a solid floor if their eyes told them they were at the edge of a cliff. We can expect that younger observers might be even more sensitive. Given that, I would be a little concerned if first-person-shooter games came to dominate the medium.

"The brain has not evolved to distinguish a compelling virtual experience from a physical experience," Bailenson at Stanford has said. He believes that we should take the power of VR experiences seriously from a moral perspective and use it to produce what he calls transformative "aha" moments. For example, he has built a VR game in which you fly around a city, Superman-style, in order to deliver insulin to a diabetic child. Another simulation his lab designed allows you to virtually inhabit the body of someone of a different gender, age, and/or ethnicity, an exercise in perspective-taking. In an exemplar of these studies, college students who "walked a mile" in the shoes of an elderly version of themselves later decided, in a hypothetical exercise, to allocate more money to retirement savings. In effect, they had cultivated empathy for their future selves.

Just as with earlier types of media, there's a worry that children will be oversensitive to the effects. We also worry just because they seem to find it so compelling. "[In experiments] we discovered that kids under three won't put on the headset," says Ken Perlin at NYU's Media Research Lab, another major VR lab. Preschoolers found it too strange, dark, heavy, and uncomfortable. But, he says, "those from four onward love it. By the age of eight or nine, the phrase that comes to mind is crack cocaine. They go nuts. They feel so completely at home. They come up with their own activities the moment they put the thing on. At a conference recently someone said, maybe this stuff isn't safe for under-thirteen-year-olds. I said, maybe it's only suitable for under-thirteen-year-olds."

I pushed back, arguing that crack cocaine is not something we think of as beneficial for children. But Perlin, an unabashed enthusiast, sees these technologies as a kind of fantastical dojo for the imagination: a place to build mental strength and flexibility by testing out possible and impossible worlds.

He makes the case by invoking our evolutionary destiny. "Our minds are protean. They're a general-purpose mechanism for working through many possible realities. Human minds evolve to deal with whatever might show up by making this general-purpose coping mechanism." And, Perlin argues, doing what we were intended by evolution to do, feels really good.

"Exercising that coping mechanism is pleasurable. We instinctively know it's helpful to expand what our minds can deal with. This is potentially a powerful way of experiencing what we know our minds are capable of." So he amends his statement; virtual realities are a food for the mind, not a drug. And extra-flexible young minds especially relish this food.

But Perlin believes that isolating, immersive VR is only ever going to be a niche market. There's a "coffee table problem"—the instant you strap on a wireless headset and enter a virtual world, your living room furniture becomes a dangerous obstacle course.

The market for solo VR may be similar to the percentage of people who could be considered hard-core PC gamers today—a tiny fraction of all players. And, no doubt, presenting the same dangers of compulsive use.

So if we're not all going to be inhabiting a virtual universe 24/7, what then is the real future of VR? Perlin likes to say, "The holodeck is other people." (The holodeck is the fictional VR environment available to characters in *Star Trek* to do things like train for sports and play games.) The experiences he and his lab are creating generally allow two or more people to interact, whether they're physically standing in the same room or separated by thousands of miles. A lot of the ones they've built so far actually resemble stations in a Montessori class-room: allowing people to collaborate on a giant immersive painting, or jam together on imaginary musical instruments in midair, or manip-ulate four-dimensional geometric shapes, or operate giant puppets, or even play catch five thousand miles apart.

To Perlin, any media experience—a novel, a TV show, a video game, or Facebook—is meaningful and compelling insofar as it pro-vokes or enhances our feelings of interaction. Here's the idea of joint engagement coming back. This could mean projection into the lives of fictional characters or communion with the imagination of an au-thor or director. But ideally it reaches its full flourishing in real-world communication with other people.

"All we care about is whatever deal is going on between me and another person," he argues. "Any medium that enriches that is suc-cessful. Any medium that replaces that is a failure."

Marching in an imaginary Day of the Dead parade alongside my kid sounds like more fun than plunking her down in front of a car-toon. If Perlin is right, multiperson VR and MR experiences, branch-ing off from the Wii and Kinect video games of today, may feel more connected than bounded screens because they move play back into a shared physical space.

As an enthusiast of the emerging genre, Perlin believes that there's another, cultural reason we should give our kids headsets and let them loose in creative environments: the mature works of VR as an art form will be created one day by today's babies and future generations.

"Linguists know that natural language is not developed by people over eight years old," he says, meaning if you encounter a new language after that age, you'll always speak it as a second language, with some awkwardness or accent. Some researchers put the age closer to ten, but the point holds.

By the same token, Perlin says, it's the people who grow up taking VR for granted who will really be fluent in it. "The Hitchcock and Spielberg of VR haven't been born yet."

AI

"Hi, what's your name? I'm Alex." Alex is a gender-ambiguous eight-year-old in a polo shirt, with medium-dark skin and hair styled in chin-length twists. In a classroom at a charter school in Pittsburgh, other third-graders sit down opposite Alex to do a science activity. Together, they have to discuss a picture of a dinosaur and figure out as much as they can about it.

Alex doesn't always seem to catch everything the other person is saying and sometimes offers inappropriate generic responses like "me too." But the illusion of a conversation is pretty good, considering Alex is an artificially intelligent avatar created at Carnegie Mellon University.

In some ways, the parenting challenges of VR and MR are easier to conceptualize because they still exist within the frame of "media"—environments and narratives designed and engineered by other human minds that you switch on and off, enter and leave, and that you understand as not being "real."

Artificial intelligence is more complex and harder to resist. The next generation of AI programs, like Alex, may start to blur the commonly understood line between interacting with a computer program and with a person. Or, perhaps, they'll establish a third category in between.

Justine Cassell, whom you've already met, has a long-standing interest in the creation of technologies that engage people socially and emotionally. More broadly, she's interested in the transactive nature of intelligence—the idea that intelligent behavior arises in dialogue, in communication, not solely inside one person's head. Over the past twenty years, she has built "listener" programs that encourage children to tell stories. Some are aimed at those on the autism spectrum, others at English language learners. Children get to create the characters that they imagine listening to them: one basketball fan chose Shaquille O'Neal. Interacting with these programs has been shown to build children's confidence and sophistication in using language, in ways that transfer to conversations with humans. (Similar kinds of therapy are done with dogs as the stand-in.) "In some ways computers are the ideal listener if they're designed well," she argues. "They're never late for work. They are infinitely available, infinitely patient."

The idea of a "lifelong learning companion" was first introduced by early AI researchers decades ago. It emphasizes the social nature of learning. Think about it: we already have access to the world's knowledge in our pockets, and it hasn't led to a demonstrable increase in smartness—in know-it-alls, maybe. But like a wise imaginary friend, learning companions could engage children socially as well as intellectually—asking questions, providing timely encouragement, offering suggestions and connections to resources, helping them talk through difficulties. Over time, the companion would "learn" more and more about what a child knows, what his or her interests are, and reflect a version of the child back to himself or herself, like a great teacher.

Alex, a research project directed by Cassell's PhD student Samantha Finkelstein, is an early step down that path. Finkelstein and Cassell were specifically curious about the phenomenon called *code-switching*. When English-language learners and other children of nondominant class and ethnic backgrounds get to school, they encounter what might be considered a foreign dialect: Standard English. Eighty percent of public school teachers are white, and the prevailing strategy in public schools is for teachers to stick to Standard English and insist that students do so as well. The children's ability to master its rules and vocabulary will help determine their success in education and in the workplace. But a student's home dialect remains the language of fluency and belonging. *Code-switching* is the term linguists coined for the agility necessary to employ the right style of language in the right context.

Finkelstein and Cassell set up an experiment around the dinosaur activity at a 99 percent black charter school in Pittsburgh. In one condition, Alex spoke Standard English the whole time. In the other, Alex spoke the children's dialect during the initial getting-to-know-you, brainstorming session. "I think we need to figure out, how do the creature, like, eat and move around and stuff," this Alex says, or "You think those spikes sharp enough to hunt the bunny?"

Then, when it's time to transition to presenting to the teacher, Alex says something like, "My teacher always like it when I use my school grammar when I gotta do presentations like this." And proceeds to speak in Standard English.

In the code-switching condition of the experiment, the children showed better verbal science reasoning, with more hypotheses supported by observations. On the other hand, Finkelstein told me, when Alex stuck to Standard English, the kids at times became pretty hostile. They baited the program with comments like "Not bad for a stupid black kid like you," or even "What kind of porn do you watch?" She thinks maybe the students were reacting to a sense of inauthenticity that came from creating a child character who looks like them but speaks like a dominant-culture adult. I know what she means. I experienced my own impulses of boundary-pushing, to try and puncture the illusion, when confronted in VR with the preternaturally placid figures of Elmo and Grover.

Sitting down with Alex makes clear that the idea of a universal lifelong learning companion is still several years away. Alex was painstakingly created for a single brief activity on a preselected topic. Almost every word and phrase it utters was based on those previously recorded on site in a Pittsburgh classroom with children this age. And still its conversation doesn't flow perfectly. To customize a program like this to hundreds of dialects, thousands of topics, not to mention in the hundred or so languages spoken in American public schools—it will take a leap forward, to say the least, in what's called *natural language processing*. (AI applications that rely on typing, not voice, have an advantage here.)

On the other hand, in the videos of the experiment I watched, the way that kids interacted with Alex seemed amazingly, for lack of a better word, natural. The kids were clear that it wasn't a real person—Cassell says when you ask them about it, they just roll their eyes—but they were willing to play along anyway. And the experimental results showed that they get very real senses of either social validation or social threat from Alex, depending on how Alex talks to them.

Most children won't encounter AI companions carefully designed in research labs for specific educational purposes, but rather commercial products like Hello Barbie, introduced for the 2015 Christmas season with eight thousand prerecorded lines of dialogue, including gems like "One place to learn a lot about outfits and clothes is school!" Customer reviews say that it's still pretty buggy.

In my anecdotal observation, kids also seem to love interacting with the first generation of voice-activated AI "assistants" designed for adults, like Amazon's Alexa and the iPhone's Siri. Anil Dash, one of the smartest commentators out there on the future of the Internet, observed in a Medium post in 2016, "The Echo's killer app for families with young kids is the timer . . . while unlocking the phone, launching a timer app, and starting a countdown is impossible for young kids to do, saying 'Alexa, set a timer for 5 minutes' is effortless."

If it seems bizarre or alienating to think about our children having relationships with computer programs, we have some clear precursors. One is the superpeer or parasocial relationships referred to earlier that children have with their favorite characters, whether superheroes, princesses, or Muppets. Another is the transitional object. That's the developmental expert Donald Winnicott's term for the teddy bear, blanket, or other lovey that most healthy children take up in infancy and may find comfort in throughout childhood. The cuddles help them transition between the early ever-presence of the mother and a gradually internalized sense of security. But those stuffed creatures also occupy an imaginary space between animate and inanimate. As the Velveteen Rabbit, a forgotten toy, says in the haunting children's book of the same title, "When a child loves you for a long, long time, not just to play with, but REALLY loves you, then you become Real."

Cassell believes we actually carry that ability to transfer affection to objects into adulthood. "It doesn't go away. I happen to think it lasts." In fact, that little beeping device you carry with you at all times might just be your lovey.

IOT

Unlike AI, the Internet of Things doesn't present the existential threat of a quasi-social intelligence. Instead, it connects us to a web that is invisible, everywhere, all the time, incrementally shaping our perceptions and interactions using software and sensors. This matrix beguiles parents in particular with the figure of the techno-nanny.

In a curious historical footnote, it was Isamu Noguchi, the renowned sculptor and designer best known for his paper lamps in geometric shapes, who created the world's first baby monitor in 1937. Called the Radio Nurse, it was manufactured in Bakelite plastic and marketed by Zenith, the American radio and television company, to capitalize on the national panic caused by the kidnapping of the baby son of Charles Lindbergh from his nursery in 1932.

Today, remote video and audio monitoring of infants in their cribs is a normal part of parenting for families at a certain level of disposable income. For example, the Infant Optics DXR-5 Portable Video Baby Monitor is one of the top 10 most popular items on Amazon baby registries.

The level of surveillance is now going up a notch, though. Remote sensor technologies, like the Owlet sock, monitor a baby's pulse and oxygen levels and transmit the information wirelessly to a phone anywhere in the world. A $1000 + "smart crib" called the Snoo, designed at MIT with the input of renowned pediatrician Harvey Karp, comes fully equipped with sensors that respond with shushing and rocking to a baby's cries and is also operable by smartphone.

We're already starting to hear about the unintended consequences of these technologies. A woman wrote to a magazine advice column in 2015 complaining that she had given her parents the password to remotely monitor their grandchild, only to have them constantly butt in. "Any time they see something on the camera that they don't approve of, they let me know. I was endlessly harassed for not putting socks on my son's feet while he was sleeping, for example. The camera has a feature allowing viewers to talk to us, so my parents randomly start talking to me or my son when we're in his room. If my son is throwing a tantrum, they will come on and say, 'Stop that crying!'"

Or for something a mite more alarming: if your baby monitor isn't properly password-protected, anyone who's interested could spy on your kid. Security expert Dan Tentler told the tech blog Ars Technica that there are likely millions of such insecure webcams out there. There have even been isolated reports of hackers taking over audio channels to harass children in their cribs. In 2015, a three-year-old boy in Washington State complained of night fears. Finally his parents heard a voice coming over his monitor saying, "Wake up little boy, Daddy's looking for you."

Poltergeist indeed.

Privacy advocates are concerned not just with pranksters but with government surveillance. In 2016, privacy groups filed a complaint with the Federal Trade Commission over the talking doll called My Friend Cayla, which had the ability to record children's conversations and transmit the information over the web to two different software companies. One of the two, Nuance, makes voice-recognition software and just happens to have a database used by law enforcement and military and intelligence agencies that matches voiceprints.

Scary, even if theoretical at this point. But another kind of threat is internal. As we adopt technologies to extend the range of parental vigilance, there's a danger of corrupting our own protective instincts into a disturbing compulsion. In other words, sometimes the spies are inside the house.

I had a friend who had a form of postpartum obsessive-compulsive disorder. She would jerk awake all night long to check that her firstborn was still breathing. She wanted to buy a breathing monitor—the one then on the market, several years ago, was embedded in a mattress pad. But her husband put his foot down. The right solution, he insisted, was meditation and therapy, maybe medication, not a digital enabler for her anxiety.

Another manifestation of this impulse is what's been called the *quantified baby*. Like the father who came into Dr. Jenny Radesky's office in Seattle several years ago with a detailed graph of his child's temperature over the past five days.

"Almost like helicopter parenting using technology," she called it, "to hyperfocus on the data rather than a whole-child picture." Or what my friend C, an engineer at Google and the dad of a young son, has jokingly nicknamed "drone parenting."

With both my babies, I used an app called Baby Connect to time and track each feeding, sleep period, and diaper change. It helped me identify their changing sleep patterns when my exhaustion wouldn't let me. And the nanny could update it, so I could check my phone to figure out when to leave work at just the right time to nurse a hungry baby.

However, in general these technologies, similar to other "quantified self" gadgets for adults like Jawbone and Up, see a major drop-off in usage after the first six months or so. And the main reason may be that they're just not that helpful in the long term, unless you have a specific circumstance, like a child on a restricted diet or one who needs regular doses of medication.

An article for the tech blog Mashable was headlined "I quantified my baby and wish I could get the time back." "Oliver has quietly generated enough stats to last a lifetime," wrote Tim Chester, "while I've missed milestones, stuck head down in a phone screen grappling with numbers. Attempting to simplify parenthood with gizmos and apps has perversely made it a lot more complicated. And as for peace of mind, forget it." He quoted another "drone parent" to the same effect: "When I paid too much attention to the app data (e.g. trying to encourage a nap at a certain time because it copied a time she slept well later), it was a distraction," she said. "It was frustrating and didn't work. At the end of the day it's only information; there's not a lot you can do with it because the source is a baby."

Babyveillance, the term used by scholars like Veronica Barassi, provides a welcome initial illusion of control. But that quickly dissolves into a confrontation with the basic unknowability of these beloved small people we share our homes with.

At the same time, the availability of these technologies creates a potential arms race, raising the social bar for what intensive mothering means. Our parents created birth announcements with the baby's weight in pounds and ounces; maybe our kids, or their in-laws, will come to expect a digital readout of the baby's respiration rates for the first three hundred days.

Parents now have to decide how closely they want to surveil their older children as well, once they are navigating both the real and virtual worlds on their own. When they're out of the house, an app called Life360, introduced in 2008, will show you where the smartphones belonging to all members of your family are on a map, and send alerts when they cross a "geofence" boundary you've set in advance. The app also integrates with the navigation system on a BMW, the better to virtually tether teen drivers. Life360 has eighty million registered users, making it just the most popular example of a genre of apps—Find My iPhone is another.

Stephen Balkam is a happy user of Life360. His teenage daughter is not. Balkam is the founder of the Family Online Safety Institute, dedicated to raising the alarm about online harassment, cyberbullying, cyberstalking, revenge porn, and other ills threatening you and your kids online. While his organization supports policies dedicated to protecting our kids from excessive commercial or government data collection or threats to their reputations, he engages in domestic surveillance of his own kid. "We had it installed in all our phones once she was driving, with her knowledge and awareness and reluctance," he told me. "We said, we're doing this so we don't have to text you. We can see you're on the Beltway, or you're on your way home or you're going to a late-night party. We're not going to stalk you, but we will use it in emergencies or where you're late or not where we thought you should be." I think about all the exciting places I, as a teenager in New Orleans, went when I should have been somewhere else.

Meanwhile, while kids are online, software called Net Nanny offers parents the power to block pornography and other objectionable material, to see a list of all the sites children have visited, set total time limits, and track children on social media, sending an alert if they post or view language associated with cyberbullying or "grooming" by sexual predators.

Because we can do these things—does that mean we should? What is the ultimate message we're sending if we enclose our children in the arms of a virtual police state?

In some ways, it's easier to set edge cases. A teenager like Griffin, whose serious difficulties in controlling his own use of technology led to his attending the Outback Unplugged wilderness therapy program, might benefit from prior restraints, an "Odysseus lashed to the mast" approach. So might his mother, Noelle, benefit from some assistance in setting those hard limits. Currently, she locks the video game system in the car overnight when she feels like her sons are going overboard.

But for Karel Baloun, the father who called in a family counselor over his wife's restrictiveneess with their teenage daughter, it was probably best that they worked out their iPhone curfew issues as a family, rather than unilaterally install a "kill switch" without negotiation.

US law in most circumstances requires law enforcement authorities to have probable cause to get a warrant for a wiretap on ordinary citizens. That warrant expires and must be renewed after a period of time. We probably should apply some similar, if not more generous, standard of liberty at home. Placing your kids on digital house arrest without prior justification is a recipe for evasion and rebellion. If we demand that kind of compliance in our homes, what message are we sending?

The technologies we adopt to increase security and peace of mind, whether Net Nannies or Radio Nurses, may end up compromising our family's safety, privacy, and sense of mutual trust instead. This is an irony insofar as it violates marketing promises, but from another point of view it's entirely to be expected. Privacy and safety, autonomy and security, trust and verification, are always and necessarily going to be in tension. This is equally true of citizens in a democracy and children in a family. Advancing information technologies just activates this tension.

As doctor and writer Atul Gawande puts it in his essential book *Being Mortal,* about the moral dilemmas of caregiving toward the end of life, the problem that faces caregivers is that each of us wants "autonomy for ourselves and safety for those we love." As parents it's our sacred duty to keep our children safe. And it's also just as sacred a duty to foster their journey toward autonomy.

Even if you resist the urge to assume the dictatorial guise of Net Nanny, it is still possible to overuse or misuse more subtle technologies of persuasion—to fall under, or put your children under, the sway of the techno-nanny.

On the morning of the day I started working on this chapter, Lulu refused to get out of bed because her Time to Wake clock hadn't yet turned green. This is an amazing gadget, recommended to all parents whose children are old enough at age three or so to grasp the concept: you set it to a predetermined time, say seven a.m., and the kid has to amuse herself in her room until the magic hour has arrived. However, the clock wasn't working correctly that morning, and it was hard to convince Lulu that I actually wanted her out of bed.

I love that Time to Wake clock. I also love the S Health app on my phone. When I was diagnosed with a prediabetic blood sugar reading in the fall of 2015, I tracked every calorie, every gram of carbohydrates, every step, for three months straight. I lost a little weight and got my blood sugar reading back into the normal range.

Quantification can clearly be a powerful tool to modify behavior. However, at the same time, when overused, these kinds of applications can become a crutch. They can interrupt the process by which people develop internal motivation and self-regulation.

This is an especially key point for parents. Developmental psychologists argue that self-regulation is a core capacity for an effective and happy life. In order to develop it, children need support in developing awareness of their surroundings and their feelings. They need a vocabulary to express what's going on around them and for them, and the security and support to know that they can express hard emotions and develop strategies to manage them. This will in turn enable them to maintain calm in challenging situations and to defer gratification so they can reach challenging goals.

The danger is that any kind of quantification—grades in school, a sticker chart at home—interrupts this process by imposing an external meter. We or our kids set our minds to gaming the system, rather than deciding for ourselves the right thing to do. As Jathan Sadowski put it in an essay on the techno-nanny: "the danger of the techno-nanny won't manifest in a brash, sudden way. It will, instead, arise through the slow creep of inertia where we incorporate Siri and other apps into our normal daily routine. The symbiotic relationship between us and our apps will be seamless; we won't even be aware of our diminishing ethical capabilities. In the worst case, smartphones will let us live without self-awareness and self-control."

This worst-case scenario isn't inevitable, though. Quantification has its purpose. The key is not to abandon our better judgment to any gadget.

To recap: Media is growing even more ubiquitous and more immersive. Technology is becoming more intrusive, more pervasive. Screen time is escaping the screens. The definition of social media may be changing as artificial intelligence improves.

The parental work of joint engagement—using screens as a basis to connect, not just check out—and authoritative mediation will become more and more important, even as the concept of "screen time" itself may fade into the background. Fostering both autonomy and connectedness has never been more important.

But there's also an intriguing, creative response to our media-saturated reality: the emergence of a consumer demand for quieter tech that helps us spend our time together better. Some of these products are being created by parents themselves.

Tristan Harris, a former design ethicist at Google, crusades for the notion of Time Well Spent. He has been trying to rally the designers who currently optimize our consumer technology for maximum addictive potential to instead pledge to "do no harm." What if user interfaces offered defaults to help us minimize distraction, like "do not disturb" settings or easier-to-use time limits?

By doing this, he's swimming upstream against the central logic flow of the Internet: the attention economy, or user eyeballs equals advertising dollars. It's a minority idea, but a compelling one, especially for parents, who might be willing to pay for a little peace and quiet.

There's a new generation of technology designed by parents to help families take control over their technological lives at home and even enhance relationships. These are at the forefront of a growing communal wisdom about putting digital media in its proper place. Designers and critics of technology are raising awareness about the moral valence of algorithms designed to hook us in, manipulate our emotions, misuse our data, and over- and misinform us. We're at the outset of these conversations and the outcome is not settled. But this debate requires a sense of moral authority that we as parents especially possess.

I'm interested in minimizing distractions by customizing the notifications on my phone. I was able to turn off the notifications from all my social networks, which puts me back in charge of how many times a day I check my phone. But I'm not able to figure out how to let through emails and messages only from key people. A gadget called Ringly is a battery-operated cocktail ring that is connected via Bluetooth to the phone and can be set to flash in a particular color when the husband or the nanny calls or texts. It's kind of pricey at $260, and styled for women, but I like the idea of being able to leave my phone in my purse at the movies or at the playground.

An app called Moment, created by developer Kevin Holesh initially as a side project to help him connect with his new bride, is an interesting way to address the issue of screen time. Log on and you can see how much time everyone in the family has spent on smartphones that day. Holesh said this inspired friendly competition between him and his wife—he got his daily average phone time down over time from ninety minutes to forty-five minutes, while she cut back in proportion, from three hours to ninety minutes. Depending on the permissions within the app, you can also set limits for family members. After they expire, an annoying notification will pop up every time they pick up the phone. And, perhaps most intriguingly, you can set a "family dinner time," where everyone's devices will disconnect for a predetermined period each day.

While this app can be used in a Net Nanny vein, it aims for more democratic family decision making. For example, Holesh says, tongue in cheek, "I made a lot of parents angry," because it gives kids as well as parents the ability to set a "family dinner."

Shelley Prevost is a psychologist who took a job several years ago as a "staff shrink" for a venture capital firm's incubator, helping tech entrepreneurs deal with the social and emotional trials of startup life. She also has three kids, ages thirteen, ten, and six. "One day I thought my oldest was sick. I took him to the doctor, and he had been up all night for six weeks playing Minecraft. So I'm coming to work in tears. I don't feel confident in my ability to manage this and interpret it." Her much-younger colleagues became her "tech sherpas," helping give her more perspective into what looked like a nasty obsession.

Therapy was in order. But influenced by her new work environment, Prevost also decided to fight tech with tech. She partnered with some designers and developers and created a "smart router" called myTorch that gives parents insight and control over Internet use at home. You can "pause" the Internet for family dinner and set a curfew at night. You can also see where kids are spending their time online by URL. "For me to have a window into my kids' online explorations is hugely valuable. It's my job as a parent to roll my sleeves up and get in there," she argues. They're currently working on a separate solution to block mobile networks as well.

Sounds pretty techno-nannyish. To be applied with caution. But even in the time that Prevost has spent developing this product, her perspective has started to shift away from outright bans and toward positive parenting with media. "These conversations have exploded with friends and now through social media. For a couple of years it was really about how do I limit it? How do I protect them? And now the conversations are shifting to how do I prepare my kids for a digital future and help them find more creative things to do with technology?" She's hoping that her company can forge content partnerships to help parents find better places for their kids to spend time online.

While some are focusing on technologies of control, others are designing technologies to fight digital distraction and foster joint engagement. As I wrote for NPR:

I'm hanging out with my 4-year-old daughter in the early evening, trying to keep her entertained and pull dinner together, when my phone buzzes.

Normally I'd feel guilty for checking it immediately, and distracted even if I didn't. But this time it's not a Twitter mention or an email from my editor. It's a timely suggestion from an app called Muse.

Here's what it says: "Try playing 'Simon Says' with L, using directional words like: behind, around, between. (ex. 'Simon Says stand between the chairs.')"

So we do. It's a ton of fun. I can even call out the commands while chopping vegetables. Win-win.

I first met Norma and Vivienne Ming, the co-creators of Muse and a wife-and-wife team, several years ago. Norma is a cognitive scientist and Vivienne a theoretical neuroscientist; both hold doctorates from Carnegie Mellon. The Mings are serial technology entrepreneurs interested in the application of artificial intelligence to human success.

As chief scientist of her previous company, a hiring platform called Gild, Vivienne Ming "built models that predicted how good people would be at jobs they'd never held." With a database of 122 million professionals, their system revealed that grades and standardized test scores were less predictive of success in a given position than were patterns indicating higher-order factors, like how easily people learn and adapt to new situations.

As I wrote for NPR:

But Vivienne Ming wasn't satisfied with using AI for evaluation or prediction. She calls this approach a "cursed crystal ball." Sometimes a little foreknowledge can be a dangerous thing: "If you tell someone, 'Hey, your daughter is going to win a Nobel Prize someday,' it makes it less likely. If you say, 'Your son is in danger of dropping out in the ninth grade,' it could make it more likely."

Instead, she wondered, can we use AI to "optimize life outcomes," by targeting small interventions to kids from birth?

Every day, the Muse app asks one yes-or-no question. That question is designed either to gather information important to a child's life outcomes, or spark reflection in a parent.

An example of the former would be, "Are you (mother) the first in your family to go to college?" and the latter is something like, "Does Jayden like to be a leader?" Ming wants future versions of the app to include the ability to upload short audio clips or pictures, say, of your kid's drawing, to customize feedback even more.

Also each day, the app provides a brief suggested activity or conversation starter. This activity usually combines learning with play.

These are geared not just to your kid's age, but to the answers you've already given about interests and abilities. If you're curious, you can tap the "why" button to learn what the activities are supposed to do.

For example, our "Simon Says" game with extra prepositions apparently "promotes the development of divergent thinking, ingenuity, adaptability, and fluid intelligence."

That's a tall order for a little game.

The idea of nudging better parental behavior through mobile phones has some evidence behind it. Since 2010, a service called Text4Baby has sent updates on topics like prenatal health and safe baby sleep guidelines timed to when mothers need them. Evaluation of this and similar "mobile health information" programs on topics like immunization has shown improved attitudes and knowledge among parents and positive impacts on children's health. In a similar vein, a tablet app called Bedtime Math provides parents with short age-appropriate word problems to talk through with their kids at night. One study (funded by the company), found that first-graders who used the app at least twice a week made significantly more progress in math over the course of a school year. And intriguingly, use of the app seemed to close a gap in performance between the children of parents who reported having their own math anxiety and those whose parents were more comfortable with math.

Povi is a different attempt at leveraging technology to build family bonds and social and emotional skills. As I wrote for NPR:

> Founder Seow Lim used to be a self-described "Tiger Mom" with a laser focus on academics. When her older son was in sixth grade, a school counselor informed her, "Your child is very smart, but he is not happy."
>
> It was a wake-up call. Lim immediately quit her high-powered tech-company executive job and immersed herself in the latest parenting literature.
>
> She learned about the importance of building empathy, perseverance, emotional regulation, resilience and growth mindset. And, in the process, she realized that parents like her were in need of some help.
>
> "People are so busy and academically focused," she explains. "Parents are worried about excessive screen time, but they don't know what to do about it. We're using technology to enhance human interaction."

Povi the character is a plush, huggable toy with a speaker inside and expressive LED eyes. It "talks" directly to kids, telling first-person stories. For example, "Today some kids at recess told me I couldn't play foursquare with them. Can you help me figure out how I feel?" "There's a lot of evidence that talking about emotions, learning about emotions, making emotions not a scary thing, helps children understand that emotions are worthwhile," explains Daphna Ram, one of Povi's advisers, who studies attachment. "With Povi, we're really focusing on ways to get parents to engage with children about emotions."

They created a toy on purpose to make the experience feel less virtual, says Lim. "At first we thought of making an animated character on a phone app, and the psychologists were like, no. We want the kid to be focusing on the parent and [the two] looking each other in the eye, not looking at the screen." There's a similar app called Vroom backed by the family foundation of Amazon founder Jeff Bezos.

So we may be headed into a future where techno-nanny meets super-nanny: technologies that seek to shape our parenting behavior to motivate more, and presumably higher-quality, real-life interactions with our kids. "It's nice to have that daily reminder," says Katie Wilson, a beta tester of Muse, who works at a large tech company in the San Francisco Bay Area and has a nearly two-year-old daughter. "Don't get stuck in your routine—a person who is learning by the second is in your house. It's a quick, welcome distraction that reminds me to put my phone down and interact with my kid." That's exactly as designed, says Vivienne Ming. "I'm not enthusiastic about educational games or apps generally," she says. "The vision here is that the kids are not engaging with the hardware at all, and the parents only for as long as it takes you to read the text."

VAST WASTELAND

Muse, Povi, Moment, and myTorch are all examples of how creative practitioners are trying to make technologies that bring families closer together instead of pushing us apart. But by pulling out these positive examples, I'm not arguing that the whole future is bright.

History holds a lesson here. There's a reason I started out this chapter with Grover. In the 1960s, a cultural panic arose over the increasingly ubiquitous "vast wasteland" that was television.

"When television is good, nothing—not the theater, not the magazines or newspapers—nothing is better. But when television is bad, nothing is worse," said FCC chairman Newton Minow in that famous 1961 speech. Joan Ganz Cooney, one of the creators of *Sesame Street*, agreed. "A word about children's programs," Cooney wrote in "The Potential Uses of Television in Preschool Education," her landmark 1967 paper. "Most of those commercially sponsored seem to be inordinately noisy and mindless affairs."

It fell to the creators of children's educational programming, the Children's Television Workshop, which produced *Sesame Street,* and Fred Rogers, the star of *Mister Rogers' Neighborhood,* to spread the countermessage that TV could be a positive and uplifting medium deserving of public support. Rogers famously testified before the US Senate Subcommittee on Communications on May 1, 1969, in defense of public television: "I give an expression of care everyday to each child."

Fred Rogers was compelling. But Newton Minow was right. Most media is not *Mister Rogers' Neighborhood* (or its reboot, *Daniel Tiger*), because most of it is commercial, created with little thought for the public interest. Rogers would probably agree. "I got into television because I hated it so," he told CNN in 2001.

Collaborations like the ones that *Sesame Street* is now pursuing with creators of both VR and AI technologies, or like the partnership between PBS Kids and ScratchJr, bring the public mission of media into the twenty-first century.

But I'm wary of how educational content, public-spirited intent, creative play, or other claims can be used as apologetics or a crutch for a less mindful use of media. And this especially tends to happen when children are the intended audience. "In my family we're trusting of PBS," parental mediation researcher Eric Rasmussen told me. That's fine as a rule of thumb, but four hours a day of solo PBS for a four-year-old is *no bueno.*

One thing that's not new about new media is that it will continue to be dominated by corporate interests. Hollywood, the TV industry, and Silicon Valley have blessed us with great art, entertainment, and edification. Still, parents have a lot of work to do if we are to advocate for media experiences for our children that stand for something other than simply profit. Armed with images of the potential drawbacks of junk-food content (real or figurative), a vision of what positive parenting looks like, and evidence about our own power to mediate, parents with agency and resources to do so will be able to act more confidently. We could use more help from policy makers and from industry-connected voices like Harris, which are all too rare.

The truth is, we and our children ultimately want parallel things from technology and media. We want to be informed and entertained, not lulled. To be engaged, not bored. To be connected, not disconnected. To consume *and* to create. We seek joy, not just the completion of tasks or momentary distraction from the unbearably mundane, day-to-day world.

Virtual realities and mobile connectedness sometimes seem to be intruding everywhere and threatening what's most human about us. Commercial interests overwhelm any sense of a public sphere. "Personalization" overwhelms the personal. Your attention is the prize; eyeballs are the money.

To say that these forces are powerful doesn't absolve us of the responsibility to do what humans do, which is to actively make choices. Assuming that the media we create and consume expresses and fulfills core human needs or interests can empower us to make our experiences even better. "Making sure that we think first of all about what we care about, what are the features that make us human," observes Cassell. "Finding ways to preserve and enhance them in this digital world is a lot of what my research is about."

Of course I worry about my children encountering the dangers and excesses of the virtual world just as I do in the real world. But children have always shown humanity how to adapt.

They can bring out our greatest love and concern, our most visceral empathy, even as they reawaken our curiosity and sense of wonder.

Confronted with this new reality of infinite information yet elusive meaning, we can call on the protective, loving awe that children bring out in us as we struggle to evolve and respond. Together, we will—we must—figure out how to build and navigate this world with our humanity intact.

These are precisely the superpowers we need to fight the robot army and construct a more humane digital world. Personally, I'm looking forward to what comes next.

10 TL;DR: THE ART OF SCREEN TIME IN FIVE MINUTES

IF YOU DON'T HAVE ANY TIME TO READ THE REST OF THIS BOOK, NO JUDGMENT. Here's what I learned writing it and what you need to know.

Enjoy screens; not too much; mostly together.

You will be more effective as a parent, and have more fun as a family, if you drop the guilt and embrace the good that screens have to offer, while balancing media with other priorities.

When in doubt, try to use media as a means of connecting.

1. On average, school-aged children today are spending more waking hours per week with electronic media than any other single activity. That includes school. Adults, meanwhile, are spending most waking hours engaged with electronic media, period.

2. Excessive exposure to media, including in the background, has small, but measurable, negative effects on children of all ages. Of these effects, the ones we have the strongest evidence for are obesity and disrupted sleep. There are small risks too of addiction, increased aggression (related specifically to violent content), attention issues, and emotional problems. There is

some evidence of larger effects when children are exposed at a younger age. There is no established safe dose and no established toxic dose—every child is different.

3. Media can have measurable positive effects too, on reading, school readiness, concentration and learning. It can be an essential resource for family bonding, discovery, creative expression, and fun.

4. Habits are often set in the preschool years, which is when parents have the most control. But it's never too late to have a positive influence; different ages require different approaches.

5. Parental rules and attitudes about technology make a measurable, positive difference through the teenage years and beyond.

6. Screens and sleep don't mix.

After going through the research and talking to dozens of experts, I found one top priority that parents, and really, people of all ages, should be paying attention to. It's sneaky and surprising, but it's the one issue with the most incontrovertible evidence.

No devices up to an hour before bedtime. Don't keep televisions in children's bedrooms, don't make screens part of the bedtime routine, and don't allow mobile devices in bedrooms overnight. Consider installing an electronic "kill switch" such as myTorch to enforce this curfew if you need it.

Poor-quality sleep, and not enough of it, aggravates every negative symptom tied to screen time. Limiting screens in the evening hits directly at the two biggest risk factors, obesity and sleep, and it helps curb tendencies toward excessive use. Call it the *Gremlins* rule, after the 1980s movie. (Don't feed them after midnight!)

7. Some families wish to enforce screen time rules. Time is a clear, understandable metric. And there are, increasingly, ways of enforcing it with apps and settings on devices. From age two through grade school, consider aiming for one to two hours on weekdays, not counting computer-based homework, and two hours on weekends. This number includes "background" TV. It doesn't necessarily need to include video chatting with family,

or audio. Occasional, out-of-routine exceptions, such as illness, travel, snow days, and holidays are fine—remember, screens are not toxic in and of themselves.

8. If you don't want to limit time, then think instead in terms of priorities and warning signals. Rather than having hard-and-fast rules, it makes sense, especially for older kids, to work toward setting limits and priorities collaboratively.

   a. Priorities: Children need to move their bodies every day, ideally outside. They need healthy meals and a calm environment in which to eat without distraction. They need face-to-face interaction with you, other caring adults, and peers. They probably need breaks from the temptations of multitasking to practice concentrating on one thing at a time. And, again, they need to sleep an appropriate amount for their age.

   b. Warning signals: Weight gain. Sleeplessness; bedtime and wakeup battles, hyperactivity, irritability. School trouble. Friendship problems. Loss of interest in other favorite activities. Mood swings, depression, aggression. All can be good cues to take a screen break for an hour, a day, or a week.

Other best practices and evidence-backed strategies:

9. To make sure kids are making good choices, and to get the best learning benefits, practice joint media engagement and active mediation at least some of the time. Get on the couch with your young child and treat a cartoon like a picture book—point out objects and name them. For older kids, discuss what is happening in the story and how characters feel, talk about their favorite discoveries on social networks, or learn from them how to play a video game. Ask "What did you see online today?" just like you ask "How was school today?" You might enlist trusted family friends and relatives as "eyes on the street" to stay connected and encourage good habits on social media without directly surveilling your kids.

From an early age, encourage creativity and expression as part of your child's media use. This could be anything from decorating greeting cards using the Paper app, to a coding app like ScratchJr, to using YouTube to research how a volcano works. Sponsor and broker your kids' learning experiences with media in school, summer camp, after school, or anywhere. Think soccer mom but for Minecraft.

10. Everyone in the family, including parents, should observe certain screen-free occasions like family dinner. Managing your own use is crucial to successfully helping your kids self-manage.

Tokens or passes (example: three passes, each good for twenty minutes of iPad time per week), chore lists (you must take out the trash and make your bed before watching TV), and family screen time contracts can all be good methods to gently shift habits and agree on a balance that works well for everyone.

The goal is to raise responsible kids in an atmosphere of trust and support. Surveillance won't achieve that. Treat online social spaces much as you would kids hanging out at a friend's house—trust, verify, and then respect their privacy.

NOTES

CHAPTER 1: DIGITAL PARENTING IN THE REAL WORLD

5 **Children today first engage with digital media:** Dimitri Christakis, "Media and Children," TED Talk, December 2011, https://www.youtube.com/watch?v = BoT7qH_uVNo.

5 **According to a Pew survey in 2015:** Pew Research Center, Social & Demographic Trends, "Parenting in America," December 17, 2015, http://www.pewsocialtrends.org/2015/12/17/parenting-in-america/.

5 **On average, children in the United States:** Victoria J. Rideout, Ulla G. Foehr, and Donald F. Roberts, "Generation M^2: Media in the Lives of 8- to 18-Year-Olds," Kaiser Family Foundation, January 2010, https://kaiserfamilyfoundation.files.wordpress.com/2013/04/8010.pdf.

6 **the American Academy of Pediatrics (AAP) rule:** *Pediatrics,* "Media Use by Children Younger than 2 Years," October 11, 2011, http://pediatrics.aappublications.org/content/early/2011/10/12/peds.2011-1753.

6 **In 2016, it was significantly altered:** *Pediatrics,* "Media and Young Minds," October 21, 2016, http://pediatrics.aappublications.org/content/early/2016/10/19/peds.2016-2591.

10 **Michael Pollan's famous maxim:** Michael Pollan, *In Defense of Food: An Eater's Manifesto* (New York: Penguin, 2009).

CHAPTER 2: THE (SOMETIMES) SCARY SCIENCE OF SCREENS

11 **The last major piece of federally funded research:** "Television and Behavior. Ten Years of Scientific Progress and Implications for

225

the Eighties. Volume I: Summary Report." National Institute of Mental Health (DHHS), 1982, https://eric.ed.gov/?id = ED222186.

14　**children still do more essentially passive video watching:** P. Sweetser et al., "Active Versus Passive Screen Time for Young Children," *Australasian Journal of Early Childhood* 37 (2012): 94–98. Victoria J. Rideout, "The Common Sense Census: Media Use by Tweens and Teens," Common Sense Media, 2015, www.commonsensemedia.org/research/the-common-sense-media-use-by-tweens-and-teens.

14　**Parental education, parental income, and parental self-efficacy:** A. M. Lampard, J. M. Jurkowski, and K. K. Davison, "Social-Cognitive Predictors of Low-Income Parents' Restriction of Screen Time Among Preschool-Aged Children," *Health Education & Behavior* 40, no. 5 (2012): 526–530; Trish Gorely, Simon J. Marshall, and Stuart J. H. Biddle, "Couch Kids: Correlates of Television Viewing Among Youth," *International Journal of Behavioral Medicine* 11, no. 3 (2004): 152–163.

15　**A 2011 survey covered nine thousand preschoolers:** Pooja S. Tandon et al., "Preschoolers' Total Daily Screen Time at Home and by Type of Child Care," *Journal of Pediatrics* 158, no. 2 (2011): 297–300.

16　**A 2003 study found that two out of three children:** Victoria J. Rideout, Elizabeth A. Vandewater, and Ellen A. Wartella, "Zero to Six: Electronic Media in the Lives of Infants, Toddlers and Preschoolers," Kaiser Family Foundation, October 1, 2003, http://kff.org/other/report/zero-to-six-electronic-media-in-the/.

16　**The most widely cited national census:** Victoria J. Rideout, "The Common Sense Census." Some researchers criticize the way this census reported results, particularly by double-counting when more than one type of media was being used at once.

17　**Humans have something called an *orienting reflex*:** E. N. Sokolov, "Higher Nervous Functions: The Orienting Reflex," *Annual Review of Physiology* 25, no. 1 (1963): 545–580.

18　**When the Children's Television Workshop:** Michael Davis, *Street Gang: The Complete History of Sesame Street* (New York: Viking, 2008), p. 144.

18　**Some media researchers posit that kids have "parasocial" relationships:** Cynthia Hoffner, "Children's Wishful Identification and Parasocial Interaction with Favorite Television Characters," *Journal of Broadcasting & Electronic Media* 40, no. 3 (1996): 389–402; Emily Moyer-Gusé, "Toward a Theory of Entertainment Persuasion: Explaining the Persuasive Effects of Entertainment Education Messages," *Communication Theory* 18, no. 3 (2008): 407–425.

18 **As child psychologist Bruno Bettelheim described:** Bruno Bettelheim, *The Uses of Enchantment* (New York: Knopf, 1976), pp. 66–70.

20 **Christakis has forced mice to spend their entire childhoods:** Dimitri A. Christakis, J. S. B. Ramirez, and Jan M. Ramirez, "Overstimulation of Newborn Mice Leads to Behavioral Differences and Deficits in Cognitive Performance," *Scientific Reports* 2 (2012): 546.

22 **One representative survey:** Jennifer Falbe et al., "Sleep Duration, Restfulness, and Screens in the Sleep Environment," *Pediatrics* 135, no. 2 (2015): e367–e375.

22 **Similar research in adults corroborates the idea:** Lanaj Klodiana, Russell E. Johnson, and Christopher M. Barnes, "Beginning the Workday yet Already Depleted? Consequences of Late-Night Smartphone Use and Sleep," *Organizational Behavior and Human Decision Processes* 124, no. 1 (2014): 11–23.

22 **exposure to light, especially blue-spectrum screen light:** Brittany Wood et al., "Light Level and Duration of Exposure Determine the Impact of Self-Luminous Tablets on Melatonin Suppression," *Applied Ergonomics* 44, no. 2 (2013): 237–240.

23 **overproduction of cortisol:** This relationship is a complex one. See Meena Kumari et al., "Self-Reported Sleep Duration and Sleep Disturbance Are Independently Associated with Cortisol Secretion in the Whitehall II Study," *Journal of Clinical Endocrinology & Metabolism* 94, no. 12 (2009): 4801–4809.

23 **She's been conducting a five-year study:** Rebecca Spencer, interview by author, November 17, 2015. A similar study is found in Amanda Cremone et al., "Sleep Tight, Act Right: Negative Affect, Sleep and Behavior Problems During Early Childhood," *Child Development,* January 27, 2017, doi: 10.1111/cdev.12717.

24 **myopia or nearsightedness has increased:** Bo-Yuan Ding et al., "Myopia Among Schoolchildren in East Asia and Singapore," *Survey of Ophthalmology* (2017), http://dx.doi.org/10.1016/j.survophthal.2017 .03.006; Brien A. Holden et al., "Global Prevalence of Myopia and High Myopia and Temporal Trends from 2000 Through 2050," *Ophthalmology* 123, no. 5 (2016): 1036–1042.

24 *computer vision syndrome:* Mark Rosenfield, "Computer Vision Syndrome (aka Digital Eye Strain)," *Optometry* 17, no. 1 (2016): 1–10.

24 **more than two hours a day watching TV:** Perrie E. Pardee et al., "Television Viewing and Hypertension in Obese Children," *American Journal of Preventive Medicine* 33, no. 6 (2007): 439–443.

24   **Obesity rates have doubled in children:** "Childhood Obesity Facts,"
     Centers for Disease Control and Prevention, January 25, 2017, https://
     www.cdc.gov/healthyschools/obesity/facts.htm.

24   **Type 1 diabetes, the genetic kind:** "How Does Type 2 Diabetes Affect
     Children?," WebMD, http://www.webmd.com/diabetes/type-2-diabetes
     -guide/type-2-diabetes-in-children#1, accessed April 23, 2017.

27   **Bobo was an inflatable doll:** Jennifer E. Lansford, "Bobo Doll Ex-
     periment," *Encyclopedia of Personality and Individual Differences,* No-
     vember 30, 2016, https://link.springer.com/referenceworkentry/10.1007
     /978-3-319-28099-8_1214-1.

28   **in addition to a whole bunch of more-long-range surveys:** Werner
     H. Hopf, Günter L. Huber, and Rudolf H. Weiss, "Media Violence and
     Youth Violence," *Journal of Media Psychology* 20, no. 3 (2008): 79–96.

28   **what is going on physiologically:** Bruce D. Perry, "The Neurodevelop-
     mental Impact of Violence in Childhood," in D. Schetky and E. Benedek
     (eds.), *Textbook of Child and Adolescent Forensic Psychiatry* (Washington,
     DC: American Psychiatric Press, 2001), pp. 221–238.

28   **"The most prevalent is desensitization":** Victor B. Cline, Roger G.
     Croft, and Steven Courrier, "Desensitization of Children to Television Vi-
     olence," *Journal of Personality and Social Psychology* 27, no. 3 (1973): 360.

28   **"fear and anxiety":** Joanne Cantor, "Fright Reactions to Mass Me-
     dia," *Media Effects: Advances in Theory and Research* 2, no. 2 (2002):
     287–306.

29   **overall murder rates are at historic lows:** John Gramlich, "5 Facts
     About Crime in the U.S.," Pew Research Center, February 21, 2017, http://
     www.pewresearch.org/fact-tank/2017/02/21/5-facts-about-crime-in-the
     -u-s/.

29   **And when you look cross-culturally:** For example, France, Sweden,
     Japan, and Korea have fewer than 1 homicide per 100,000 people com-
     pared to 8 per 100,000 in the United States. See "Intentional Homicides
     (per 100,000 People)," Indexmundi.com, June 30, 2016, http://www
     .indexmundi.com/facts/indicators/VC.IHR.PSRC.P5/compare?country
     = oe#country = ca:fr:oe:se:us.

30   **TV Parental Guidelines system:** "The TV Parental Guidelines," http://
     www.tvguidelines.org/. In order from most to least appropriate, the rat-
     ings are TVY, TVY7, TVY7FV, TVG, TVPG, TV14, and TVMA. Objec-
     tionable content is D for dialogue, L for crude language, S for sexuality,
     V for violence, and FV for "fantasy violence."

31   **Patti Valkenburg:** J. T. Piotrowski and P. M. Valkenburg, "Finding Or-
     chids in a Field of Dandelions: Understanding Children's Differential

Susceptibility to Media Effects," *American Behavioral Scientist* 59 (2015): 1776–1789, doi: 10.1177/0002764215596552.

CHAPTER 3: EMERGING EVIDENCE

37 ***Four Arguments for the Elimination of Television:*** Jerry Mander, *Four Arguments for the Elimination of Television* (New York: Morrow, 1978).

38 **nine out of ten American children:** Amanda Lenhart et al., "Teens, Video Games, and Civics," Pew Research Center, Internet & Technology, September 16, 2008, http://www.pewinternet.org/2008/09/16/teens -video-games-and-civics/.

38 **about 8 percent meet enough categories:** M. R. Hauge and D. Gentile, "Video Game Addiction Among Adolescents: Associations with Academic Performance and Aggression," poster presented at the 2003 Society for Research in Child Development Biennial Conference, Tampa, FL, 2003.

38 **These are the types of questions:** Lauren A. Jelenchick et al., "The Problematic and Risky Internet Use Screening Scale (PRIUSS) for Adolescents and Young Adults: Scale Development and Refinement," *Computers in Human Behavior* 35 (2014): 171–178.

39 **In Japan, China, and South Korea:** These are not without controversy. One "center, in Shandong Province, made headlines in September after one of its patients killed her mother in retribution for abuse she had purportedly suffered at the camp during a forced detox regimen." See Mike Ives, "Electroshock Therapy for Internet Addicts? China Vows to End It," *New York Times,* January 13, 2017, https://www.nytimes .com/2017/01/13/world/asia/china-internet-addiction-electroshock therapy.html; and Martin Fackler, "In Korea, a Boot Camp Cure for Web Obsession," *New York Times,* November 18, 2007, https://www.nytimes.com /2007/11/18/technology/18rehab.html.

39 **Taiwan has even gone so far:** Sara Malm, "Does Your Toddler Play on an iPad? Taiwan Makes It Illegal for Parents to Let Children Under Two Use Electronic Gadgets . . . and Under-18s Must Limit Use to 'Reasonable' Lengths," *Daily Mail Online,* January 29, 2015, http://www.daily-mail.co.uk/news/article-2929530/Does-toddler-play-iPad-Taiwan-makes -ILLEGAL-parents-let-children-two-use-electronic-gadgets-18s-limit-use -reasonable-lengths.html.

39 **Victoria Dunckley is a child psychiatrist:** Victoria L. Dunckley, *Reset Your Child's Brain: A Four-Week Plan to End Meltdowns, Raise Grades, and Boost Social Skills by Reversing the Effects of Electronic Screen-Time* (Novato, CA: New World Library, 2015).

39   **The 2016 book *Glow Kids*:** Nicholas Kardaras, *Glow Kids: How Screen Addiction Is Hijacking Our Kids—and How to Break the Trance* (New York: St. Martin's Press, 2016).

40   **Dopamine is released when the brain seeks:** Ethan S. Bromberg-Martin, Masayuki Matsumoto, and Okihide Hikosaka, "Dopamine in Motivational Control: Rewarding, Aversive, and Alerting," *Neuron* 68, no. 5 (2010): 815–834.

40   **Studies showing the release of dopamine:** M. J. Koepp et al., "Evidence for Striatal Dopamine Release During a Video Game," *Nature* 393, no. 6682 (1998): 266–268.

40   **in similar studies, dopamine releases:** Glen R. Van Loon, Leonard Schwartz, and Michael J. Sole, "Plasma Dopamine Responses to Standing and Exercise in Man," *Life Sciences* 24, no. 24 (1979): 2273–2277; Valorie N. Salimpoor et al., "Anatomically Distinct Dopamine Release During Anticipation and Experience of Peak Emotion to Music," *Nature Neuroscience* 14, no. 2 (2011): 257–262; Bridgit V. Nolan et al., "Tanning as an Addictive Behavior: A Literature Review," *Photodermatology, Photoimmunology & Photomedicine* 25, no. 1 (2009): 12–19.

41   **dopamine levels in the brain:** Benjamin Rolland et al., "Pharmacology of Hallucinations: Several Mechanisms for One Single Symptom?" *BioMed Research International* 2014 (2014): 1–9, http://dx.doi.org/10.1155/2014/307106.

41   **This, along with the typical bright, flashing lights:** A. Must and S. M. Parisi, "Sedentary Behavior and Sleep: Paradoxical Effects in Association with Childhood Obesity," *International Journal of Obesity* 33, suppl. 1 (2009): S82–S86.

41   **older kids are sneaking under the covers:** Laura Holson, "Vamping Teenagers Are Up All Night Texting," *New York Times,* July 3, 2014, https://www.nytimes.com/2014/07/06/fashion/vamping-teenagers-are-up-all-night-texting.html.

42   **Her first study on the topic:** Jenny S. Radesky et al., "Infant Self-Regulation and Early Childhood Media Exposure," *Pediatrics* 133, no. 5 (2014): e1172–e1178.

43   **Experts attribute much of this rise:** Jon Hamilton, "Jump in Autism Cases May Not Mean It's More Prevalent," NPR, March 27, 2014, http://www.npr.org/sections/health-shots/2014/03/27/295317351/higher-autism-numbers-may-not-mean-more-kids-actually-have-it.

43   **in one study of 2.5-year-olds:** Micah O. Mazurek and Colleen Wenstrup, "Television, Video Game and Social Media Use Among Children

with ASD and Typically Developing Siblings," *Journal of Autism and Developmental Disorders* 43, no. 6 (2012): 1258–1271.

43 **in 2006 a single paper was published:** Michael Waldman et al., "Autism Prevalence and Precipitation Rates in California, Oregon, and Washington Counties," *Archives of Pediatrics & Adolescent Medicine* 162, no. 11 (2008): 1026.

44 **Karen Heffler, an ophthalmologist:** Karen Frankel Heffler and Leonard M. Oestreicher, "Causation Model of Autism: Audiovisual Brain Specialization in Infancy Competes with Social Brain Networks," *Medical Hypotheses* 91 (June 2016): 114–122.

45 *applied behavior analysis:* According to this meta-analysis, "long-term, comprehensive ABA intervention leads to (positive) medium to large effects in terms of intellectual functioning, language development, acquisition of daily living skills and social functioning in children with autism." Javier Virués-Ortega, "Applied Behavior Analytic Intervention for Autism in Early Childhood: Meta-Analysis, Meta-Regression and Dose–Response Meta-Analysis of Multiple Outcomes." *Clinical Psychology Review* 30, no. 4 (2010): 387–399.

45 **Shannon Rosa:** Her blog is at http://www.squidalicious.com/.

46 **Ron Suskind:** Ron Suskind, *Life, Animated: A Story of Sidekicks, Heroes, and Autism* (Disney Electronic Content, 2016).

46 **A small but intriguing 2014 study:** Yalda T. Uhls et al., "Five Days at Outdoor Education Camp Without Screens Improves Preteen Skills with Nonverbal Emotion Cues," *Computers in Human Behavior* 39 (2014): 387–392.

47 **In the 1970s, laws of consumer:** Edmund L. Andrews, "F.C.C. Adopts Limits on TV Ads Aimed at Children." *New York Times,* April 10, 1991, http://www.nytimes.com/1991/04/10/business/the-media-business-fcc-adopts-limits-on-tv-ads-aimed-at-children.html.

47 **Diane Levin and Nancy Carlsson-Paige:** Nancy Carlsson-Paige and Diane E. Levin, *The War Play Dilemma: Balancing Needs and Values in the Early Childhood Classroom* (New York: Teachers College Press, 1987); Nancy Carlsson-Paige, *Taking Back Childhood: Helping Your Kids Thrive in a Fast-Paced, Media-Saturated, Violence-Filled World* (New York: Hudson Street Press, 2008).

48 **A representative study in this field:** Sarah M. Coyne et al., "Pretty as a Princess: Longitudinal Effects of Engagement with Disney Princesses on Gender Stereotypes, Body Esteem, and Prosocial Behavior in Children," *Child Development* 87, no. 6 (2016): 1909–1925.

49 **High school graduation is at an all-time high:** Jennifer L. DePaoli et al., "Building a Grad Nation: Progress and Challenge in Ending the High School Dropout Epidemic," Johns Hopkins University, October 4, 2016.

49 **Teen car crash rates are down since 1999:** "Teenagers," Insurance Institute for Highway Safety, April 16, 2017, http://www.iihs.org/iihs /topics/t/teenagers/fatalityfacts/teenagers.

49 **Dangerous drug and alcohol use has plunged:** "Monitoring the Future Survey: High School and Youth Trends," National Institute on Drug Abuse, December 2016, https://www.drugabuse.gov/publications /drugfacts/monitoring-future-survey-high-school-youth-trends.

49 **Teen pregnancy rates are down 44 percent since 1991:** "Trends in Teen Pregnancy and Childbearing," US Department of Health and Human Services, June 2, 2016, https://www.hhs.gov/ash/oah/adolescent -development/reproductive-health-and-teen-pregnancy/teen-pregnancy -and-childbearing/trends/index.html.

49 **Compared to the 1990s, fewer high school students:** "Trends in the Prevalence of Sexual Behaviors and HIV Testing, National YRBS: 1991– 2015," Centers for Disease Control and Prevention, https://www.cdc.gov /healthyyouth/data/yrbs/pdf/trends/2015_us_sexual_trend_yrbs.pdf.

49 **HIV rates are down:** R. Kachur et al., "Adolescents, Technology, and Reducing Risk for HIV, STDs, and Pregnancy," Centers for Disease Control and Prevention, 2013, https://www.cdc.gov/std/life-stages-populations /adolescents-white-paper.pdf.

49 **The Crimes Against Children Research Center:** David Finkelhor and Lisa Jones, "Have Sexual Abuse and Physical Abuse Declined Since the 1990s?" Crimes Against Children Research Center, November 2012, http://www.unh.edu/ccrc/pdf/CV267 % 20Have % 20SA % 20PA % 20Decline % 20FACT % 20SHEET % 2011-7-12.pdf.

49 **the Bureau of Justice Statistics reported a 64 percent drop:** Michael Planty et al., "Female Victims of Sexual Violence, 1994–2010," US Department of Justice, March 2013, https://www.bjs.gov/content/pub/pdf /fvsv9410.pdf.

49 **Arrests of teens for all crimes also plunged:** "Juvenile Arrest Rate Trends," US Department of Justice, Office of Juvenile Justice and Delinquency Prevention, March 27, 2017, https://www.ojjdp.gov/ojstatbb /crime/JAR_Display.asp?ID = qa05201.

49 **The incidence of eating disorders appears stable:** "Overview and Statistics," National Eating Disorders Association, https://www.nationaleating

disorders.org/learn/by-eating-disorder/osfed/overview, accessed April 19, 2017.

49   **On a national health survey given annually by the CDC:** Summary Health Statistics: National Health Interview Survey, 2015.

50   **only about 7 percent of teens in one large survey:** "How Many Teens Are Actually Sexting?" Center for Innovative Public Health Research, January 26, 2015, https://innovativepublichealth.org/blog/how-many -teens-are-actually-sexting/.

50   **In a second, retrospective survey that came out in 2015:** Elizabeth Englander, "Coerced Sexting and Revenge Porn Among Teens," Virtual Commons, Bridgewater State University, 2015, http://vc.bridgew.edu /psychology_fac/69/.

50   **in the most recent nationally representative federal survey:** "Student Reports of Bullying and Cyber-Bullying: Results from the 2013 School Crime Supplement to the National Crime Victimization Survey." National Center for Education Statistics, US Department of Education, April 2015, https://nces.ed.gov/pubs2015/2015056.pdf.

50   **In a second national survey published in 2016:** Amanda Lenhart et al., "Online Harassment, Digital Abuse, and Cyberstalking in America," Data & Society Research Institute, November 21, 2016, https://www .datasociety.net/pubs/oh/Online_Harassment_2016.pdf.

50   **danah boyd, the author of *It's Complicated*:** danah boyd, *It's Complicated: The Social Lives of Networked Teens* (New Haven, CT: Yale University Press, 2014).

51   **And more social media use correlates:** G. S. O'Keeffe and K. Clarke-Pearson, "The Impact of Social Media on Children, Adolescents, and Families," *Pediatrics* 127, no. 4 (2011): 800–804.

51   **a striking rise in self-reports of narcissism:** Jean M. Twenge et al., "Egos Inflating over Time: A Cross-Temporal Meta-Analysis of the Narcissistic Personality Inventory." *Journal of Personality* 76, no. 4 (2008): 875–902.

52   **Sara Konrath at the University of Michigan:** Sara H. Konrath, Edward H. O'Brien, and Courtney Hsing, "Changes in Dispositional Empathy in American College Students over Time: A Meta-Analysis." *Personality and Social Psychology Review* 15, no. 2 (2011): 180–198.

52   **separate studies show that more narcissistic people:** Such as L. E. Buffardi and W. K. Campbell, "Narcissism and Social Networking Web Sites." *Personality and Social Psychology Bulletin* 34, no. 10 (2008): 1303–1314; and David G. Taylor and David Strutton, "Does Facebook Usage

Lead to Conspicuous Consumption?" *Journal of Research in Interactive Marketing* 10, no. 3 (2016): 231–248.

52 **undergraduates using Snapchat:** Joseph B. Bayer et al., "Sharing the Small Moments: Ephemeral Social Interaction on Snapchat," *Information, Communication & Society* 19, no. 7 (2016): 956–977.

53 **The AAP issued revised guidelines in the fall of 2016:** "American Academy of Pediatrics Announces New Recommendations for Children's Media Use." American Academy of Pediatrics, October 21, 2016, https://www.aap.org/en-us/about-the-aap/aap-press-room/pages/american-academy-of-pediatrics-announces-new-recommendations-for-childrens-media-use.aspx.

54 **a couple of small observational studies:** Elisabeth McClure and Rachel Barr, "Building Family Relationships from a Distance: Supporting Connections with Babies and Toddlers Using Video and Video Chat," in Rachel Barr and Deborah Nichols Linebarger (eds.), *Media Exposure During Infancy and Early Childhood* (New York: Springer, 2017), pp. 227–248.

54 **The AAP cites some small studies:** R. A. Richert et al., "Word Learning from Baby Videos," *Archives of Pediatric & Adolescent Medicine* 164, no. 5 (2010): 432–437.

CHAPTER 4: YOU HAVE THE POWER: POSITIVE PARENTING WITH MEDIA

59 **In several huge studies, watching *Sesame Street*:** See, for example, Melissa Kearney and Phillip Levine, "Early Childhood Education by MOOC: Lessons from *Sesame Street*," National Bureau of Economic Research, Working Paper no. 21229, June 2015, http://www.nber.org/papers/w21229.

59 **A newer study by Eric Rasmussen:** Eric E. Rasmussen et al., "Relation Between Active Mediation, Exposure to *Daniel Tiger's Neighborhood,* and US Preschoolers' Social and Emotional Development." *Journal of Children and Media* (2016): 1–19.

59 **In the past decade and a half:** Heather L. Kirkorian, Ellen A. Wartella, and Daniel R. Anderson, "Media and Young Children's Learning," *Future of Children* 18, no. 1 (2008): 39–61; Shalom M. Fisch, H. Kirkorian, and D. Anderson, "Transfer of Learning in Informal Education," in Jose P. Mestre (ed.), *Transfer of Learning: Research and Perspectives* (Charlotte, NC: Information Age, 2005), pp. 371–393; Heather L. Kirkorian and Daniel R. Anderson, "Learning from Educational Media," in Sandra L. Calvert and Barbara J. Wilson (eds.), *The Handbook of Children, Media, and Development* (Malden, MA: Wiley-Blackwell, 2008), pp. 188–213.

59 **Fast-paced video games have been shown:** Sandro Franceschini et al., "Action Video Games Make Dyslexic Children Read Better," *Current Biology* 23, no. 6 (2013): 462–466.

60 **Fast-paced video games can also help:** C. S. Green and D. Bavelier, "Learning, Attentional Control, and Action Video Games," *Current Biology* 22, no. 6 (2012): R197–R206.

60 **Active video games:** J. L. Rowland et al., "Perspectives on Active Video Gaming as a New Frontier in Accessible Physical Activity for Youth with Physical Disabilities," *Physical Therapy* 96, no. 4 (2015): 521–532.

60 **video games that resemble biofeedback simulators:** Jyoti Mishra et al., "Video Games for Neuro-Cognitive Optimization," *Neuron* 90, no. 2 (2016): 214–218.

60 **In one game, instead of crashing a fast car:** Bjorn Carey, "Stanford Experiment Shows that Virtual Superpowers Encourage Real-World Empathy," Stanford News, January 31, 2013, http://news.stanford.edu /news/2013/january/virtual-reality-altruism-013013.html.

60 **Other VR simulations are being tested:** Emily F. Law et al., "Video-game Distraction Using Virtual Reality Technology for Children Experiencing Cold Pressor Pain: The Role of Cognitive Processing," *Journal of Pediatric Psychology* 36, no. 1 (2011): 84–94.

60 **"Technology is neither good nor bad; nor is it neutral":** Melvin Kranzberg, "Technology and History: 'Kranzberg's Laws,'" *Technology and Culture* 27, no. 3 (1986): 544–560. Worth reading in its entirety. I also recommend L. M. Sacasas, "Kranzberg's Six Laws of Technology, a Metaphor, and a Story," The Frailest Thing, August 25, 2011, https:// thefrailestthing.com/2011/08/25/kranzbergs-six-laws-of-technology-a -metaphor-and-a-story/.

CHAPTER 5: AN HOUR AT A TIME: HOW REAL FAMILIES NAVIGATE SCREENS

94 **In this, we're fairly typical:** "The Nielsen Total Audience Report: Q4 2016," Nielsen.com, April 3, 2017, http://www.nielsen.com/us/en/insights /reports/2017/the-nielsen-total-audience-report-q4-2016.html.

94 **Similarly, Common Sense Media found in 2016:** "The Common Sense Census: Plugged-In Parents of Tweens and Teens 2016," Common Sense Media,https://www.commonsensemedia.org/research/the-common-sense -census-plugged-in-parents-of-tweens-and-teens-2016, accessed April 25, 2017.

98 **A blogger who uses the handle NarrowbackSlacker:** Narrowback-Slacker, "How I Limited Screen Time by Offering My Kids Unlimited

Screen Time," May 13, 2014, https://narrowbackslacker.com/2014/05/13
/how-i-limited-screen-time-by-offering-my-kids-unlimited-screen-time/.

104 **Lynn Schofield Clark at the University of Denver:** Lynn Schofield
Clark, *The Parent App: Understanding Families in the Digital Age* (Oxford,
UK: Oxford University Press, 2013).

108 **A 2014 study gave parents information and counseling:** R. Maddison
et al., "Screen-Time Weight-Loss Intervention Targeting Children at
Home (SWITCH): A Randomized Controlled Trial," *International Journal of Behavioral Nutrition and Physical Activity* no. 11 (2014): 111,
doi:10.1186/s12966-014-0111-2. Also see Lei Wu et al., "The Effect of
Interventions Targeting Screen Time Reduction: A Systematic Review
and Meta-Analysis," *Medicine* 95, no. 27 (2016): e4029.

CHAPTER 6: SCREENS AT SCHOOL

118 **Mark Zuckerberg or Bill Gates:** In "A Letter to Our Daughter," Facebook founder Zuckerberg and his wife, Priscilla Chan, pledged to give
away 99 percent of their Facebook shares or $45 billion to a variety of
causes including "personalized learning." "Can you learn and experience
100 times more than we do today?" they asked their infant daughter.
"You'll have technology that understands how you learn best and where
you need to focus. You'll advance quickly in subjects that interest you
most, and get as much help as you need in your most challenging areas . . .
personalized learning can be one scalable way to give all children a better
education and more equal opportunity." Mark Zuckerberg and Priscilla
Chan, "A Letter to Our Daughter," Facebook, December 1, 2015, https://
www.facebook.com/notes/mark-zuckerberg/a-letter-to-our-daughter
/10153375081581634/. In a 2013 keynote at the South by Southwest Education ed-tech conference, Bill Gates of Microsoft noted, "In just the
past few years technology has finally become part of our schools in a
big way, and it's only getting bigger." Anya Kamenetz, "Bill Gates Gives
South By Southwest Education Conference Keynote, Cites $9 Billion 'Tip-
ping Point' in Education," *Fast Company,* March 6, 2013, https://www
.fastcompany.com/3006708/creative-conversations/bill-gates-gives-sxsw
-education-conference-keynote-cites-9-billion-ti.

118 **a magical "robot tutor in the sky":** Eric Westervelt, "Meet the Mind-
Reading Robo Tutor in the Sky," NPR, October 13, 2015, http://www.npr
.org/sections/ed/2015/10/13/437265231/meet-the-mind-reading-robo
-tutor-in-the-sky.

119 **In the early 1960s, a South African mathematician:** Anya Kamenetz,
"Remembering a Thinker Who Thought About Thinking," NPR, Au-

gust 5, 2016, http://www.npr.org/sections/ed/2016/08/05/488669276 /remembering-a-thinker-who-thought-about-thinking.

120 **"Every seventh grader should have a laptop computer":** "Seymour Papert at Bates College—2000," Vimeo, January 31, 2010, https://vimeo .com/9106174. Found via The Daily Papert, a rich multimedia archive of Papert's works maintained by Gary Stager.

121 **Hirsh-Pasek can tell you:** Kathy Hirsh-Pasek et al., "Putting Education in "Educational" Apps: Lessons from the Science of Learning," *Psychological Science in the Public Interest* 16, no. 1 (2015): 3–34.

121 **For example, in one study:** Stephan Schwan and Roland Riempp, "The Cognitive Benefits of Interactive Videos: Learning to Tie Nautical Knots," *Learning and Instruction* 14, no. 3 (2004): 293–305.

122 **For example, a 2013 study by Hirsh-Pasek and others:** Julia Parish-Morris et al., "Once Upon a Time: Parent-Child Dialogue and Storybook Reading in the Electronic Era," *Mind, Brain, and Education* 7, no. 3 (2013): 200–211.

122 **children as young as eighteen months:** Alice Ann Howard Gola et al., "Building Meaningful Parasocial Relationships Between Toddlers and Media Characters to Teach Early Mathematical Skills," *Media Psychology* 16, no. 4 (2013): 390–411.

123 **Warren Buckleitner has been devoted:** Children's Technology Review, http://www.childrenstech.com.

124 **Common Sense Media has more than two thousand free ratings:** Common Sense Media, https://www.commonsensemedia.org.

124 **The Programme for International Student Assessment:** Actually 1.8 to 1. "Students, Computers and Learning: Making the Connection," Organization for Economic Cooperation and Development, http:// www.oecd.org/pisa/keyfindings/PISA-2012-students-computers-us.pdf, accessed April 27, 2017.

124 **In 2016 alone, US K–12 districts:** "Sales of Mobile PCs into the US K–12 Education Market Continue to Grow, as OS Battle Heats Up," Futuresource Consulting, March 2, 2017, https://www.futuresource-consulting .com/Press-K-12-Education-Market-Qtr4-0317.html.

125 **Google's free suite of apps:** Kyle Wiggers, "Google's G Suite for Education App Platform Now Has Over 70 Million Users," Digital Trends, January 24, 2017, http://www.digitaltrends.com/web/google-g-suite-70-million/.

126 **the classroom market share of Apple products:** Kif Leswing, "Apple iPads Are Getting Crushed in a Key Market by What Tim Cook Calls 'Test Machines,'" Business Insider, June 4, 2016, https://finance.yahoo.com /news/apple-ipads-getting-crushed-key-140000709.html.

127 **In a large 2014 survey:** "Primary Sources, Third Edition," Scholastic, http://www.scholastic.com/primarysources/, accessed June 16, 2016.

128 **But a comprehensive 2015 report by PISA:** Ismael Peña-López, "Students, Computers and Learning. Making the Connection," OECD, September 15, 2015, http://www.oecd.org/publications/students-computers-and-learning-9789264239555-en.htm.

129 **Neil Selwyn is a professor of education:** Neil Selwyn and Scott Bulfin, "Exploring School Regulation of Students' Technology Use—Rules That Are Made to Be Broken?" *Educational Review* 68, no. 3 (2016): 274–290.

131 **Sonia Livingstone published a book:** Sonia Livingstone and Julian Sefton-Green, *The Class: Living and Learning in the Digital Age* (New York: NYU Press, 2016).

132 **Today, almost two hundred thousand children and teenagers:** Gary Miron and Charisse Gulosino, "Virtual Schools Report 2016," National Education Policy Center, April 20, 2016, http://nepc.colorado.edu/publication/virtual-schools-annual-2016.

132 **even the charter school lobby:** "A Call to Action to Improve the 132 of Full-Time Virtual Charter Public Schools," National Alliance for Public Charter Schools, June 16, 2016, http://www.publiccharters.org/publications/call-action-improve-quality-full-time-virtual-charter-public-schools/.

132 **all over Africa and Asia:** Catrina Stewart, "Bridge International Academies: Scripted Schooling for $6 a Month Is an Audacious Answer to Educating the Poorest Children Across Africa and Asia," *The Independent,* July 28, 2015, http://www.independent.co.uk/news/world/africa/bridge-international-academies-scripted-schooling-for-6-a-month-is-an-audacious-answer-to-educating-10420028.html.

132 **the nation of Liberia:** Graham Brown-Martin, "Education in Africa: The Uberfication of Education by Bridge International Academies," Learning imagined, Medium, June 20, 2016, https://medium.com/learning-re-imagined/education-in-africa-1f495dc6d0af.

132 **80 percent of bricks-and-mortar charter schools:** Kate Zernike, "How Trump's Education Nominee Bent Detroit to Her Will on Charter Schools," *New York Times,* December 12, 2016, https://www.nytimes.com/2016/12/12/us/politics/betsy-devos-how-trumps-education-nominee-bent-detroit-to-her-will-on-charter-schools.html.

133 **In February 2016, the University of Central Florida:** Gabrielle Russon, "Hack at UCF Compromises 63,000 Social Security Numbers,"

Orlando Sentinel, February 4, 2016, http://www.orlandosentinel.com /features/education/os-ucf-data-hack-students-20160204-story.html.

133 **Most current agreements:** Gennie Gebhart, "Spying on Students: School-Issued Devices and Student Privacy," Electronic Frontier Foundation, April 13, 2017, https://www.eff.org/wp/school-issued-devices-and -student-privacy.

133 **One such security program I reported on for NPR:** Anya Kamenetz, "Software Flags 'Suicidal' Students, Presenting Privacy Dilemma," NPR, March 28, 2016, http://www.npr.org/sections/ed/2016/03/28 /470840270/when-school-installed-software-stops-a-suicide.

134 **the Electronic Privacy Information Center's student privacy project:** https://epic.org/privacy/student/.

134 **In 2009, at a migrant-worker camp in Baja California, Mexico:** Anya Kamenetz, "A Is for App: How Smartphones, Handheld Computers Sparked an Educational Revolution," *Fast Company*, April 1, 2010, https:// www.fastcompany.com/1579376/app-how-smartphones-handheld -computers-sparked-educational-revolution.

134 **At the World Maker Faire in Queens in 2014:** Anya Kamenetz, "Three Rs for the Digital Age: Rockets, Robots and Remote Control," NPR, September 24, 2014, http://www.npr.org/sections/ed/2014/09/24/350645620 /three-r-s-for-the-digital-age-rockets-robots-and-remote-control.

135 **And in the fall of 2015:** Anya Kamenetz, "E Is for Experimental and Entrepreneur," NPR, November 13, 2015, http://www.npr.org/sections /ed/2015/11/13/454313355/the-incubator-school-e-is-for-experimental -entrepreneur.

137 **The Computer Science Teachers Association:** Anya Kamenetz, "The President Wants Every Student to Learn Computer Science. How Would That Work?" NPR, January 12, 2016, http://www.npr.org/sections/ed /2016/01/12/462698966/the-president-wants-every-student-to-learn- computer-science-how-would-that-work.

138 **A version called ScratchJr:** Anya Kamenetz, "A Kids' Coding Expert Says We're Making Computer Class Way Too Boring," NPR, December 11, 2015, http://www.npr.org/sections/ed/2015/12/11/458782056/a -kids-coding-expert-says-were-making-computer-class-way-too-boring.

138 **Marina Umaschi Bers:** Elizabeth R. Kazakoff and Marina Umaschi Bers, "Put Your Robot In, Put Your Robot Out: Sequencing Through Programming Robots in Early Childhood," *Journal of Educational Computing Research* 50, no. 4 (2014): 553–573.

CHAPTER 7: THE MOM WITH HER PHONE AT THE PLAYGROUND

141   **Now you are pushing your baby in the swing:** Tonya Ferguson, "Dear Mom on the iPhone," 4LittleFergusons, November 14, 2012, https://4littlefergusons.wordpress.com/2012/11/14/dear-mom-on-the-iphone/.

142   **Millennial parents, in particular, spend more time online:** "Millennials Grow Up: New Study Explores the First Generation of Digitally Native Moms & Dads," Crowdtap, January 26, 2016, http://www.businesswire.com/news/home/20160126006022/en/Millennials-Grow-Study-Explores-Generation-Digitally-Native.

142   **As my friend Jennifer Bleyer:** Jennifer Bleyer, "I Need My Cell Phone, But It Doesn't Make Me a Bad Parent," Babble, July 13, 2011.

143   **She got worldwide media coverage:** Jenny S. Radesky et al., "Patterns of Mobile Device Use by Caregivers and Children During Meals in Fast Food Restaurants," *Pediatrics* 133, no. 4 (2014): e843–e849.

144   **parents who watch more TV:** Amy Bleakley, Amy B. Jordan, and Michael Hennessy, "The Relationship Between Parents' and Children's Television Viewing," *Pediatrics* 132, no. 2 (2013): e364–e371.

145   **In June 2015, three siblings drowned:** "Mom Arrested After Children Drowned Bonds Out of Jail," CBS DFW, July 10, 2015, http://dfw.cbslocal.com/2015/07/10/family-supports-mom-arrested-after-children-drowned/.

145   **Between 2007, when the iPhone was introduced:** Ben Worthen, "The Perils of Texting While Parenting," *Wall Street Journal,* September 29, 2012.

145   **In a paper published in 2014:** Craig Palsson, "That Smarts!: Smartphones and Child Injuries," Department of Economics, Yale University, October 7, 2014, http://www.palssonresearch.org/wp-content/uploads/2014/10/smartphone_v17.pdf.

146   **Car crashes are the leading cause of death:** Nagesh N. Borse et al., "CDC Childhood Injury Report: Patterns of Unintentional Injuries Among 0–19 Year Olds in the United States, 2000–2006," Centers for Disease Control and Prevention, December 2008, https://www.cdc.gov/safechild/images/cdc-childhoodinjury.pdf.

146   **cell phones are currently estimated:** Gabrielle Kratsas, "Cellphone Use Causes over 1 in 4 Car Accidents," *USA Today,* March 28, 2014, https://www.usatoday.com/story/money/cars/2014/03/28/cellphone-use-1-in-4-car-crashes/7018505/.

146   **Traffic deaths have been trending upward:** Neal E. Boudette, "U.S. Traffic Deaths Rise for a Second Straight Year," *New York Times,* February 15, 2017, https://www.nytimes.com/2017/02/15/business/highway-traffic-safety.html.

146 **Meanwhile, in a 2014 survey:** Michelle L. Macy et al., "Potential Distractions and Unsafe Driving Behaviors Among Drivers of 1- to 12-Year-Old Children," *Academic Pediatrics* 14, no. 3 (2014): 279–286.

146 **There is a video of a psychological experiment:** "Still Face Experiment: Dr. Edward Tronick," YouTube, November 30, 2009, https://www.youtube.com/watch?v = apzXGEbZht0.

147 **Edward Tronick at the University of Massachusetts Boston:** Edward Tronick et al., "The Infant's Response to Entrapment Between Contradictory Messages in Face-to-Face Interaction," *Journal of the American Academy of Child Psychiatry* 17, no. 1 (1978): 1–13.

148 **Research by Dr. Dimitri Christakis:** Dimitri A. Christakis et al., "Audible Television and Decreased Adult Words, Infant Vocalizations, and Conversational Turns," *Archives of Pediatrics & Adolescent Medicine* 163, no. 6 (2009): 554.

148 **We know that lower-income, less-educated parents:** Dimitri A. Christakis et al., "Television, Video, and Computer Game Usage in Children Under 11 Years of Age," *Journal of Pediatrics* 145, no. 5 (2004): 652–656.

148 **parenting styles that emphasize compliance:** Jacob E. Cheadle and Paul R. Amato, "A Quantitative Assessment of Lareau's Qualitative Conclusions About Class, Race, and Parenting," *Journal of Family Issues* 32, no. 5 (2011): 679–706.

148 **studies of immigrant families:** Sandra L. Calvert et al., "Interaction and Participation for Young Hispanic and Caucasian Girls' and Boys' Learning of Media Content," *Media Psychology* 9, no. 2 (2007): 431–445.

149 **A small 2014 study:** Martin Pielot, Karen Church, and Rodrigo De Oliveira, "An In-Situ Study of Mobile Phone Notifications," in *Proceedings of the 16th International Conference on Human-Computer Interaction with Mobile Devices & Services* (New York: ACM Digital Library, 2014), pp. 233–242.

149 **Natasha Dow Schüll's 2012 book:** Natasha Dow Schüll, *Addiction by Design: Machine Gambling in Las Vegas* (Princeton, NJ: Princeton University Press, 2012).

150 **The British pediatrician and psychoanalytic psychologist Donald Winnicott:** She "starts off with an almost complete adaptation to her infant's needs, and as time proceeds she adapts less and less completely, gradually, according to the infant's growing ability to deal with her failure." Savithiri Ratnapalan and Helen Batty, "To Be Good Enough," *Canadian Family Physician* 55, no. 3 (2009): 239–240.

150 **Sociologist Sharon Hays, in her 1996 book:** Sharon Hays, *The Cultural Contradictions of Motherhood* (New Haven, CT: Yale University Press, 1996).

150 **"A child-centered, expert-guided, emotionally absorbing, labor intensive ideology":** Deirdre D. Johnston and Debra H. Swanson, "Constructing the "Good Mother": The Experience of Mothering Ideologies by Work Status," *Sex Roles* 54, no. 7–8 (2006): 509–519.

150 **Sociologist Annette Lareau focused on the related idea:** Annette Lareau, *Unequal Childhoods: Race, Class and Family Life* (Berkeley: University of California Press, 2003).

151 **David Lancy's *The Anthropology of Childhood*:** David F. Lancy, *The Anthropology of Childhood: Cherubs, Chattel, Changelings* (New York: Cambridge University Press, 2015).

151 *attachment parenting*: William Sears and Martha Sears, *The Attachment Parenting Book: A Commonsense Guide to Understanding and Nurturing Your Baby* (Boston: Little, Brown, 2001).

151 **Attachment Parenting International:** "API's Eight Principles of Parenting," Attachment Parenting International, http://www.attachment parenting.org/principles/api, accessed June 16, 2017.

152 **just over half of American children:** "Basic Facts About Low-Income Children," National Center for Children in Poverty (NCCP), Columbia University Mailman School of Public Health, February 2016, http://www.nccp.org/publications/pub_1145.html.

153 **We are the only developed country:** "Parental Leave: Where Are the Fathers?" Organization for Economic Cooperation and Development Policy Brief, March 2016, https://www.oecd.org/policy-briefs/parental-leave-where-are-the-fathers.pdf.

153 **the only one with no guaranteed paid sick leave:** One hundred forty-five countries mandate some paid vacation days. See Alison Earle, Jeffrey Hayes, and Jody Heymann, "The Work, Family, and Equity Index: How Does the United States Measure Up?" Institute for Health and Social Policy, January 2007, https://www.worldpolicycenter.org/sites/default/files/Work%20Family%20and%20Equity%20Index-How%20does%20the%20US%20measure%20up-Jan%202007.pdf

153 **the only one with no mandated vacation days:** Alexander E. M. Hess, "On Holiday: Countries with the Most Vacation Days," *USA Today*, June 8, 2013, https://www.usatoday.com/story/money/business/2013/06/08/countries-most-vacation-days/2400193/.

153 **two thirds of workers tell Gallup pollsters:** Jim Harter, "Should Employers Ban Email After Work Hours?" Gallup Organization, September

9, 2014, http://www.gallup.com/businessjournal/175670/employers-ban -email-work-hours.aspx.

153 **Labor regulators are considering cracking down:** Jim Harter, "Should Employers Ban Email After Work Hours?" Gallup Organization, September 9, 2014, http://www.gallup.com/businessjournal/175670/employers -ban-email-work-hours.aspx.

153 **"Our best—and very time-consuming—ideas":** Alain de Botton et al., "The Sorrows of Competition," The Book of Life, http://www.thebook oflife.org/the-sorrows-of-competition/.

154 **"Put the cellphone away!":** "Put the Cellphone Away! Fragmented Baby Care Can Affect Brain Development," University of California, Irvine, January 5, 2016, https://news.uci.edu/health/put-the-cellphone -away-fragmented-baby-care-can-affect-brain-development/.

155 **The witness's statement that Allen was texting:** James Ragland, "Irving Mother of Three Drowned Children Still Grieving, and Fighting to Get Surviving Kids Back Home," *Dallas Morning News,* November 17, 2015.

155 **a certified nurses' aide:** Jim Douglas, "Drowning Victims' Mom: 'They Can Swim. I Can Swim,'" *Journal News,* August 10, 2015. Salary information via Payscale.com.

156 **Postnatal insomnia:** See, for example, Leslie M. Swanson et al., "An Open Pilot of Cognitive-Behavioral Therapy for Insomnia in Women with Postpartum Depression," *Behavioral Sleep Medicine* 11, no. 4 (2013): 297–307.

156 **mothers multitask more:** S. Offer and B. Schneider, "Revisiting the Gender Gap in Time-Use Patterns: Multitasking and Well-Being Among Mothers and Fathers in Dual-Earner Families," *American Sociological Review* 76, no. 6 (2011): 809–833.

157 *More Work for Mother:* Ruth Schwartz Cowan, *More Work for Mother: The Ironies of Household Technology from the Open Hearth to the Microwave* (New York: Basic Books, 1983).

158 **Time-use studies since the 1960s:** "Parental Time Use," Pew Research Center, http://www.pewresearch.org/data-trend/society-and-demographics /parental-time-use/, accessed June 16, 2017.

159 **Adrienne Rich published *Of Woman Born*:** Adrienne Rich, *Of Woman Born: Motherhood as Experience and Institution* (New York: Norton, 1995).

162 *Dear Parent: Caring for Infants with Respect:* Magda Gerber, *Dear Parent: Caring for Infants with Respect* (Los Angeles: Resources for Infant Educarers, 1998).

163 **Janet Lansbury:** Janet Lansbury's Respectful Parenting Guide, http:// www.janetlansbury.com.

CHAPTER 8: MODERN FAMILIES: PARENTS AND SCREENS

168 **a 2013 market research study:** "Report Finds Pregnancy Apps More Popular Than Fitness Apps," MobiHealthNews, February 14, 2013, http://www.mobihealthnews.com/20333/report-finds-pregnancy-apps -more-popular-than-fitness-apps.

168 **new mothers in America post 2.5 times as many:** Christopher Heine, "You Already Knew Parents Post on Facebook More Than Others. Now Find Out How Much," Adweek, January 11, 2016, http://www.adweek .com/digital/you-already-knew-parents-post-facebook-more-others-now -find-out-how-much-168932/.

168 **A 2016 survey by a UK-based nonprofit:** Alicia Blum-Ross, "'Sha-renting:' Parent Bloggers and Managing Children's Digital Footprints," Parenting for a Digital Future, June 17, 2015, http://blogs.lse.ac.uk /parenting4digitalfuture/2015/06/17/managing-your-childs-digital-foot print-and-or-parent-bloggers-ahead-of-brit-mums-on-the-20th-of-june/.

168 **In a Pew poll released in the winter of 2015:** "Parenting in America: Outlook, Worries, Aspirations Are Strongly Linked to Financial Situation," Pew Research Center, December 17, 2015, http://www.pewsocialtrends .org/files/2015/12/2015-12-17_parenting-in-america_FINAL.pdf.

172 **"On some accounts the play takes on a more malicious tone":** Blake Miller, "The Creepiest New Corner of Instagram," *Fast Company,* September 23, 2014, https://www.fastcompany.com/3036073/the-creepiest -new-corner-of-instagram-role-playing-with-stolen-baby-photos.

172 **Lacey Spears was sentenced to twenty years in prison:** Lee Higgins, "Lacey Spears Gets 20 Years In Son's Poisoning Death," *Journal News,* April 7, 2015, http://www.lohud.com/story/news/crime/2015/04/07 /lacey-spears-sentenced-death-son-poison-court-rockland-new-york /25431741/.

172 ***Munchausen by proxy:*** Scholars have also coined the term *Munchausen by Internet* to describe people who fake illnesses online, either their own or family members', in an apparent bid for sympathy and attention. Marc D. Feldman, "Munchausen by Internet: Detecting Factitious Illness and Crisis on the Internet," *Southern Medical Journal* 93, no. 7 (2000): 669–672.

173 **If the disease is caught before symptoms appear:** Patricia K. Duffner et al., "Newborn Screening for Krabbe Disease: The New York State Model," *Pediatric Neurology* 40, no. 4 (2009): 245–252.

173 **Schuman is a St. Louis–based author:** Sample quote: "The reasons I take and post these pictures are varied. I crave emotional release after hours of increasingly desperate nursing, jiggling, rocking, walking, and, my per-

sonal favorite, walk-nursing (all wriggling, self-torpedoing 22 pounds of her)." Rebecca Schuman, "How Wrong Am I to Flip Off My Sleeping Infant? A Philosophical Inquiry," *Slate*, August 26, 2015, http://www.slate .com/articles/life/family/2015/08/i_give_my_baby_the_middle_finger _parenting_ethics_101.html.

174 **a conversation like this can easily be misinterpreted:** Alice E. Marwick and danah boyd, "I Tweet Honestly, I Tweet Passionately: Twitter Users, Context Collapse, and the Imagined Audience," *New Media & Society* 13, no. 1 (2011): 114–133. Quote: "Some techniques of audience management resemble the practices of 'micro-celebrity' and personal branding, both strategic self-commodification."

175 **Lindy West is a feminist writer:** "If You Don't Have Anything Nice to Say, Say IT IN ALL CAPS," *This American Life,* January 23, 2015, https://www.thisamericanlife.org/radio-archives/episode/545/if-you -dont-have-anything-nice-to-say-say-it-in-all-caps.

175 **West nonetheless announced that she'd quit Twitter:** Lindy West, "I've Left Twitter. It Is Unusable for Anyone but Trolls, Robots and Dictators," *The Guardian,* January 3, 2017, https://www .theguardian.com/commentisfree/2017/jan/03/ive-left-twitter-unusable -anyone-but-trolls-robots-dictators-lindy-west.

175 **These companies enjoy immunity under US law:** "Section 230 of the Communications Decency Act," Electronic Frontier Foundation, https:// www.eff.org/issues/cda230, accessed April 27, 2017.

175 **Law enforcement is often ill-informed:** Margaret Talbot, "The Attorney Fighting Revenge Porn," *New Yorker,* December 5, 2016, http://www .newyorker.com/magazine/2016/12/05/the-attorney-fighting-revenge-porn.

175 **Katherine Clark, a Democratic congressperson:** Ann Friedman, "Trolls Have Swatted, Doxxed, and Threatened to Kill Katherine Clark. She's Still Going After Them," *Elle,* July 13, 2016, http://www.elle.com /culture/tech/a37728/katherine-clark-harassment-abuse-legislation/.

176 **"What if my bad parenting choices go viral?":** Rebecca Schuman, "I Am Terrified of Taking My Child Literally Anywhere," *Slate,* July 25, 2015, http://www.slate.com/articles/life/family/2015/07/crying_toddler_in _maine_diner_i_m_afraid_my_parenting_could_go_viral_too.html.

177 **A single study published in a prominent British medical journal:** Matt Ford, "*The Lancet* retracts paper linking MMR vaccines and autism," Ars Technica, February 3, 2010, https://arstechnica.com/science/2010/02 /the-lancet-retracts-paper-linking-mmr-vaccines-and-autism/.

177 **Vaccination rates have dropped dramatically:** Charles McCoy, "Why Are Vaccination Rates Dropping in America?" *New Republic,* July 24, 2015,

https://newrepublic.com/article/122367/why-are-vaccination-rates
-dropping-america.

178 **Cases of measles, considered eliminated in the year 2000:** Melinda
Wenner Moyer, "Measles and Mumps Rebound," *Discover,* January–
February 2013, http://discovermagazine.com/2013/jan-feb/57-measles
-and-mumps-rebound.

178 **The president, who has a strong affinity for conspiracy theories:**
Arthur Allen, "RFK Jr. says Trump Still Wants 'Vaccine Safety Commission,'" Politico, February 15, 2017, http://www.politico.com/story/2017
/02/robert-f-kennedy-jr-trump-vaccine-safety-commission-235058.

178 **the media reported that someone infected with measles:** Erin All-
day, "Peninsula BART Rider with Measles Exposes Other Passengers," *San
Francisco Chronicle,* February 26, 2015, http://www.sfgate.com/bayarea
/article/A-Peninsula-BART-rider-with-measles-may-have-6103759.php.

179 **As DiResta argued in a 2016 piece for *Fast Company*:** Renée DiResta,
"Social Network Algorithms Are Distorting Reality by Boosting Conspiracy
Theories," *Fast Company,* May 11, 2016, https://www.fastcompany.com
/3059742/social-network-algorithms-are-distorting-reality-by-boosting
-conspiracy-theories.

179 **In 2015 Google announced:** They noted that one in twenty searches
are health-related. "A Remedy for Your Health-Related Questions: Health
Info in the Knowledge Graph," Google Blog, February 10, 2015, https://
googleblog.blogspot.com/2015/02/health-info-knowledge-graph.html.

181 **According to the *Financial Times*:** "Financial Worth of Data Comes In
at Under a Penny a Piece," *Financial Times,* June 12, 2013, https://www
.ft.com/content/3cb056c6-d343–11e2-b3ff-00144feab7de.

181 **This is why companies like Target:** Charles Duhigg, "How Companies Learn Your Secrets," *New York Times Magazine,* February 16, 2012,
http://www.nytimes.com/2012/02/19/magazine/shopping-habits.html.

182 **"In the world of contemporary Internet companies":** Janet Vertesi,
"How Evasion Matters: Implications from Surfacing Data Tracking Online," *Interface* 1, no. 1 (2015): 13.

182 **A few weeks before giving birth:** Janet Vertesi, "My Experiment Opting Out of Big Data Made Me Look Like a Criminal," *Time,* April 30,
2014, http://time.com/83200/privacy-internet-big-data-opt-out/.

184 **French and German police have publicly warned parents:** "Ger-
man Police Warn Parents over Facebook Pictures of Children," BBC,
October 15, 2015, http://www.bbc.com/news/technology-34539059;
David Chazan, "French Parents 'Could Be Jailed' for Posting Children's
Photos Online." *The Telegraph,* March 1, 2016, http://www.telegraph

.co.uk/news/worldnews/europe/france/12179584/French-parents-could
-be-jailed-for-posting-childrens-photos-online.html.

185   **A University of Michigan study in 2016:** Alexis Hiniker, Sarita Y.
Schoenebeck, and Julie A. Kientz, "Not at the Dinner Table: Parents' and
Children's Perspectives on Family Technology Rules," in *Proceedings of
the 19th ACM Conference on Computer-Supported Cooperative Work & Social Computing* (New York: ACM Digital Library, 2016), pp. 1376–1389.

186   **In a 2016 review of the research:** Deborah Lupton, Sarah Pedersen,
and Gareth M. Thomas, "Parenting and Digital Media: From the Early
Web to Contemporary Digital Society," *Sociology Compass* 10, no. 8
(2016): 730–743.

187   **One of the articles calling him out:** Haley Overland, "Ryan Reynolds
Slammed for Making a Parenting Mistake," Today's Parent, July 8, 2015,
https://www.todaysparent.com/blogs/ryan-reynolds-parenting/.

188   **The Huffington Post is one of the top-trafficked sites:** David Segal,
"Arianna Huffington's Improbable, Insatiable Content Machine." *New York
Times Magazine,* June 30, 2015, https://www.nytimes.com/2015/07/05
/magazine/arianna-huffingtons-improbable-insatiable-content-machine
.html?_r = 0. While HuffPostParents still chugs along, Huffington has
turned over a new leaf, of sorts, authoring books on the importance of
sleep and work-life balance, and leaving the website to start a company
called Thrive Global dedicated to wellness and productivity.

189   **the 70 percent of the economy:** Rick Mathews, "US GDP Is 70 Percent
Consumer Spending: Inside the Numbers," Mic, September 21, 2012, https://
mic.com/articles/15097/us-gdp-is-70-percent-personal-consumption
-inside-the-numbers#.jVBxmVVwr.

189   **controlled by women:** Estimates vary. "Buying Power: Women in the
US," Catalyst.org, May 20, 2015, http://www.catalyst.org/system/files
/buying_power_women_0.pdf.

189   **fourteen million mothers:** Elizabeth Segran, "On Winning the Hearts—
and Dollars—of Mommy Bloggers," *Fast Company,* August 14, 2015, http://
www.fastcompany.com/3049137/most-creative-people/on-winning-the
-hearts-and-dollars-of-mommy-bloggers.

189   **As far back as 2008, Walmart recruited:** Jessica Ramirez, "Are Mommy
Bloggers Corporate Sellouts?" *Newsweek,* July 14, 2009, http://www
.newsweek.com/tech-are-mommy-bloggers-corporate-sellouts-82155.

189   **In 2009, General Mills created its own network:** Karlene Lukovitz, "General Mills Network Taps Blogger Moms," *Marketing Daily,* April 29, 2009,
https://www.mediapost.com/publications/article/105092/general-mills
-network-taps-blogger-moms.html?edition = .

189   **In 2015** *Fast Company* **profiled Susan Petersen:** Elizabeth Segran, "On Winning the Hearts—and Dollars—of Mommy Bloggers," *Fast Company,* August 14, 2015, http://www.fastcompany.com/3049137/most -creative-people/on-winning-the-hearts-and-dollars-of-mommy-bloggers.

192   **a study published by Pace University in 2015:** Katerina Lup, Leora Trub, and Lisa Rosenthal, "Instagram# instasad?: Exploring Associations Among Instagram Use, Depressive Symptoms, Negative Social Comparison, and Strangers Followed," *Cyberpsychology, Behavior, and Social Networking* 18, no. 5 (2015): 247–252.

CHAPTER 9: THE FUTURE OF DIGITAL PARENTING

195   **It happened on a visit:** Stanford University Virtual Human Interaction Lab, https://vhil.stanford.edu.

195   **Facebook announced the purchase of a startup called Oculus Rift:** In the official announcement, on Facebook of course, Mark Zuckerberg wrote, "After games, we're going to make Oculus a platform for many other experiences. Imagine enjoying a courtside seat at a game, studying in a classroom of students and teachers all over the world or consulting with a doctor face-to-face—just by putting on goggles in your home." Mark Zuckerberg, Facebook, March 25, 2014, https://www.facebook.com /zuck/posts/10101319050523971.

195   **Facebook's CEO, Mark Zuckerberg, came to this lab:** Lance Ulanoff, "The VR Experience That May Have Convinced Mark Zuckerberg to Buy Oculus," Mashable, March 26, 2014, http://mashable.com/2014/03/26 /zuckerberg-tried-stanford-vr-oculus-rift/#wc1RlHR.Kaql.

196   **Pokémon Go, which became the top-downloaded paid application:** Maureen Morrison, "Pokémon Go Goes Viral with No Big Marketing Blitz," *Ad Age,* July 11, 2016, http://adage.com/article/digital/pokemon -go-viral-marketing/304905/.

197   **Owlet, a "smart sock" that monitors an infant's pulse:** http://www .owletcare.com.

198   **the Lumière brothers' 1895 film of a train:** A famous 2004 essay by two German media scholars calls this story "cinema's founding myth." Martin Loiperdinger and Bernd Elzer, "Lumière's Arrival of the Train: Cinema's Founding Myth," *Moving Image* 4, no. 1 (2004): 89–118.

198   **A VR game in which you fly around a city:** Robin S. Rosenberg, Shawnee L. Baughman, and Jeremy N. Bailenson, "Virtual Superheroes: Using Superpowers in Virtual Reality to Encourage Prosocial Behavior," *PLOS ONE* 8, no. 1 (2013): e55003.

198   **In an exemplar of these studies:** T. Sims, J. Bailenson, and L. L. Carstensen, "Connecting to Your Future Self: Enhancing Financial Planning Among Diverse Communities Using Virtual Technology," paper presented at the annual meeting of the Gerontological Society of America, Orlando, FL, 2015.

200   **A lot of the ones they've built so far:** See Ken Perlin's blog at https://mrl.nyu.edu/~perlin/.

201   **"Hi, what's your name? I'm Alex":** Samantha Finkelstein et al., "Investigating the Influence of Virtual Peers as Dialect Models on Students' Prosodic Inventory," Institute for Creative Technologies, University of Southern California, 2012, http://ict.usc.edu/pubs/Investigating % 20the % 20Influence % 20of % 20Virtual % 20Peers % 20as % 20Dialect % 20Models % 20on % 20Students % 20Prosodic % 20Inventory.pdf; Samantha Finkelstein et al., "Alex: A Virtual Peer That Identifies Student Dialect," in *Proceedings of the Workshop on Culturally-Aware Technology Enhanced Learning in Conjunction with EC-TEL 2013,* Paphos, Cyprus, September 17. 2013.

202   **Eighty percent of public school teachers are white:** "The State of Racial Diversity in the Educator Workforce, 2016," US Department of Education, July 2016, https://www2.ed.gov/rschstat/eval/highered/racial-diversity/state-racial-diversity-workforce.pdf, p. 1.

202   *Code-switching* **is the term linguists coined:** Most often attributed to John J. Gumperz, *Discourse Strategies,* Vol. 1 (New York: Cambridge University Press, 1982).

203   **The idea of a universal lifelong learning companion:** Tak-Wai Chan and Arthur B. Baskin, "Studying with the Prince: The Computer as a Learning Companion," in *Proceedings of the International Conference on Intelligent Tutoring Systems* (1988), pp. 194–200.

203   **Hello Barbie, introduced for the 2015 Christmas season:** Lauren Walker, "Hello Barbie, Your Child's Chattiest and Riskiest Christmas Present," *Newsweek,* December 15, 2015, http://www.newsweek.com/2015/12/25/hello-barbie-your-childs-chattiest-and-riskiest-christmas-present-404897.html.

204   **Anil Dash, one of the smartest commentators:** Anil Dash, "Amazon Echo and Alexa Really Matter," Medium, June 22, 2016, https://medium.com/@anildash/amazon-echo-and-alexa-really-matter-dcc6d817ad6b.

204   **The transitional object:** D. W. Winnicott, "10. Transitional Objects and Transitional Phenomena: A Study of the First Not-Me," *Essential Papers on Object Relations* (1986): 254.

205   **Isamu Noguchi, the renowned sculptor:** Rebecca Onion, "The World's First Baby Monitor: Zenith's 1937 'Radio Nurse.'" *Slate*, February 7, 2013, http://www.slate.com/blogs/the_vault/2013/02/07/zenith_s_radio _nurse_designed_by_isamu_noguchi_was_the_world_s_first_baby.html.

205   **Infant Optics DXR-5 Portable Video Baby Monitor:** "Amazon Most Wished For." No. 6 as of April 2017. https://www.amazon.com/gp/most -wished-for/baby-products/ref=zg_bsnr_tab_t_mw.

205   **the Snoo, designed at MIT:** Rachel Rothman and Good Housekeeping Institute, "Snoo Smart Sleeper," Good Housekeeping Product Reviews, November 2016, http://www.goodhousekeeping.com/childrens-products /a41743/snoo-smart-sleeper-review/.

205   **A woman wrote to a magazine advice column in 2015:** Emily Yoffe, "Dear Prudence: Mom and Dad Are Watching," *Slate*, June 25, 2015, http://www.slate.com/articles/life/dear_prudence/2015/06/dear_prudence _i_gave_my_parents_remote_access_to_our_baby_monitor_oops.html.

205   **the tech blog Ars Technica:** J. M. Porup, "'Internet of Things' Security Is Hilariously Broken and Getting Worse," Ars Technica, January 23, 2016, https://arstechnica.com/security/2016/01/how-to-search-the -internet-of-things-for-photos-of-sleeping-babies/.

206   **In 2015, a three-year-old boy in Washington State:** "Seen at 11: Cyber Spies Could Target Your Child Through a Baby Monitor," CBS New York, April 21, 2005, http://newyork.cbslocal.com/2015/04/21/seen-at -11-cyber-spies-could-target-your-child-through-a-baby-monitor/.

206   **In 2016, privacy groups filed a complaint:** "In the Matter of Genesis Toys and Nuance Communications," Federal Trade Commission, December 6, 2016, https://epic.org/privacy/kids/EPIC-IPR-FTC-Genesis -Complaint.pdf.

207   **in general these technologies:** Gina Neff and Dawn Nafus, *Self-Tracking* (Cambridge, MA: MIT Press, 2016).

207   **"I quantified my baby and wish I could get the time back":** Tim Chester, "I Quantified My Baby and Wish I Could Get the Time Back," Mashable, October 15, 2015, http://mashable.com/2015/10/15/quantified -baby-infant-tracking/.

207   *Babyveillance:* Veronica Barassi, "BabyVeillance: Digital Parents, Online Surveillance and the Construction of Babies' Digital Profiles," *Social Media & Society*, May 19, 2017, http://journals.sagepub.com/doi/full/10.1177 /2056305117707188.

208   **Life360 has eighty million registered users:** www.crunchbase.com. Accessed August 10, 2017.

208 **Net Nanny offers parents the power:** "NetNanny (for iPhone)," *PC-Mag*, March 23, 2016, http://www.pcmag.com/review/342827/net-nanny -for-iphone.

209 **Placing your kids on digital house arrest:** "Electronic Surveillance," Legal Information Institute, Cornell University Law School, https://www .law.cornell.edu/wex/electronic_surveillance, accessed June 16, 2017.

209 **As doctor and writer Atul Gawande puts it:** Atul Gawande, *Being Mortal: Medicine and What Matters in the End* (New York: Macmillan, 2014), p. 106.

210 **Developmental psychologists argue that:** Bruce Duncan Perry, "Self-Regulation: The Second Core Strength," Scholastic, http://teacher .scholastic.com/professional/bruceperry/self_regulation.htm, accessed June 16, 2017.

210 **As Jathan Sadowski put it in an essay:** Jathan Sadowski, "Reign of the Techno-Nanny," New Inquiry, October 5, 2012, https://thenewinquiry .com/reign-of-the-techno-nanny/.

211 **Tristan Harris, a former design ethicist:** See Time Well Spent, http:// www.timewellspent.io/.

212 **A gadget called Ringly:** Ringly Smart Jewelry, http://www.ringly.com.

212 **An app called Moment:** Moment, https://inthemoment.io/.

213 **I'm hanging out with my 4-year-old daughter:** Anya Kamenetz, "Apps That Aim to Give Parents Superpowers," NPR, June 8, 2016, http://www.npr.org/sections/ed/2016/06/08/480593689/apps-that-aim -to-give-parents-superpowers.

215 **Text4Baby:** William Douglas Evans, Jasmine L. Wallace, and Jeremy Snider, "Pilot Evaluation of the Text4Baby Mobile Health Program," *BMC Public Health* 12, no. 1 (2012): 1031; Danielle A. Naugle and Robert C. Hornik, "Systematic Review of the Effectiveness of Mass Media Interventions for Child Survival in Low- and Middle-Income Countries," *Journal of Health Communication* 19, suppl. 1 (2014): 190–215.

215 **a tablet app called Bedtime Math:** Eric Westervelt, "Where the Wild Fractions Are: The Power of a Bedtime (Math) Story," NPR, October 8, 2015, http://www.npr.org/sections/ed/2015/10/08/446490524/where -the-wild-fractions-are-the-power-of-a-bedtime-math-story.

215 **Seow Lim used to be a self-described "Tiger Mom":** Anya Kamenetz, "Apps That Aim to Give Parents Superpowers," NPR, June 8, 2016, http://www.npr.org/sections/ed/2016/06/08/480593689/apps-that-aim -to-give-parents-superpowers.

217 **"When television is good, nothing":** Laurie Ouellette and Justin Lewis,

"Moving Beyond the "Vast Wasteland" Cultural Policy and Television in the United States," *Television & New Media* 1, no. 1 (2000): 95–115.

217   **her landmark 1967 paper:** Joan Ganz Cooney, "The Potential Uses of Television in Preschool Education," 1967, http://www.joanganzcooney center.org/wp-content/uploads/2014/01/JGC_1966_report.pdf.

217   **"I give an expression of care everyday to each child":** Jeana Lietz, "Journey to the Neighborhood: An Analysis of Fred Rogers and His Lessons for Educational Leaders," Loyola University Chicago, 2014, http:// ecommons.luc.edu/cgi/viewcontent.cgi?article = 2096&context = luc _diss.

217   **"I got into television because I hated it so":** "Mr. Rogers Neighborhood to Air Last Show," CNN, August 31, 2001, http://transcripts.cnn.com /TRANSCRIPTS/0108/31/lad.09.html.

CHAPTER 10: TL;DR: THE ART OF SCREEN TIME IN FIVE MINUTES

221   **1.:** See chapter 1.

221   **2.:** See chapters 2 and 3.

222   **3., 4., 5.:** See chapter 4.

222   **6.:** See chapter 2.

222   **7., 8.:** See chapter 5.

223   **9.:** See chapter 4.

224   **10.:** See chapter 7.

INDEX

Anya Kamenetz is an education correspondent for NPR, where she also cohosts the *Life Kit* parenting podcast. She speaks, writes, and thinks about learning and the future. She is the author of three books on education and technology, *Generation Debt, DIY U,* and *The Test.* She lives in Brooklyn with her family.